The TRINITY in the
STONE-CAMPBELL MOVEMENT

The TRINITY in the STONE-CAMPBELL MOVEMENT

Restoring
the Heart of
Christian Faith

KELLY D. CARTER

THE TRINITY IN THE STONE-CAMPBELL MOVEMENT
Restoring the Heart of Christian Faith

Copyright 2015 by Kelly D. Carter

ISBN 978-0-89112-596-9

Printed in the United States of America

ALL RIGHTS RESERVED
No part of this publication may be reproduced, stored in a retrieval system, or transmitted in any form by any means—electronic, mechanical, photocopying, recording or otherwise—without prior written consent.

Scripture quotations, unless otherwise noted, are from The Holy Bible, New International Version. Copyright 1984, International Bible Society. Used by permission of Zondervan Publishers.

Cover and interior text design by Sandy Armstrong, Strong Design

Abilene Christian University Press
ACU Box 29138
Abilene, Texas 79699

1-877-816-4455 toll free | www.acupressbooks.com

15 16 17 18 19 20 / 7 6 5 4 3 2 1

Table of Contents

Preface and Acknowledgements 7

1. Introduction 13
2. The Trinity among the Early Disciples—
   Thomas and Alexander Campbell 27
3. The Trinity in the Writings of Barton Stone:
   Stone's Quasi-Arianism 89
4. The Historical/Theological Roots of Early
   Restorationist Trinitarianism 139
5. The Impact of Prior Trinitarian Perspectives on
   Trinitarian Theology in the Later Stone-Campbell Movement 185
6. The Need For Reassessing Stone-Campbell
   Trinitarian Perspectives 223
7. Toward A Stone-Campbell Trinitarian Theology:
   A Summary Proposal 255

Bibliography 273

Preface and Acknowledgements

Although I had become conversant with Trinitarian scholarship at an academic level while completing a master of arts thesis on the theology of Jürgen Moltmann in 1986, I had done little serious reflection on the significance of the doctrine of the Trinity *for Stone-Campbell churches* prior to beginning a fifteen-year ministerial stint with the Shelbourne St. Church of Christ in Victoria, British Columbia. Much of what I now think concerning the relationship between the Father and the Son and the active ministry of the Holy Spirit was framed while working among these dear friends as a young minister, so it can be quite accurately said that my personal Trinitarian theology was forged in the crucible of ministry in Churches of Christ (a cappella)—hereafter abbreviated CCa—specifically in Victoria.

As will be seen below, this is a bit ironic, given the sparseness of Trinitarian thought within CCa and their hesitancy to make Trinitarian theology of central concern. It is also ironic given my own personal theological stance, which is essentially classically Trinitarian, and the strong presence in the Shelbourne St. Church of a Barton Stone-like perspective on the Trinity. Nonetheless, there has been synergy between my ecclesiastical context and ministry experience in CCa and my interest in academic systematic theology, including my study of and understanding of the doctrine of the Trinity. This synergy has enriched, and continues to enrich, both my theology and my praxis, and I am thankful to those in Victoria and now those from the Calgary Church of Christ for the opportunity I have had to think reflectively about theology and Trinitarianism, all the while attempting to minister in CCa in ways that reflect the unity, love, and mutual service present between the Father, Son, and Spirit.

In this book, I hope in some small way to help create a similar synergy for Stone-Campbell (hereafter abbreviated SC) churches. Prior to leaving Victoria and Vancouver Island in 2001 to move to Dallas, Texas to undertake a PhD in systematic theology at Southern Methodist University, I had occasion to spend a weekend with the elders and ministers of the Calgary (Alberta) Church of Christ, the church that, coincidentally, I now serve. Our time together included my proposal that taking seriously the doctrine of the Trinity, and applying a Trinitarian theological understanding in their life as a church, would not only benefit their particular congregation, but would also make them progenitors of what I predicted would be a renaissance of Trinitarian thinking within CCa. Given this scenario, ecclesiastical, ministerial renewal would occur, in part because of a reconsideration of the place of the doctrine of the Trinity among SC churches.

It is too early to tell, but there are indications (see Chapter One and Chapter Five) that the time may have come for Trinitarian studies to impact SC churches in the way I predicted on that first trip to Calgary. I am hoping this is the case. Were the Independent Christian Churches/Churches of Christ and Churches of Christ (a cappella) (hereafter abbreviated as the ICC/CC and CCa) to think seriously about the Trinity, allowing such reflection to impact our understanding and praxis of ministry in the world and the manner in which we think of and experience ecclesial life with fellow believers, we would come closer to living out the Trinitarian unity, love, and mutual service that is demonstrated for us, that should define us, and that should infuse us as representatives of our Trinitarian God. Trinitarian reflection would be for us, then, something other than an ethereal, intangible, impractical exercise avoided by most because they have neither the time nor the inclination to think about something that has so little (apparent) impact on daily efforts to live out Christianity. They would instead see that a close look at the Trinity specifically allows theological reflection to most directly touch Christian life and praxis. I am grateful that I now have opportunity to help fulfill in Calgary what I there suggested several years ago should be the future for SC churches.

In addition to the churches I have served in Victoria and Calgary, we were able to find a church home with the Greenville Oaks Church of Christ in Allen, Texas during the portions of 2001–2006 that our family was in Dallas at SMU. Space does not permit me opportunity to express to them all that the Carter family owes them. God could not have done better than by quite literally leading us to their front door. Thank you to these wonderful brothers and sisters for being genuine family to us.

I wish, also, to thank several who made contributions to this project by offering input about Trinitarian thought within ICC/CC and CCa, including Jack Cottrell, John Castelein, Douglas Foster, John Mark Hicks, Ron Highfield, Mark Love, Mark Powell, and Johnny Pressley. Thank you, too, to Hans Rollmann, whose service to SC churches with the construction of his Restoration Movement (hereafter abbreviated as RM) website (now moved to Abilene Christian University) has been invaluable and monumental, and to Craig Churchill and Carisse Berryhill at ACU's Center for Restoration Studies for being so willing to return e-mails and offer assistance in tracking down obscure works and references.

Although there are three decades separating the publishing of this volume and the days I spent at Abilene Christian University as an undergraduate and master's student, in many ways the influence of faculty and friends from those days is as impactful on the present volume as anything else. As the primary example, without the mentorship and guidance of Tom Olbricht, who first introduced me to systematic theology, biblical theology, and theological reading and prioritizing, I might never have come to love the church, ministry, and theology as I do. His influence on a whole generation of ministers and theological scholars puts the CCa in his debt in a way that can be said of few, and this profoundly applies to me. I need also to thank Tom for reading this manuscript and making much needed suggestions.

The customary nature of the acknowledgements of a writer's family should in no way diminish the expression of my heartfelt appreciation to my own family for what they endured while their husband and father worked on the dissertation on which this book is based, and then on this book. You were uprooted, inconvenienced, and frequently dragged between Canada and the United States, and you selflessly tolerated it all. Adam, Ryan, and Meghan, thank you for being the most tolerant and encouraging children in the world. To Robin, especially, who has unselfishly sacrificed more, simply as a gift of her life to me, than I can hardly believe, I extend my deepest appreciation and love, and I dedicate this work specifically to you, R.D.

If Karl Barth may be taken as any kind of authority, there is merit in the synergy I described above between ministry and scholarship and in what I have suggested I have had the privilege of doing: working out and applying theology in an ecclesiological and ministerial context. As part of a lengthy introduction prior to launching into his specific treatment of the Trinity, Barth writes in *Church Dogmatics:*

> Church proclamation has to be accompanied and confronted by Church theology, especially dogmatics. In distinction from all scattered answers to irrelevant questions, theology, and especially dogmatics, is the concentrated care and concern of the church for its own most proper responsibility. In making its proclamation the raw material of dogmatics, it does the one thing it really needs apart from proclamation itself and the prayer that it may be right, the one and only thing it can do as the Church in relation to the obvious centre of its life.[1]

These words are framed, hanging in my church office a step away from where I sit as I continue to work in the church, while also serving students in an academic environment at Alberta Bible College—now in the shadow of the majestic Canadian Rockies when the sun sets, rather than within ear shot of Vancouver Island Pacific breakers. It is hoped that just because the current academic and theological project is being completed in the context of church ministry, there will be an appropriate richness in its application of Trinitarian theology to—and for—*the church*.

Note

[1] Karl Barth, *Church Dogmatics,* 1:1, 76.

Introduction

A book examining both what the individual, earliest SC leaders thought about the Trinity and the subsequent general theological orientation with respect to the Trinity of the Stone-Campbell Movement (hereafter abbreviated SCM) will not amount to a re-exploration of issues adequately addressed by others. In fact, no published full-length scholarly monographs give an adequate account of the early Restorationists' Trinitarian tendencies or more generally assess Trinitarianism within the SCM. Although some circumscribed accounts address the Trinity from a Restorationist perspective, key issues and questions largely remain unexplored.[1] It is the goal of this book to provide both a comprehensive examination of early Restorationist Trinitarian thought and an assessment of the place of the doctrine of the Trinity in the SCM in general. For a sizable group of Christian thinkers—namely, those who write, teach, preach, pastor, and otherwise lead by doing theology within the SC tradition—a study of the Movement's

Trinitarianism will help to fill gaps which currently exist within both historical studies of Restorationist theology and Restorationist theology.[2]

The fact that there are relatively few published materials written by either early or later Restorationists that directly address the subject of the Trinity is not happenstance. This absence fits with a pervasive hesitancy to "speculate on the incomprehensible Jehovah,"[3] so that philosophical and systematic theology have been, by far, the most neglected of the standard theological disciplines among Restorationists. Alexander Campbell's attitude regarding speculation on the Trinity is discernible in his seventeenth- and eighteenth-century theological/historical predecessors and contemporaries, pervading not only his attitude but those of his father (despite Thomas Campbell's willingness to use language concerning the Trinity that his son considered "speculative") and of Barton Stone.[4] Nonetheless, the Campbells and Stone did on occasion address Trinitarianism, so an understanding of their positions may be delineated even while their hesitancy to formulate Trinitarian theology and doctrine is examined.

My hope is that this study will significantly contribute to an understanding of the history and theology of the SCM by assessing Restorationist Trinitarian thought and offer significant suggestions concerning the role an overtly delineated Trinitarianism could play wherever it is lacking in SC churches and their theologies. The intention is to correct a foundational theological error, including its practical ramifications. An avoidance of Trinitarian doctrine left SC theology incomplete and inappropriately centered, negatively impacting its ecclesiology and praxis. Thus, this book will be historically descriptive and both theologically and ecclesiologically constructive.

In addition to the historical, theological, and ecclesiastical significance of the subject, at least four factors indicate the *timeliness* of an in-depth examination of SC Trinitarianism. First, this project is being undertaken on the heels of, in response to, and as part of the ongoing, unprecedented work of a number of historians and historical theologians at the close of the twentieth century and beginning of the twenty-first. Leonard Allen, Michael Casey, James Duke, Douglas Foster, David Edwin Harrell, Richard Hughes, John Mark Hicks, Hiram Lester, Thomas Olbricht, Richard Phillips, Hans Rollmann, Ernie Stefanik, Mark Toulouse, D. Newell Williams, and numerous others have since the early 1980s offered illuminating insights into the intellectual, ecclesiastical, and theological history of the SCM and American biblical primitivism. Those efforts are significantly shaping the preaching, teaching, and ministries of those who conduct their spiritual lives in a SC ecclesiastical context. Such efforts apply and build upon the earlier work of W. E. Garrison, W. H. Hanna, Lester McAllister, and others who performed the same function for previous generations.

A second factor indicating the timeliness of this book is the ecclesiastical ferment present within the traditionally most conservative branch of the SCM—the CCa—where my own spiritual heritage lies. In the past four decades, the CCa has been in great flux, as churches that previously clearly understood who they were and what they believed began to question the validity of some of their key beliefs and practices, leading in some cases to significant alterations in doctrinal understanding, ecclesiastical character, and liturgical patterns. Changes in the intellectual landscape of North America, including what is generally referred to as post-modernism, have given rise in CCa to questions concerning the character of Scripture, the ways in which Scripture's authority should influence belief and practice, its interpretation, its central theological themes and their importance, and its application both in churches and in the lives of individual Christians. The growth of evangelicalism in North America—including the dissolving of denominational rigidity between conservative Christians, the ascendancy and influence of megachurches, the amazing multiplication of conservative, unaffiliated community churches with whom CCa have increasing contact, and the tremendous expansion of evangelical publishing—has created a climate in which denominational isolation is virtually impossible, and contact with others has led many in CCa to entertain changes in perspectives and practices.

The result of the above ecclesiastical ferment in CCa is routinely termed an "identity crisis." It is not just that there now exists a broad spectrum of beliefs and practices among CCa in the world, so that one cannot know exactly what will occur when visiting any particular congregation on a Sunday morning. It is that many individual congregations have lost the practical and theological moorings which previously created for them a self-identity and justification for their existence. Among the vast array of religious and theological options available, what comprises the foundational system of beliefs that sustains the existence and particularity of the fellowship of CCa? What, now, is the rationale for their existence in distinction from other groups of conservative Christians; are the differences between themselves and others sufficient to justify continued separation? What purposes derive from what central theological values, so that churches can identify not only who they are but what purposes they serve? It is partially in light of such questions that the current book finds its justification.

Third, exploring Trinitarianism within the SCM is required by some relatively recent overtures made by thinkers in the movement toward the actual doing of Trinitarian theology. Of note first are the publications of Roy Lanier, Ed Myers and J. J. Turner, and Lonzo Pribble, all of which attempt to address the subject of the Trinity in an ecclesiastical context historically reticent to do so. They are in this sense welcome aberrations. These writers and their publications demonstrate great variance in intention, scope, theological acuity, and theological orientation, but they share treatments of a common theme, published within a few years of each other, after decades of relative silence on the subject of the Trinity. Mention should also be made of Leonard Allen and Danny Swick's *Participating in God's Life: Two Crossroads for Churches of Christ*. While not written as systematic theology or as a monograph on the Trinity (as are the previously mentioned works), Allen and Swick's assessment of and contribution to practical ecclesiology gives an account of the significance of Trinitiarian theology for CCa.

In fact, it is Allen and Swick's work which points toward a fourth factor indicating the appropriateness of this study. Theologians may have overstated both the scarcity of Trinitarian thinking prior to the publication of Volume 1, Part 1 of Barth's *Church Dogmatics* and the apparent renewal of Trinitarian studies since that point, but it is difficult to miss how much more frequently systematic theologians have directed their attention toward Trinitarian theology since 1967, when Karl Rahner's *The Trinity* was published. Works by Boris Bobrinsky, David Cunningham, Robert Jenson, Catherine LaCugna, Jürgen Moltmann, Wolfhart Pannenberg, Ted Peters, Kathryn Tanner, T. F. Torrance, Miroslav Wolf, John Zizioulas, and numerous others have explicated Trinitarian perspectives that not only make central the doctrine of the Trinity but also bear ramifications for

SC adherents willing to test contemporary theological waters. Allen and Swick explored these waters by applying the Trinitarian views of Catherine LaCugna in their work. This project seeks to encourage Restorationists to undertake other similar investigations and applications of contemporary Trinitarian theology at a time when many have reasserted the importance of Trinitarian doctrine within Christian theology.

Some SCM adherents still commonly profess the historical/doctrinal position which asserts that the progenitors of the RM relied on few precedents aside from Scripture and no predecessors for their "no creed but the Bible" foundation. For them, it is as if early Restorationists' primitivistic approaches to theology and ecclesiastical practice had no parallels or roots prior to the efforts that began early in the nineteenth century. In this view, Restorationists developed wholly new hermeneutical practices, new views of the character and authority of Scripture, new concerns for individual religious liberty and for establishing and restoring the primitive beliefs and practices of the biblical church, a devotion to Christian unity unprecedented among English-speaking Protestants, and a unique aversion to denominational Christianity and the statements of faith, confessions, and creeds that identified distinct fellowships.

Such a perspective is being challenged today by the unprecedented work of a number of historians and historical theologians who have identified intellectual, theological, and ecclesiastical parallels between Restorationists and others and delineated the common roots arising out of this milieu. Foundational SC documents have been carefully and critically examined, so that Restorationist thought can be viewed in context, complete with an understanding of the origins of key Restorationist ideas. The simplistic, unhistorical, somewhat naïve perspective that depicted Restorationist thought as uniquely revolutionary has been superseded by critical understanding and careful research, leading not to a depreciation of the value of the ideas of SC progenitors, but to a deeper appreciation of their ability to reflect on contemporary theology, their awareness of intellectual trends, and their willingness to apply new ideas to their own theological and ecclesiastical contexts. They were children of their age, but not naively so. To think of them as uneducated, ignorant, backwater, anti-intellectual preachers unaware of theological trends of their day is to misperceive and underestimate their abilities, experiences, and contributions.

Many now acknowledge the impact of the Reformation on Restorationists, and the philosophical, historical, and denominational roots of early Restorationists have been carefully traced—specifically with reference to the Irish/Scottish/American Presbyterian background of Thomas and Alexander Campbell, Walter Scott, and Barton Stone and to the influence of the Baconian, Lockean, Newtonian intellectual world of the late seventeenth and early eighteenth centuries. However, I contend that the debt early Restorationists owed to both their contemporary Protestant theological climate and to specific theologians and their writings needs further explication, especially with reference to the Trinity. Restorationists' perceptions about the Trinity were neither unique nor formulated in a theological vacuum, justifying a careful look at the theological impulses that led them to their conclusions. This study is historical and descriptive in that it will include (1) a description of Trinitarianism among early Restorationists, and (2) the intellectual and, especially, the *theological* background that serves as the catalyst for what develops from Thomas Campbell, Alexander Campbell, and Barton Stone concerning the Trinity.[5]

Understanding what the Campbells and Stone did with Trinitarian doctrine and the Trinitarian ethos of the SCM in general will be enhanced by an understanding of some of the basic issues concerning classical Trinitarian discussion. These include questions related to:

- Monarchianism; monarchian alternatives offered in Sabellianism
- Modalism; the views of Novatian; the views of Arius of Antioch, who described the Son as "created"
- Arius's Alexandrian counterparts Alexander and Athanasius who thought of the Son as being completely God
- The foundational Trinitarian statements from Nicea in AD 325 and Constantinople in AD 381, including the creedal usage of *homoousios;* the delineations of the Cappadocian fathers concerning *ousia* and *hypostasis*
- The eternality of the Son, his pre-existence, and his status as begotten from the Father

- The definition of and rise of Socinianism around the time of the Reformation
- The impact of non-Trinitarian views on eighteenth-century English Presbyterians, including the Independents and English dissenters.

This book will not offer an introduction to such matters here, so it is suggested that readers unacquainted with this theological history consult the many works that do. The *International Standard Bible Encyclopedia* in both its early and revised editions offers such material, and numerous introductory works and overviews, including various websites, provide both this information and bibliography for studying these matters.[6]

The closest connection between these classical Trinitarian issues and the founders of the SCM concerns the question of the relationship between the Father and Son. There may be a relatively insignificant disagreement between the positions of the Campbells and that of classical Nicean-Constantinoplean Trinitarianism; with Thomas Campbell one sees a mild subordination of the Son and with Alexander Campbell questions arise concerning the eternality of the Son and the incorrectness of referring to the λόγος by using Father-Son terminology. With Barton Stone there is a definite move in the direction of Arianism, whereby the Son finds his origin in the Father at a specific time prior to natural history, meaning that the Son cannot be identical with the one and only true God, who alone is eternal.

Chapters Two and Three will provide an examination into the Trinitarian thinking of three of the SCM patriarchs—Alexander Campbell (1788–1866), Thomas Campbell (1763–1854), and Barton Stone (1772–1844). Reference will also be made to Robert Richardson (1806–1876) and a few other early Restorationists. These two chapters and an examination in Chapter Four of the historical and theological roots from which these leaders derived their positions will form the backdrop that makes it possible to see how these early writers impacted the subsequent treatment of the Trinity among Restorationists, which is the subject of Chapter Five. At that point, the foundation will have been provided for framing a reassessment of classical Trinitarianism among Restorationist churches.

Chapter Six will progress from assessing how the movement's ecclesiastical and theological heritage have impacted current Restorationists toward a proposal to explicitly apply biblical, historical, and contemporary systematic Trinitarianism to SC theology. That chapter will delineate the theological and ecclesiastical—even practical—values SC churches can gain by reflecting at length on Trinitarianism (or on SC non-Trinitarianism!).

Finally, Chapter Seven will close the study with a summary proposal suggesting steps ICC/CC and CCa can take as they go about overtly adopting classical Trinitarianism.

An Excursus: The Trinity among the Disciples of Christ

Although it would be tangential to include here a detailed description of the differences between the Disciples of Christ (Christian Church) and the ICC/CC and CCa, it is worth noting that the Disciples of Christ have tended to be more willing to interact in theological dialogue with thinkers and writers from beyond the SCM. The Disciples have been more willing to see value in and to conform theologically and ecclesiastically to traditional Protestantism as manifested among the mainline denominations. In some cases, this has impacted their willingness to accept theological moves that would be considered too biblically aberrant or theologically liberal to be made by ICC/CC and CCa, such as official communal agreements with mainline denominations, the widespread ordination of women to serve as senior pastors or elders, and a more accepting perspective toward the LGBT community and homosexual practices. In other cases, it simply means taking a more positive stance toward traditional Christian theology, so that the ways systematic theology has developed in Christianity through time have been more readily addressed by those among the Disciples than by those in ICC/CC and CCa.

Although it would be a mistake to say that the Disciples have been captivated by traditional Trinitarian doctrine or by the developments in Trinitarianism over the last four decades, their willingness to engage with contemporary Trinitarian discussion has meant that the doctrine of the Trinity plays a more overtly central role for some among the Disciples than is typically found among those from the ICC/CC and CCa. It goes beyond the intentions of the current project to treat at length the doctrine of the

Trinity found among the Disciples after the nineteenth century, but perhaps it will be helpful to briefly examine one example of systematic theology coming from the Disciples in which the Trinity actually plays a decisive role. This occurs in the systematic theology of Joe R. Jones, specifically from his work, *A Grammar of Christian Faith: Systematic Explorations in Christian Life and Doctrine*.[7]

Jones gives more centralized attention to the Trinity as part of his theological program than any SC theologian of which I am aware, and he does so as part of the most extensive work in systematic theology written by anyone with roots in the SCM, aside perhaps from Jack Cottrell. Jones summarizes his theological program in terms of "three normative identifying references as to who God is"—following a Trinitarian pattern of organizing his thoughts, with the content of his *identifying references* being inherently Trinitarian, similar to the centrality of the Trinity for Barth[8]—and gives a preeminent place to the Trinity as "professed and described from the perspective of Jesus Christ as the definitive self-revelation of God."[9] For Jones, Barth's Trinitarian Christocentricity is foundationally central, and while Wittgenstein's language-games and Lindbeck's grounding of theological doctrine in the grammar of communities help to shape Jones's theological perspective, it is the Bible's Trinitarian priorities filtered through Barth's Trinitarian Christocentricity that primarily influences Jones's *Grammar*.

Epistemically, Jones overtly and intentionally grounds his Trinitarian identification of God in what is revealed in the economic Trinity and what he calls "*God's triune self-identifying being-in acts*"[10]—citing God's activity in choosing and walking with Israel, his self-revelation in the person Jesus of Nazareth, and his involvement in the church through the Spirit as the three normative identifying references that communicate God to humankind. Of these three—following Barth—Jones prioritizes God's activity in Jesus Christ, calling it the "definitive self-revelation of God."[11]

In discussing the matter of God's unity and multiplicity, Jones first applies what he calls the *person-subject model* to God's unity. For Jones, neither describing God's unity in terms of common essence nor as a unity or community of persons adequately holds together the singularity of God and the full divinity of all three persons. Instead, he chooses, like Barth, to speak of three modes-of-being, where a mode is a way of being-in-action undertaken by God who is the divine, supreme Person-Subject.[12] However, the three modes of God whereby God acts as God are each fully and equally God, and Jones will have nothing of the idea that the Father serves as source of the other two modes of God's being or that the Spirit—as in Barth's view—finds his instantiation as merely the source and force of loving unity between the Father and Son.[13] In each of the three modes, God is the "I" that he is, with real distinctions between the Three requiring that although One, God is a *"self-differentiating...complex person-subject"* who includes within himself the Three. The traditional simplicity of God, then, must be seen in God's "self-identicalness...throughout all God's self-differentiating life with the world" that is a "special sort of simplicity that allows for a special sort of complexity."[14] Here the idea of God as complex Person-Subject permits the modes of God to be both distinct and interrelated, with each mode being what it is only in the context of a relationship of love with the other two.[15]

Regarding God's immanence and economy, Jones views God's immanent existence prior to creation as necessary if God's freedom is truly to be maintained. This immanent existence and its conjoined activity in the economy of God's *being-in-acts* with his creation are delineated by Jones using the concepts of God's essence and actuality, which Jones says must be differentiated in order for God's free, self-determined existence and his appearance in Jesus Christ to cohere.[16] However, rather than viewing *essence* as the basic reality of God, according to Jones, God's essence includes only those elements that are the necessary and unchanging constituents that must be present in God in order for God to be God. His *actuality*, or his real existence, is not simply his essence but consists of his actual loving and living in the three modes of being-in-act and is, in fact, God's basic reality. Where God's *essence* is immutable, God's *actuality*, consisting first of the primordial relationality of the Three—the *Primordial Trinity* or *Primordial Actuality of God* or God the *triune primordial Subject*—sequentially becomes the *Actual Economic Trinity*, whereby God's being-in-act extends to creation and to relationship with creation, without which God's actuality would not be what it is.

There is much in Jones's *A Grammar of the Christian Faith* and in his grounding of his theology in the triune existence of God that commends itself to those in the SCM interested in Trinitarian theology and in examining how one writer within the SCM heritage has approached systematic theology. That his systematic explorations give to the Trinity a foundational role warrants examination by those in the ICC/CC and CCa, even while his delineation of God's essence and actuality deserves the attention of the wider scholarly community. What is perhaps most significant for the purposes of this book is to see that Trinitarian doctrine can and should have a central place within the systematic theological explorations of those within the SCM heritage. Jones has allowed the results of contemporary Trinitarian thought to help him establish his own theological course, so that a concern for biblical revelation and the theological grammar, created in his mind by Scripture's witness to God's interaction with humankind, is supplemented and massaged by contemporary Trinitarian theology, illuminating rather than obfuscating the revelation of God and his activity that is offered in Scripture.

Notes

[1] For accounts of the Trinity from an SC perspective, see Douglas Foster, "Christology in the Stone-Campbell Movement"; John Mark Hicks, "Christological Reflections"; Alfred Thomas DeGroot, *Disciple Thought*; Ron Highfield, "Does the Doctrine of the Trinity Make a Difference?"; Mark C. Black, *Theology Matters*, 15–26; C. Leonard Allen and Danny Swick, *Participating in God's Life*; and Jack Cottrell, *What the Bible Says About God the Redeemer and The Faith Once for All*. Three treatments of the Trinity by Church of Christ authors are Lonzo Pribble, *Theology Simplified: God, His Son, and His Spirit*; Roy H. Lanier, *The Timeless Trinity for the Ceaseless Centuries*; and J. J. Turner and Edward P. Myers, *The Doctrine of the Godhead*. In addition, Richard T. Huber's unpublished master's thesis, *The Doctrine of the Trinity in the Thought of Thomas and Alexander Campbell*, moved in this direction. His work is to be appreciated, but its analysis is insufficient both in historical backgrounds and theological acuity.

[2] The current volume represents a reworking of my 2012 PhD dissertation, "The Trinity in the Stone-Campbell Movement: Historical/Theological Analysis and Constructive Proposal," written at Southern Methodist University. It has been modified for the church, having been originally written to complete academic requirements. I hope it now successfully adheres to the standards of academic rigor while also being of substantial benefit to those SCM leaders who want to understand how Trinitarian doctrine may enhance the church's ministry.

[3] Alexander Campbell, *The Christian Baptist*, 333. The page numbers used throughout this work for references to *The Christian Baptist* are from the 1835 single volume version of the journal edited by D. S. Burnet.

[4] Of course, the anti-speculation mindset seen among Restorationists, their predecessors, and their contemporaries has a notable heritage, being seen both among the Reformers—especially Calvin—and in the continuum that runs through Bacon and Locke. Nonetheless, it is interesting that this aversion to speculation beyond what can be said to be "known" from the "facts" can lead those holding such a position to radically different conclusions about the Trinity. Calvin wanted his theology to adhere to biblical language and biblical "facts" (although I am not sure he would put it quite like that), and yet his Trinitarian thoughts and language are in line with traditional Trinitarianism. Campbell's desire to stick with the "facts" of revelation as found in Scripture moves him to denigrate traditional Trinitarian language. Calvin and Campbell may both wish to reject "speculation," but their ways of carrying out this principle of doing theology drastically diverge, as seen in their conclusions concerning the usefulness of traditional Trinitarian categories. Calvin rejects speculative, scholastic questions like "What is God?" (the roots of an anti-speculative bent can be seen in his rejection of such a question; in this sense he is the antecedent of Bacon and Locke) but accepts the traditional depiction of the Trinity as cohering to answer the question, "Who is the God that is revealed?" However, Campbell views even traditional Trinitarian language as speculative, as there is no direct, explicitly stated antecedent in Scripture.

[5] Anyone familiar with the roots of the SCM will note the absence of Walter Scott from the list of early Restorationists whose Trinitarian thoughts are being investigated here. Scott, as much as any of the progenitors of the SCM, singled out one Person within the divine Trinity when he chose to write at length on the Holy Spirit; other than this, he made no substantial contribution to SC Trinitarian thought. This aspect of his contribution to early SC theology has received attention from historical theologians and

so does not require treatment here. Scott's focus on the Spirit was substantially free from many of the questions of traditional Trinitarian theology.

⁶E.g., see *International Standard Bible Encyclopedia*, s.v. "Trinity"; *New International Dictionary of the Christian Church*, rev. ed., s.v. "Trinity"; Jaroslav Pelikan, *Emergence of the Catholic Tradition*, 172–225; Justo Gonzalez, *From the Beginnings*, 1:268–343. Edward R. Hardy, *Christology of the Later Fathers*, 15–38; Alistair McGrath, *Understanding the Trinity*; William G. Rusch, *Trinitarian Controversy*, 8–30.

⁷Joe R. Jones, *A Grammar of Christian Faith*.
⁸Ibid., 150, 182ff.
⁹Ibid., 181–82.
¹⁰Ibid., 187.
¹¹Ibid., 182.
¹²Ibid., 191.
¹³Ibid., 192.
¹⁴Ibid., 193.
¹⁵Ibid., 194–96.
¹⁶See *Grammar*, 204–15 for Jones's discussion of essence and actuality.

2

The Trinity among the Early Disciples
THOMAS AND ALEXANDER CAMPBELL

Historians of the SCM universally recognize that Thomas Campbell, Alexander Campbell, Walter Scott (1796–1861), and Barton Stone are the four major architects of early SCM thought. The Campbells and Scott initiated both the unity efforts and the trademark primitivistic restoration of the ancient order that became synonymous with the early "Disciples" side of the SCM . Thomas Campbell's *Declaration and Address*[1] provided their constitutional foundation and set forth the basic features of their anticreedal, primitivistic plea for unity. Alexander Campbell's journals *The Christian Baptist*[2] and *The Millennial Harbinger*,[3] along with works such as *The Christian System*[4] and *Christian Baptism, with Its Antecedents and Consequents*,[5] expanded the influence of the SCM and established its central tenets regarding doctrine, polity, epistemology, hermeneutical style, and ecclesiological practice. Walter Scott, mainly through his itinerant preaching and contributions in Alexander Campbell's journals, disseminated what the three regarded as the Movement's central message—the ancient gospel restored.[6] With time, Alexander Campbell's voice became the most authoritative of the three, and his preaching, debating, authorship, and journal editing did more to solidify Restorationists into a movement than did any other influence. Campbell's application of biblical primitivism and his opinions and teaching on various doctrines and theological topics became decisive as the Movement grew.

Meanwhile, followers of Barton Stone, a leader among renegade Presbyterians, were finding a voice they could trust in his preaching; the journals he edited, such as *The Christian Messenger*;[7] and the pamphlets he published, including *The Last Will and Testament of the Springfield Presbytery*[8] and *An Address to the Christian Churches*.[9] Among those early SCM leaders, Stone felt the most compelled to address the topic of Trinitarian theology. While SCM adherents largely avoided the Trinitarian debates that were taking place on the American frontier in the first half of the nineteenth century, Stone addressed the doctrine of the Trinity with some frequency, especially prior to the 1832 union between the Stone and Campbell camps. If an explicitly stated non-Trinitarian impulse is present anywhere among early Restorationists, vis à vis an avoidance and intentional silence on the subject, it is present with Barton Stone.

Subsequent theologians, preachers, and teachers often looked to these four for assistance in determining their own doctrinal positions and, therefore, in determining the theological direction of what became the SCM. Not that later SC writers and thinkers were apt either first to look to the positions of others for their dogma—their inherently primitivistic perspective caused them first to look to Scripture and the example of the early church—or to write prolifically about the Trinity, Christology, or any number of theological issues. They typically viewed discussion of such matters as tending toward speculation. But when doctrinal matters arose or when their thoughts turned toward topics typically treated in classical theology, the approaches and opinions of the Campbells, Scott, and Stone often served as the fertile soil in which the thoughts of later Restorationists germinated and grew. For this reason, Chapters Two and Three will address Trinitarian doctrine as discussed within the writings of three of these four early leaders. The remainder of Chapter Two will address Trinitarian thought within the writings of Thomas and Alexander Campbell; Chapter Three will focus on Barton Stone.[10]

Thomas Campbell (1763-1854)

Thomas Campbell was nurtured in a religious world that was experiencing significant upheaval. His family was affiliated with the Church of Ireland, which at the end of the eighteenth century evinced its traditional heritage in Anglicanism but also included characteristics of the pietistic and evangelical renewal associated with the Wesleys, Whitefield, and the growing movement of the Dissenters. Although it is historically inaccurate to ignore the differences in definition, origin, and affiliation of the groups associated with the designations Methodism, Independency, Dissent, and Latitudinarianism,[11] they each were generally concerned with reform, with de-emphasizing the formalities and institutionalism of the traditional state-affiliated denominational bodies, and with emphasizing the needs for genuine conversion and the experience of personal forgiveness through the gospel of Christ. Many were beginning to think of the long-standing hierarchies and extensively developed polities and creeds as unnecessary encumbrances, believing identification with such structures was secondary to individual faith and piety. The number of Independents was on the rise, with many of the leaders, preachers, and teachers of dissent, having first been ordained by the Church of Ireland, choosing to leave traditional Anglicanism for something they considered more biblically oriented.[12]

Thomas Campbell and his brothers Archibald and James made their first ecclesiastical move laterally from the Church of Ireland to Irish Antiburgher Seceder Presbyterianism and the Synod of Ulster. Their father, Archibald, who had left Roman Catholicism for the Church of Ireland as a younger man, remained an Anglican the rest of his life, dying in that communion at age eighty-eight.[13] Thus, for his first twenty-six years, Thomas shared with his family a commitment to the *Thirty-Nine Articles* of Anglicanism, including the statements found there that referenced its traditional Trinitarianism.[14] Following his move to Presbyterianism, he completed in 1792 undergraduate work at the University of Glasgow (without taking a degree), and then, over five summers, he completed ministerial training at the Anti-burgher Seceder seminary at Whitburn, Scotland, being ordained in 1798.¹⁵ As a licensed pastor among the Anti-burgher Seceder Presbyterians, Campbell subscribed to the Westminster Confession of Faith, including its provisions for a Trinitarian perspective.¹⁶ He labored among the Anti-burgher Seceder Presbyterians for ten years, first in Ireland and then, for about a year in the United States.

As will be seen in Chapter Four, during his time as an Anglican and a Presbyterian, Thomas Campbell was afforded significant exposure to reform movements that included anti-Trinitarian perspectives. In addition to the general sense of Latitudinarianism present among Presbyterians and the Church of Ireland, there was a significant openness to reform in the counties of Armagh and Down, where Thomas Campbell spent the majority of his early years and served as a Presbyterian pastor. Methodists, Dissenters, and Independents frequently were found preaching in Ulster, and Thomas made direct contact with some of these.¹⁷ As his own attitudes progressed, Thomas was centered enough upon reform and the promotion of nonsectarian Christianity that even prior to his immigration to the United States he participated in remonstrances among the Anti-burgher Seceder Presbyterians, being formally commissioned by the Synod of Ulster in 1804 to work toward the unity of Burgher and Anti-burgher Seceder Presbyterians in Ireland and Scotland. Alexander Campbell says of his father: "in Europe he had been, for many years, an advocate of reformation in the Secession Church standards and proceedings, as well as in their lives and behavior."¹⁸ In addition, he had:

> formed a largely extended acquaintance with the onward movements of the General Assembly of [the Anti-burgher Presbyterians] both in Scotland and Ireland, he sympathized with these movements. . . . He had, indeed, outside of his own Church and Presbytery, many highly influential friends and brethren who cordially sympathized with his views of reform, both in doctrine and discipline.¹⁹

Given the general religious climate of the day and his contacts and work as a reformer among the Irish and Scottish Presbyterians, it is not surprising that Thomas Campbell would eventually travel away from formal denominationalism and into extensive Latitudinarianism. However, it would be a mistake to think he would automatically accept the additional move made by many Latitudinarians who rejected a Trinitarian position in favor of what eventually became Unitarianism.

Lifelong Trinitarianism

There is significant evidence that Thomas Campbell's belief in the Trinity, stated in traditional language, was maintained throughout his life. First, Thomas Campbell's ordination and standing in the Irish Anti-burgher Seceder Presbyterian Church required him to accept the Westminster Confession of Faith, and, unlike with Barton Stone, there is no record that Thomas Campbell then hesitated concerning any points of the Confession.[20]

Second, and more telling, is what Alexander Campbell says when describing how Thomas had for many years before coming to the United States been an advocate in Ireland and Scotland of reformation within the Secession branch of the Presbyterian Church. He writes of his father:

> He objected not so much to the doctrines of the Secession creed and platform, as a doctrinal basis, but to the assumption of any formula of religious theories or opinions, as the foundation of the Church of Christ; alleging that the holy Scriptures, Divinely inspired, were all-sufficient for all the purposes contemplated by the Author . . . But in advocating the paramount claims of the Bible, and especially the all-sufficiency and alone sufficiency of the Christian Scriptures for the edification and perfection of the Christian Church, he was compelled to remonstrate against "the doctrines and commandments of men," as having usurped, more or less, in all the Protestant forms of the Christian profession, and undue and unconstitutional influence and authority; in many instances making void the teachings and the preachings of the divinely commissioned apostles and evangelists of Jesus Christ.[21]

Then, after Thomas Campbell's immigration to the United States, in a letter of protest and appeal before the Associate Synod of North America to his censure by the Presbytery of Chartiers of Washington County, Pennsylvania, Thomas Campbell wrote:

> I dare not venture to trust my own understanding so far as to take upon me to teach anything as a matter of faith or duty but what is already expressly taught and enjoined by Divine authority; and I hope it is no presumption to believe that in saying and doing the very same things that are said and done before our eyes on the sacred page, is infallibly right, as well as all-sufficient for the edification of the Church, whose duty and perfection it is to be in all things conformed to the original standard. It is, therefore, because I have no confidence, either in my own infallibility or in that of others, that I absolutely refuse, as inadmissible and schismatic, the introduction of human opinions and human inventions into the faith and worship of the Church.[22]

The point of the above two quotations, taken together, is to demonstrate that although Thomas Campbell disagreed with the legitimacy of constructing and using a creedal confession or any other humanly constructed summation of a doctrinal position as a standard for belief and practice, during the time he was Presbyterian *he did not necessarily disagree with the content* of the Westminster Confession of Faith. It is, therefore, not surprising he would continue to be essentially orthodox Trinitarian in belief, because "He objected not so much to the *doctrines* [emphasis added] of the Secession creed and platform, as a doctrinal basis."

Further, in the asterisked note at the bottom of page sixteen of *Memoirs of Elder Thomas Campbell*, Alexander Campbell writes that at the time of Thomas Campbell's censure by the Associated Synod of North America, in 1808, "and long after, Father Campbell was as sound a Calvinist as any man I then knew in Scotland or Ireland; as strong in that system as the most orthodox in the Presbyterian Church."

Such adherence to Calvinism would, of course, include belief in the Trinity in line with the Westminster Confession of Faith, even if Thomas Campbell repudiated the creedal authority of the Confession or the existence of creeds. Lester McAllister offers a summary of the charges brought against Thomas Campbell by the Presbyterian Associated Synod of North America.[23] They accused him of several non-Calvinist improprieties: (1) "occasional hearing," which apparently means not only that he was open to hearing the preaching of Independents but that he did on occasion go listen to such non-Calvinist preaching; (2) offering the Lord's Supper to non-Seceder Presbyterians; (3) moving away from a Calvinistic, Holy Spirit-authored "conversion experience"; and (4) encouraging ruling elders to gather the people, read Scripture, and pray in the absence of ordained clergy. Among these charges put forth by a group clearly trying to do their punctilious utmost to level charges, there is no mention of any concerns regarding Thomas Campbell's Trinitarian theology, or lack thereof. It is reasonable, then, to conclude that Thomas Campbell was still at that point traditionally Trinitarian in his belief.

If evidence from his early life makes it clear that Thomas Campbell was an orthodox Trinitarian, there is evidence that near the close of life, despite all he had done to disparage the use of creedal formulations and nonbiblical language when formulating Christian doctrine, he was still willing to define the nature of deity using some of the traditional language he had accepted as a young Anglican and Presbyterian. Thomas Campbell's farewell address of 1851 in the Bethany Meeting-House, when he was 88 years-old, indicates his apparent lifelong acceptance of the doctrine of the Trinity:

> How rich and precious are these promises of our blessed Lord! But, my brethren, why should we doubt, since we already have the greatest gift—even the Holy Spirit—the Comforter, or Advocate, whom our blessed Savior promised he would send to abide with his disciples forever. And this is "the earnest of our inheritance," given to us who believe in Christ, "in whom, also" says the Apostle Paul, "after that ye believed, ye were sealed with that Holy Spirit of promise, which is the earnest of our inheritance until the redemption of the purchased possession, unto the praise of his glory;" and again, "Know ye not that ye are the temple of God, and that the Spirit of God dwelleth in you?" Thus, my brethren, we are thoroughly furnished unto every good word and work. God our heavenly Father, hath not withholden from us even his Holy Spirit, a part of the Trinity in Unity; so that Father, Son, and Holy Spirit, are all graciously and mercifully united in providing, procuring, and effecting our salvation.

> The Holy Spirit, by the law and the prophets, puts us into possession of the salvation provided for us by the Father, in sending his well-beloved and only begotten Son into the world, to die for our sins. It is through the Spirit that we have been furnished with this Divine illumination, and from it alone have we derived all definite and reliable knowledge of the adorable character and attributes of our Creator, of our duties to him, and our own future and everlasting destiny.[24]

Particularly telling are Alexander Campbell's supportive comments in response to his father's message, likely made in direct response to the fact that his father had used the word "Trinity," which may have been as surprising to Alexander as it is to a modern reader of early Restorationists. As part of reflections on the happiness and blessed fellowship that may be anticipated of heaven because of the nature of the God who had watched over the life and ministry of his father for over 60 years, the son says,

> Without *society*, according to all our most vivid conceptions of happiness, there is no such thing. Hence, in the godhead, in JEHOVAH ELOHIM, there must essentially be a plurality of personalities. This is the loftiest and the most aggrandizing theme within the whole circle of human reason, or of human imagination. It is the mightiest, the grandest, and the most aggrandizing theme in creation's broadest, loftiest, and most profound conception. Hence, in harmony with this conception, we are divinely taught, that there are three distinct personalities in Jehovah: THE FATHER, THE WORD, AND THE HOLY SPIRIT. These three are, and these three alone constitute, Jehovah.[25]

Such language is significant. By the time *Memoirs of the Elder Thomas Campbell* was published in 1861, ten years after Thomas's *Farewell Discourse*, Alexander Campbell had been intentionally avoiding nonbiblical language and speculative theological doctrinal conceptions for about fifty years. But this does not prevent him here from using language such as "in the godhead, in JEHOVAH ELOHIM, there must essentially be a plurality of personalities," "there are three distinct personalities in Jehovah," and "these three alone constitute, Jehovah." Aside from the names and titles and the King James language of "godhead," none of this is specifically biblical language directly quoted from biblical statements about the Three.[26] Most striking of all is that Alexander Campbell specifically says that the notion of "a plurality of personalities" and "three distinct personalities in Jehovah" is "divinely taught."

Although we may wonder at exactly what Alexander means by "divinely taught," the whole course of Alexander Campbell's theology, and that of his father, leads to the conclusion that he could only mean by this that *Scripture* taught these very concepts, including the idea that "These three are, and these three alone constitute Jehovah." This passage will be examined further in the next section focusing on Alexander Campbell, but here it should be said that, although Alexander seems to be admitting his own concession regarding nonbiblical language when he uses the words "human reason, or of human imagination," he also seems convinced of and is comfortable with his father's Trinitarian stance, even using his father's reference to the Trinity to make his own theological point. This is most likely because at this point in his life Alexander believed the language of "godhead" in English translations biblically authorized the use of such language in reference to God, allowing him to write as he does of God's influence on the communal aspect of the church. He further believed that "plurality of personalities," "there are three distinct personalities in Jehovah," and "these three alone constitute, Jehovah" were statements in line with biblical teaching. If he failed to see biblical justification for writing in this way, it is difficult to imagine him doing so, given the whole tenor of his theological life. Clearly father and son felt the freedom to apply nonbiblical language in at least one area of Christian doctrine, no doubt because they believed such language was orthodox, cohering with the witness of the Bible.

Writings on the Trinity

It is important to analyze further what Thomas Campbell did actually write with respect to the Trinity. In the above quote from his *Farewell Discourse*, he mentions the soteriological impact of the Father, Son, and Spirit and specifically mentions the "Trinity" in identifying how the three work in salvation. This is, of course, in the context of his remarks about the Holy Spirit, and it is interesting that this former Calvinist feels free to use extrabiblical soteriological language like "Divine illumination" in describing the work of the Spirit. Thomas is here "doing theology," specifically in the area of soteriology, applying the doctrine of the Trinity to a major theme within systematic theology.

On August 31, 1816, Thomas read a statement he had prepared regarding his perspective on the Trinity before a meeting of the Redstone Baptist Association, at Cross Creek, Brooke County, Virginia (an area that would become West Virginia). Lester McAllister indicates that Campbell was assigned this topic because "the Baptist preachers were very anxious to hear what the Campbells had to say on this subject."[27] It is likely that the Redstone Baptist Association was wanting to know if the brand of Latitudinarianism or Independency espoused by the Campbells was Trinitarianly orthodox. As will be discussed more in Chapter Four, the fact that the Campbells had come out of Presbyterianism would perhaps have done little to calm the fears of the Redstone Baptist Association concerning the orthodoxy of their Trinitarianism, even if they knew that the Campbells were not *English* Presbyterians.

The Circular Letter of 1816. Only sixteen pages in length, this letter is as lengthy and comprehensive a statement of a Trinitarian position as one finds within the early SCM. It was first published as part of a larger work in Appendix A in Robert Richardson's *Memoirs of Alexander Campbell*.[28] Of course, for SC historians, the 1816 meeting of the Redstone Baptist Association is most famous for Alexander Campbell's presentation of his *Sermon on the Law*, later published in *The Millennial Harbinger*.[29] But for the purposes of this book, Richardson's record of Thomas Campbell's part of the meeting is most interesting. In recording a list of actions that occurred at the meeting, Richardson says the "circular letter prepared by brother T. Campbell was read and accepted without amendment."[30] He goes on to say:

> It appears, further, that Thomas Campbell presented, on this occasion, the circular letter which he had been appointed to prepare at the meeting the year before. The subject given to him was the "TRINITY," upon which the Baptist preachers were very anxious to elicit the views entertained by the reformers. This circular letter, it seems, was so entirely satisfactory that even the

keen vision of the most orthodox enemies in the Association could find no ground of objection, and it was accordingly accepted, we are told, "without amendment," and printed at the close of the minutes as the letter of the Association. . . . [31]

As the circular letter above referred to presents the views of both [Thomas and Alexander] upon the most profound subject in the Bible, as it forms a part of the history of the times and of the persons described, and illustrates how entirely sufficient the Scriptures themselves are for the elucidation of the most difficult questions, so far as these can be at all comprehended by the human mind, it deserves to be rescued from the oblivion which would soon engulf the few remaining copies. It will therefore be found in the Appendix to the present volume.[32]

Robert Richardson's efforts, then, have preserved for SCM historians one of the key documents for assessing the early Restorationists' perspectives on the Trinity, giving us a text, the historical context of its writing, and some assessment of its significance from one intimately familiar with its author and the circumstances under which it was written. Richardson's own view of the writing is interesting in that he clearly is apologetic on Thomas Campbell's behalf for Campbell's use of traditional, technical, nonbiblical language in stating his Trinitarian views:

In it, this profound subject is treated in a highly interesting manner, and mainly in the simple and express terms of Scripture. In condescension, however, probably to the modes of thought and speech current amongst the party with which he was now associated, the author employs some of the terms of scholastic divinity, such as essence, triune and person, but the word "Trinity" does not once occur in the document. The use of such terms was not in harmony with the principle of the Reformation, which required that Bible things should be spoken of in Bible words—not in "the words that man's wisdom teacheth," but in those which the Holy Spirit has employed. Under the circumstances, however, it gives evidence of a remarkable advance toward soundness of speech on the part of one long accustomed to the language of the schools, and who now addressed a people to whom its terms would have been much more familiar, and doubtless much more acceptable, than those employed in Holy Writ.[33]

Implicit in Richardson's comments is the rejection on his part of "the terms of scholastic divinity" and a preference for the "simple and express terms of Scripture." He clearly believes Thomas Campbell's use of traditional Trinitarian language is an accommodation and a departure from what Richardson would wish to have used, making it clear that the use of such language violated one of the cardinal principles of Restorationism—that only biblical language should be used with reference to biblical doctrine. Hence his pains to point out that Campbell did not use the word "Trinity."

What is significant here is that Campbell was actually willing to make such concessions and to make them in the manner in which he did. He was willing to compromise on the vocabulary used to present his position, choosing to use traditional Trinitarian language that he clearly believed was appropriate. This is telling. The entire tenor of Thomas Campbell's approach to theology, hermeneutics, and restoration would necessitate that he entertain only theological positions he believed to be entirely biblical. In fact, he preferred to state his positions using the plain language of the Bible. Wishing to enter into fellowship with the Redstone Baptist Association, Campbell used the language he thought most appropriate and efficacious under the circumstances, but he also used language that represented the position *he believed to be in line with biblical doctrine.* Certainly, if Thomas Campbell thought the traditional language he used in the *Circular Letter* was inconsistent with the teaching of Scripture, he would have chosen other words to express his view.

Telling, also, is Richardson's comment that the letter presents the views of both Thomas and Alexander "upon the most profound subject in the Bible." Robert Richardson was Alexander Campbell's dear friend and biographer, and he clearly took the *Circular Letter* of 1816 to be an accurate statement of what *Alexander* Campbell also believed with respect to the Trinity. In conveying their doctrinal beliefs, neither father nor son wished to use language other than that specifically used in the Bible, but in this case, rather than just passing such language off as speculative, both Campbells, according to Richardson, believed such language accurately depicted a biblical position about the Trinity. Traditional Trinitarian language, then, was not *mistaken* in what it expressed of Trinitarian doctrine, it was simply not language directly discernible among the pages of the Bible, and therefore, was typically not acceptable for Restorationists to use in discussing the Trinitarian nature of God.

Thomas Campbell's piece on the Trinity employs a very large percentage of traditional, creedal, nonbiblical language and argument to define his position. His classically Trinitarian discussion about inherent plurality in *elohim*, and his use of "intelligent agent," "subsistence," "nature," "divine nature," "same common nature," "individual essence," "being," "divine nature," "tri-theism," "essentiality," "essential relations," "co-existence," "economy of salvation," "mutual essential relation," "relative subordination," "divine energy," and "efficient will" are striking. Additionally, he gives consideration to the appropriateness of using πρόσωπον/*persona* to describe the three individualities, finally asserting, in line with ancient usage, its use as acceptable. This is an oft-repeated discussion among Trinitarians, going back to the fourth century, which has also found a place in Trinitarian discussion during the last few decades.[34] One finds here a discussion about the economical versus essential character of the Trinity, an issue on which, of course, the Scriptures say nothing. Campbell also defends the view that refuses to accept that Christ is a "creature," an obvious allusion to Arianism, and his view on the interaction of the three persons in revealing and working includes the concepts that stand behind the technical terms "appropriation" and *perichoresis*, although he uses neither term. Campbell specifically argues for the Spirit deriving from both Father and Son, an obvious reference to the *filioque* controversy, a subject on which he takes a typically Western stance. Referring to Trinitarian errors, he describes and rejects both Modalism and Tri-theism, speaks against those who deny relative subordination, and says he wants nothing to do with talking of the "eternal generation of the Son, and procession of the Holy Ghost [although he has already essentially argued in favour of *filioque*]; nor yet with that semi-Arian doctrine about the pre-existence of the human soul of the Redeemer, before the creation of the world; nor with any such vain speculations."[35]

Further, Thomas's brief paper includes a description of the "Spirit of wisdom and revelation" as Jehovah; an ascription of divine works to Father, Son, and Spirit; a discussion of and acceptance of the "real internal essential relations" in the Godhead vis-à-vis the economic Trinity; and a specific rejection of Unitarianism. Campbell does express a kind of relative subordinationism, but he immediately follows these comments by identifying the Father, Son, and Spirit as sharing the same nature and essence.[36] Although he is apparently careful to make no reference to accepting ancient creedal statements, Thomas Campbell presents himself as being fully Trinitarian in orientation, and on page 550 he specifically dissociates himself from Arianism, accepting a position that conforms to Nicea, even if he refuses to use ὁμοούσιος.[37]

What we have seen, then, is that in 1816, in the context of a Baptist conference interested in the Campbells' orthodoxy, Thomas Campbell is compelled to use the *speculative language* that many of a Latitudinarian ilk had by now been denigrating for over a century. While he does not directly refer to other authors, it seems as if Campbell had in front of him a classic statement of Trinitarian issues in current and ancient theology, and he simply addresses them one by one, frequently using the Trinitarian jargon of his predecessors. In fact, the evidence in the *Circular Letter* points toward Thomas Campbell being quite classically Trinitarian—which might be expected of a former Anglican turned Presbyterian—one who finds the biblical position to coincide with the classical Trinitarianism he learned as a young man, and he is not afraid to use such Trinitarian language, despite the general Latitudinarian tenor of his theological perspective.[38]

As was mentioned in Chapter One, the early Restorationists were not simple, uneducated, backwoods amateur theologians unfamiliar with rigorous theology. Thomas Campbell was academically trained, familiar with the classics and the classical languages. He was well-versed in the philosophies of John Locke and Thomas Reid. The Anglicanism and Presbyterianism of his early years, including his acceptance of the Westminster Confession of Faith, put him in a position to understand well the language, history, and argumentation that characterized Trinitarian theology both before and during his theological career. Trinitarian doctrine was of special interest to Presbyterians of all stripes in England, Ireland, and Scotland during Thomas Campbell's training in Scotland and his ministry in Ireland. The language of traditional Trinitarian theological argumentation in the *Circular Letter* was very familiar territory for him, and he no doubt had embraced just such language when as a younger man he worked to forge his own theological stance.

Prospectus of a Religious Reformation. In Thomas Campbell's *Prospectus of a Religious reformation; The object of which is The restoration of primitive apostolic christianity in letter and spirit—in principle and practice* (1829), there is a brief section entitled ANALYSIS OF THE GREAT SALVATION, in which Campbell simply writes:

> *First of its concurring causes.* 1. The prime moving or designing cause—the love of God. 2. The procuring cause—the blood of Christ. 3. The efficient cause—the Holy Spirit. 4. The instrumental cause—the Gospel and Law of Christ, or, the word of truth.[39]

The obvious Trinitarian way in which the *causes* of Christian salvation are listed here is significant for those interested in how much Thomas Campbell viewed the Trinity as decisive for other areas of Christian doctrine. Here the issue is soteriology, with Campbell listing in bullet form what he considers to be the divine bases for Christian salvation. Because the *Prospectus* is simply a brief outline and introductory description of the current "reformation," readers are left to wonder at how Thomas Campbell would have expounded on his bullet points. For example, did he think that the causal powers of each of the members of the Trinity were equal in significance in authoring salvation? As it is, one gets a sense here of a mild subordinationism in Campbell's statement of the primacy of the love of God as the "moving or designing cause." This expression in reference to God is, of course, so close to being Aristotelian that it is difficult to shed the impression that Campbell placed some sort of priority on "God" as "the prime moving or designing cause" in salvation, over the Son and Spirit.[40]

In addition, Campbell makes no specific effort here to separate what he considers the instrumental cause of salvation—"the Gospel and Law of Christ, or, the word of truth"—from the causal force directly linked to the members of the Trinity. While it is inappropriate to make too much of such a brief reference, it is nonetheless interesting that Campbell gives "Gospel and Law of Christ, or, the word of truth" a place similar to the one he gives to the Trinitarian causes of salvation. This is striking. Does this represent a devaluing of Trinity by Campbell, or is this an almost Barthian-like "super-valuing" of the proclaimed gospel and word? Or, are both in some sense the case? At the very least, Thomas Campbell did not automatically think he necessarily needed to place the soteriological, causal power of the Trinity above and separate from every other source of salvation. And, since it is unlikely that gospel and word and the notion of proclamation in Campbell's soteriology would approach the role they play in Barth's theology, one could say the Trinity is actually de-valued by Campbell compared to those whose theologies are inherently and intentionally Trinitarianly centered. This being the case, there is something that early Restorationists like Thomas Campbell could have learned from Karl Barth.

Millennial Harbinger articles. It is in a series of three articles Thomas Campbell published in the *Millennial Harbinger* in 1839 that we find him at his Trinitarian best, not just explicating the Trinity *per se*, as in the *Circular Letter* of 1816, but applying Trinitarian theology to life in the Christian church.[41] As he begins the first essay, Thomas describes his task in terms of helping his readers understand the life of holiness, but in doing so, he uses language that echoes the standard categories of classic systematic theology, saying:

> We should distinctly and duly consider their moral and religious documents, that by a distinct and intelligent apprehension of these, we might be duly furnished for a life of holiness. Now *these*, we presume, may be evidently reduced to the following topics, viz.—1st. The knowledge of God. 2d. Of man. 3d. Of sin. 4th. Of the Saviour. 5th. Of his salvation. 6th. Of the principle and means of enjoying it. 7th. Of its blissful effects and consequences. That *these* are the grand comprehensive doctrinal topics, which the scriptures were specially designed to teach; and that in the knowledge, belief, and practical influence of

these consists our present salvation, is evident both from the express contents of the Book, and also from the explicit intention of the salvation it exhibits; which is to turn men to God, and thus to fit them for heaven."[42]

In the remainder of the essay, Thomas expands on the need for faithful Christians to develop "a more perfect knowledge of these all-important topics," including, "the essential properties of his nature, viz.—His knowledge, power, wisdom, goodness; justice, truth, holiness; love, mercy, and condescension;—his self-existence, independence, eternity, immensity, and immutability."[43]

Again, these divine traits, especially the latter five in the list, sound more like attributes and characteristics of the divine nature as established by systematic theologians reflecting on Scripture than they do exegetical results. He further alludes to being "engaged in learning and contemplating the divine character," and says that as Christians, "we should not only make it our solemn intention and constant practice to search the scriptures daily, to ascertain the amount of the instruction they afford, upon each of the aforesaid topics; but we should also exercise ourselves unto godliness in frequent meditation and religious conversation on those all-important subjects."[44]

Is it going too far to say that to "exercise ourselves" in "frequent meditation and religious conversation on those all-important subjects" intimates systematic theology? Perhaps. But if he not only used the categories of classical systematic theology for delineating life in the church but also turned to the epitome of systematic themes—the concept of the Trinity—as a theological guidepost, it would not be surprising if Thomas was in fact influenced by his reading of some unnamed systematician or by his theological training. In the remainder of the series, Thomas does just exactly this, exemplifying the application of Trinitarian theology to life in the church.

First, in the second essay, Thomas discusses the bases for Christian holiness, but here he grounds it not in obedience to individual propositions, but in the "constraining influence of the love of God the Father, and of Christ, and of the Holy Spirit."[45] For Thomas this is: "the New Covenant relation in which we stand to God as our Father-to Christ as our Redeemer, our Lord and Saviour—and to the Holy Spirit as the immediate Author of our spiritual life; and of our salvation from under the deadly influence and dominion of sin."[46]

This is nothing less than Trinitarian theology being applied to the sanctified life.

Second, Thomas not only identifies the work of the Son as the instrumental means for the relationship human beings have with God, but also indicates the relationship between Father and Son is the pattern for that relationship, so that the Trinitarian connection between Father and Son becomes for us the source and prototype of our own relationship with God. Our relationship with God is thoroughly christologically grounded. Loving, obeying, and honoring the Son means loving, obeying, and honoring the Father. At this point, Thomas's specific language is quite striking. He briefly comments on his suggestion that there is to be mutual love for Father and Son and rhetorically wonders if there is a conflict or "embarrassment" in the fact that our love and obedience would be directed to both divine persons. His conclusion, of course, is that this is no embarrassment—but, note his language: "Nor is there any embarrassing difficulty in adjusting those distinct claims of supreme and infinite obligation; for the economical and essential unity of the divine claimants completely obviate this: for he who loves, honors, and obeys the Son, in so doing honors and obeys the Father who sent him."[47]

The justification that permits mutual love and obedience from human respondents to be directed equally at both Father and Son is the *"economical and essential unity of the divine claimants"* for that love and obedience! It would be difficult for Thomas to more clearly express his dependency upon the kinds of discussions that interest systematic theologians, both in the middle of the nineteenth century and at the beginning of the twenty-first. Οἰκονομία notwithstanding, one will be hard pressed to find in the New Testament delineated discussion of the economic and essential, or economic and immanent, Trinity. I find Thomas's language here to be theologically accurate and immensely interesting, but on this point he is far from simply calling Bible things by Bible names. The man who could be described as the chief initiator of the SC plea for biblical primitivism at this point is engaging in nothing short of *classical systematic Trinitarian theology.*

If the reference to the economic and essential Trinity were not enough, Thomas proceeds in the very next point in the third essay to discuss the third person of the Trinity, and to again do so in poignantly *systematic* fashion. Thomas says:

> Nor is our devotion and submission to the Holy Spirit, in his official dictations by the holy Apostles and Prophets, (who all spoke as they were moved by him,) less imperative and obligatory; or less consistent with our supreme love and absolute devotion to the Father, and to the Son, for he proceeds from both; being the authoritative messenger and efficient agent of both;—our divine Regenerator, Tutor, and immediate Advocate; so that whoever rejects or blasphemes him in the execution of his new covenant office, rejects both the Father and the Son; and, of course—the enjoyment of the great salvation which they have provided.[48]

It is noteworthy that in referring to the obligatory life of the believer now devoted to the Spirit, Thomas sees the necessary response of Christians to the Spirit to be no "less imperative and obligatory; or less consistent with our supreme love and absolute devotion to the Father, and to the Son...." This is a direct application of Trinitarian theology to the pneumatological presence in the life of the church. But what is even more striking is Thomas's justification for the mutual devotion that should be directed to the Spirit, "*for he proceeds from both; being the authoritative messenger and efficient agent of both.*" Just as in the *Circular Letter,* Thomas has applied the language of traditional, classical Trinitarian discussion, typically associated with discussion of *filioque,* taking a stance in line with the western church. These three essays were published in the *Millennial Harbinger* twenty-three years after Thomas appeared before the Redstone Baptist Association; during this period, his willingness to openly use traditional Trinitarian language—*and to be classically Trinitarian*—seems not to have diminished.

Third, Thomas Campbell offers a summation of what he considers "the great fundamental truths of the gospel," in which he includes specific mention of each person of the Trinity, saying that our devotion consists in nothing but:

> the grave, serious, and sober effect, of the due scriptural conviction and consideration of the great fundamental truths of the gospel; namely, the love of the Father, the grace of the Son, the remission of sins, the adoption of sons, the fellowship of the Spirit, the glorious resurrection, and the blissful immortality, which the blessed gospel presents to our faith and to our hope.[49]

These words are interesting on two grounds: (1) Campbell is clearly summarizing and prioritizing what he takes to be the heart of Christianity and its theological center, purposefully and intentionally including the Trinity in this summation. That he specifically mentions each Person of the Trinity near the end of the *Millennial Harbinger* articles affirms that he intended to give the concept of the Trinity a central role throughout these submissions. (2) In this brief summary of the gospel, there is a kind of soteriological or even chronological ordering of the benefits received from God, so that we first experience the Father's love, which manifests itself in the grace of the Son, leading to the remission of sins and our adoption as sons, whereby we enter into the fellowship of the Spirit, leading to our glorious resurrection, and, ultimately, our blissful immortality. Again, he intentionally works the Trinitarian source of these benefits into the listing of what God has done on behalf of humankind when no scriptural precedent forces him to do so; he is choosing to summarize the gospel's theological benefits to humankind by delineating the Trinity's central role in these benefits.

To briefly summarize, this explication of Thomas Campbell's Trinitarian position points toward him being largely orthodox in the classical sense. He likely maintained such a position from his earliest days as a member of the Church of Ireland, through his Presbyterian years, and into his many years as a founder and member of the Disciples of Christ, as demonstrated by the above selections, which stem from 1816, 1829, 1839, and 1851. Although he is a classically orthodox Trinitarian, Thomas Campbell seems to have subscribed to a mild subordinationism, but without in any way compromising the full deity of the Son. His position allowed him to use traditional language in describing the Trinity, apparently because he saw that language as coherent with biblical teaching.

Alexander Campbell (1788-1866)

Alexander Campbell's theological orientation was a product of his father's Latitudinarian thinking, the religious, theological, denominational context in which he was raised, and his combined experiences and study both in Glasgow in 1807–1808 and in the new world after he immigrated to the United States in 1809. This is not meant to minimize Alexander's own theological independence or his contribution to the framing of SC theology, both of which were extensive. His contribution to subsequent Restorationist thinking significantly outweighed that of his father or Barton Stone, particularly concerning Trinitarian doctrine. Although Chapter Four will provide additional detail to the factors that shaped Alexander's thoughts on the Trinity, here it should at least be remarked that Alexander Campbell was quite hesitant to write concerning the Trinity, viewing Trinitarian theology as a major contributor to disunity among Christians. Thus, Alexander Campbell was responsible for eventually reducing the amount of attention that other Restorationists, including Barton Stone, gave in written form to Trinitarian doctrine.

Alexander Campbell's Hesitantly Stated Trinitarianism

Because reference has been made earlier in this chapter to Alexander Campbell's response to Thomas Campbell's 1851 *Farewell Discourse,* we will begin by reiterating the points made there. In his *Discourse,* Thomas Campbell used the word "Trinity," saying all three persons of the Trinity have soteriological import. Rather than openly questioning his father's use of unbiblical language, as one might expect from his own personality and history, Alexander Campbell positively reflects on Thomas's comments, asserting the significance of Trinitarian community within "the godhead,"[50] and saying, "This is the loftiest and the most aggrandizing theme within the whole circle of human reason, or of human imagination. It is the mightiest, the grandest, and the most aggrandizing theme in creation's broadest, loftiest, and most profound conception."[51]

Clearly, whatever his apprehensions about using nonbiblical language, Alexander's theological affinities lay on the side of Trinitarian theology and Trinitarian community as he prescribes such a lofty place for Trinitarian reflection. It may be that in writing "human reason, or of human imagination"

Alexander is in his own mild way letting his readers know that his father's use of "Trinity" is a departure from the principle of using only divine, biblical language in relation to Christian doctrine; nonetheless, he proceeds to assert the significance of the "societal" aspect of Trinitarian theology. In fact, he makes a point concerning "society" within the Trinity that is comparable to that made by John Zizioulas and Miroslav Volf 150 years later.[52]

In addition, in responding to his father, Alexander uses the expressions "a plurality of personalities" and "three distinct personalities in Jehovah," saying such depictions of the godhead are "divinely taught."[53] Such descriptions use language that is absent from the biblical text, but Alexander freely makes a theological application with these. Given his history of arguing against just this kind of theologizing with nonbiblical language, how can Alexander Campbell allow himself such an "indiscretion"? First, he must have thought such language to be in line with biblical teaching or he simply would not have stooped to using it. Second, my sense is that 72- or 73-year-old Alexander is at this point—the publishing of the *Memoirs of the Elder Thomas Campbell* in 1861—simply recognizing after years of reflection the need to state clearly *the theological and biblical centrality of the triune nature of God*. Given its theological significance and the Bible's somewhat veiled way of speaking of the Trinity (in comparison with the plain clarity with which Scripture speaks of other prominent theological themes), Alexander Campbell chooses, with full understanding of the irony of what he is now doing, to relax his position and compromise his language at a place where he deems it most justified.

Response to "Timothy"

Eleven years after Thomas Campbell's *Circular Letter* of 1816, Alexander Campbell was asked by "Timothy" in *The Christian Baptist* about his views on "the Trinity," in light of a previous conversation about John 1:1.[54] In that conversation, Campbell had offered some comments concerning "the Word" with which those present "were much delighted." This question led to a response from Campbell[55] and then to an exchange between Alexander Campbell and Barton Stone on the pages of *The Christian Baptist* and Stone's *The Christian Messenger*. The "official" joining together of Campbell's "Disciples" and Stone's "Christians" did not occur until 1832, but they knew of each other and carried on public correspondence through their journals before that date. Fortuitously for those interested in early SC Trinitarianism, this short Trinitarian discussion between these two most significant early Restorationists was public and recorded, making it easily accessible. The series includes Campbell's original response to "Timothy" (*The Christian Baptist*, May 7, 1827, 333–335); Barton Stone's response to Campbell (*Christian Messenger*, July 1827, 204–209); Campbell's response to Stone (*The Christian Baptist*, October 1, 1827, 378–381); and Stone's second response to Campbell (*Christian Messenger*, November 1827, 6–13). Stone's contributions to the discussions will be treated in Chapter Three.

In response to Timothy, Alexander indicates his hesitation "to speculate on the incomprehensible Jehovah," which is not surprising, but then he also describes the nature of Trinitarian doctrine as "in common estimation so awfully sacred," that "if a man did not speak in a very fixed and set phrase on this subject, he endangered his whole Christian reputation and his own usefulness." He says that his aversion to speculating on the Trinity concerns the judgment that would come upon him from orthodox others were he to "depart even in one monosyllable from the orthodox views." He further says that he wished not to speculate on the Trinity:

> because, if I differed in the least from the orthodox, I introduced something like a new theory, or something that would be treated as such, and either approved or rejected on theoretic grounds. If, however, you will neither make a new theory out of my expositions, nor contend for any speculations on the subject, nor carry the views further than where I leave off, I will gratify you and other friends with my views of the first sentence in John's Preface to his Testimony.[56]

Prior to an exposition of Alexander's view of the Trinity as disclosed in *The Christian Baptist*, it must be noted that his hesitancy to speak on the Trinity derives first from his view of the Trinity as mystery and from the lack of definitive biblical language about the incomprehensible Triune One. He also hesitates because of how he predicts others will react to his thoughts, whether by judgmentally disagreeing or by making a new "system" out of his views. Campbell did not fear judgment from others or worry they would think poorly of him, but he was concerned about giving them an excuse to designate his new unity movement as another "ism" that would stand alongside Unitarianism, Socinianism, or any other "obnoxious ism" they would wish to name.

Alexander Campbell's response to "Timothy" in *The Christian Baptist* may serve as one example of his thoughts on the Trinity. It is significant that Campbell is initially willing to discuss the doctrine of the Trinity not so much as an isolated theological doctrine but in the course of presenting his thoughts on John 1:1.[57] It would appear that Timothy knew Campbell well enough to know he could not easily be convinced to violate his principles concerning speculative doctrine, but that being asked to provide an interpretation of John 1:1 was a different matter.

It is also notable that despite his unwillingness to be "speculative," as Campbell moves into the discussion his first two numbered points are more directly concerned with a critique of "Calvinistic doctrine of the Trinity" than with an exegesis or interpretation of John 1:1. In fact, although presented under the umbrella of an interpretation of John 1:1, both the numbered paragraphs and the balance of Campbell's remarks address Calvinism, Arianism, relationality, and the eternal nature of the immanent Trinity vis à vis the economic relations of Father and Son; and they include speculation concerning why God would choose λόγος to depict the eternal relationship between himself and his Word. Strikingly, it seems as if Alexander Campbell, similar to his father, could not help but participate in at least some provisional way in the types of doctrinal discussions he so vehemently denounced and attempted to avoid. Neither father nor son were able absolutely to avoid such discussions, perhaps not only because they needed to use the vocabulary of those around them, but also because *the Bible is not entirely silent when it comes to the Trinitarian nature of God.* Alexander says that he wishes only to "gratify [Timothy] and other friends with my views of the first sentence in John's Preface to his Testimony."[58] But, clearly, to share in the exegesis and interpretation of this Scripture *necessarily* meant that Campbell could not entirely refrain from discussing the Trinitarian ramifications offered by the Scripture. Alexander could not fully comment on John 1:1 and avoid what he saw as the obvious significance of this verse concerning the relationship between God and His Word, nor could he ignore what he saw as the conflict between John 1:1 and other Trinitarian views.

Although Alexander Campbell makes much of his unwillingness to speculate on God's Trinitarian character, he is drawn into the discussion out of a desire to "give him [Christ] more glory than the Calvinists give him," because in his view the Calvinist position places Christ as far below his real glory, depicted in John 1:1, as do the heretical views of the Arians and Socinians.[59] His concern is that when Calvinists call the Savior Jesus, Messiah, Only Begotten Son, or Son of God, they are actually expressing something about the Savior which is only the case *after* the Incarnation, without having said anything meaningful of his *pre-existence*. They improperly speak of the pre-existent relationship between Father and Son, when in actuality such a familial relationship did not exist prior to the birth of Jesus of Nazareth. Therefore, in speaking of an *eternal Son*, Calvinists are speaking incorrectly, since to speak of the pre-existent, eternal *Son* is to speak about a relationship that did not eternally exist.[60] He says:

> The names Jesus, Christ, or Messiah, Only Begotten Son, Son of God, belong to the Founder of the christian religion, and to no one else. They express not a relation existing before the christian era, but relations which commenced at that time. To understand the relation betwixt the Saviour and his Father, which existed before time, and that relation which began in time, is impossible on either of these theories.[61]

In addition, relational language used for created things, even language used to describe human relationships, is insufficient for describing "the original relation between God and the word of God."[62] "Created relation" stands apart from "uncreated relation," in the same way that creature stands apart from that which is uncreated.[63] Here Campbell is doing something more than just extrapolating the typical orthodox objection to Arianism—that it is improper to imply that the λόγος was at some point in time created—to the God/Word relation, although he is, indeed, also making that application. He is concerned that the Father/Son relation first takes place in time as a created relationship and is, therefore, not eternal, and is thus inadequate by itself to describe the eternal relation between God and Word. In addition, he argues that the relation between Father and Son bears the imprint of that which is created, in that "Father" and "Son" are terms of human relation accurately applied only after the Son had taken the form of created humanity. For Campbell:

> There was no Jesus, no Messiah, no Christ, no Son of God, no Only Begotten, before the reign of Augustus Cesar. The relation that was before the christian era, was not that of a son and a father, terms which always imply disparity; but it was that expressed by John in the sentence under consideration.[64]

To use only the language of human, creaturely relation (Father/Son; language that is entirely appropriate in describing the relation between God and λόγος after the Incarnation) to describe the eternal, pre-existing relation between God and the Word means a degradation, in that relation, of the eternal λόγος described in John 1:1.

This denial of the eternal, pre-existing Father-Son relationship clearly does not constitute for Alexander Campbell a denial of the eternal pre-existence of the second person of the Trinity or a denial of the eternal, spiritual relation between God and the Word. Exactly the opposite is the case, in that an adequate, fully biblical presentation of the pre-existence of the λόγος and His eternal relationship to God is what Alexander says he fails to see within Calvinism, causing him to reject Reformed Trinitarianism. For Alexander, the biblically defined relationship between the Savior and his Father, before the Incarnation, is one between God and the *Word* of God, a relation "quite different from that of a father and a *son*—a relationship perfectly intimate, equal, and glorious."[65] He places the "God and Father" in relation to the Savior anterior to the birth of Jesus, so that, Word and Savior may be considered with reference to a pre-Incarnational relationship to God which is "uncreated and unoriginated," even if the Father-Son relationship began only in the days of Augustus Caesar.[66]

Continuing, Campbell asserts that only a "mental" or "spiritual," non-carnal description of the relationship between the eternal Savior and God is appropriate, so that God chose to express this relationship in terms of God and "Word" of God, the "most suitable," "best, if not the only" term that could have been chosen "in the whole vocabulary of human speech at all adapted to express that relation that existed 'in the beginning,'" and one specifically selected by the Holy Spirit to describe in John 1:1 the one who saves humankind.[67] Campbell's notion of the Trinity, then, is one substantially dependent upon John's use of λόγος.

In order to elaborate on the appropriateness of the Holy Spirit's choice of λόγος to describe the eternal Savior and the relation between the Savior and God, Campbell applies in his argument John Locke's conception of words as expressions of ideas.

> A word is a sign or representative of a thought or an idea, and is the idea in an audible or visible form. It is the exact image of the invisible thought which is a perfect secret to all the world until it is expressed. . . . Hence it follows that the word and the idea which it represents, are co-etaneous, or of the same age or antiquity . . . the word is just as old as the idea. . . . An idea cannot exist without a word, nor a word without an idea. . . . He that is acquainted with the word, is acquainted with the idea, for the idea is wholly in the word.[68]

He further says of the relation between ideas and words that,

> It is a relation of the most sublime order; and no doubt the reason why the name Word is adopted by the apostle in this sentence [John 1:1] was because of its superior ability to represent to us the divine relation existing between God and the Saviour prior to his becoming the Son of God. By putting together the above remarks on the term word, we have full view of what John intended to communicate. As a word is an exact image of an idea, so is "The Word" an exact image of the invisible God. As a word cannot exist without an idea, nor an idea without a word, so God never was without "The Word," nor "The Word" without God; or as a word is of equal age, or coetaneous with its idea, so "the Word" and God are co-eternal. And as an idea does not create its word nor a word its idea; so God did not create "The Word," nor the "Word" God.[69]

Again, what is clear in Campbell's description of the relation between idea and word and, therefore, between God and the λόγος, is that he believes

Calvinism confuses the biblical depiction of the eternal relation between God and the Word by using Father/Son language, without giving due place to John's use of λόγος. "Eternal filiation," "eternal generation," and "eternal Son" are inadequate expressions of the biblical depiction in that the adjective "eternal" is biblically fitting only when conjoined with λόγος.[70] For Campbell, the relation between God and the eternal, pre-existent Word of God is one of identity and co-existence, as closely connected to one another as are idea and word in human thought processes and the generation of language. As long as one recognizes the connection between ideas and words, and as long as John's language is taken seriously, there will be no question about the eternality of the Savior or of the absolute identification between God and the Savior. Neither will there be doubt of the connection between the λόγος and the Son of God, in that it is the λόγος who in time became the Son of God, in flesh, Emmanuel, even if the title "Son" is technically and biblically inappropriate for describing the eternal character of the Savior.[71]

Besides the distinction Campbell draws between a generated Son and the eternal Word, and his use of Locke, what is most notable in Alexander's initial response to Timothy is his insistence at the end of the article that he goes no further in his thoughts than what he sees as being directly derivable from the words of Scripture. "I could, indeed, amplify considerably, and perhaps obviate some difficulties by following up farther the hints submitted," he says, "but such are my views of the import of the beginning of John's testimony."[72] He is convinced that in staying within these bounds he has given the Savior a far loftier place of eminence than either the Arians, Socinians, or Calvinists, believing his view gives the Savior the loftiest position, with the Calvinists next, followed by the Arians, and, finally the Socinians.[73] His basis for reaching this conclusion, he says, is "no other authority than my own reasonings," although he is careful to assert he would neither dispute with anyone over such issues, because of their speculative nature, nor he consider them part of a *system* to be upheld.[74]

Response in Christian Baptist

As mentioned above, Alexander Campbell's response to "Timothy" in *The Christian Baptist* was read by Barton Stone, who responded to Campbell in his own *The Christian Messenger*. To this, Campbell then responded in *The*

Christian Baptist in October 1827, reiterating that he wished completely to avoid speculation and theorizing and suggesting that Stone should do the same, remarking that he "regrets" Stone has insisted on carrying on with Trinitarian debate.[75] As part of his initial comments, Campbell references Stone's own unorthodox view and notes that some Baptists have rejected Stone because they consider him a heretical Arian. However, Campbell says he will accept Stone as a brother if Stone would be willing to "conscientiously and devoutly pray to the Lord Jesus Christ as though there was no other God in the universe than he," noting that "they who tell me that they supremely venerate, and unequivocally worship the King my Lord and Master, and are willing to obey him in all things, I call my brethren."[76]

Here Campbell clearly presents himself as one committed to the full divinity of Christ and identifies Christ with the one God beside whom there is no other. He rejects Trinitarian theorizing but accepts Christ as God. This, of course, coincides with the level of glory Campbell saw fit to give to the eternal Word in his initial response to Timothy. In this second installment, Campbell says he was trying in the original article to "examine into the ideas attached to the *term* employed by the Holy Spirit to designate the relation existing between him that '*was made flesh*,' and sent into the world, and him who sent him."[77]

At this point in his second article, Alexander launches into a treatment of the use of human reason in the interpretation of the Bible and the formulation of Christian doctrine, and it at first appears he has taken an aside from his discussion of Trinitarian theology. For him, Scripture presents "evidences" received by human reason as "first principles" to be accepted and "from which we are to reason as from intuitive principles in any human science."[78] Reason is the arbiter of the scriptural things taught us by God, allowing human beings to interpret and understand. However, Campbell immediately applies this point about reason to Trinitarian doctrine, asserting that those who claim there is unreasonableness in the idea of three persons being but one God are themselves thinking unreasonably. He says:

> The strongest objections urged against the Trinitarians by their opponents are derived from what is called the unreasonableness, or the absurdity of three persons being but one God, and that

each of these three is the Supreme God. Now as you know I am not at all disposed either to adopt the style nor to contend for the views of the Trinitarians, any more than I am the views of the Socinians or Unitarians of any grade: you will bear with me when I tell you that no man as a philosopher, or as a reasoner, can object to the Trinitarian hypothesis, even should it say that the Father, the Word, and the Spirit, are three distinct beings, and yet but one God. There is nothing unreasonable in it. . . . Your error is this: you know nothing of the existence of spirits at all. All bodies you know anything of occupy both time and place; consequently, it would be absurd to suppose that three beings whose modes of existence are such as to be governed by time and space, could be one being. But inasmuch as we do know nothing about the mode of existence of spirits, we cannot say that it would be incompatible with their nature, or modes of existence, that three might be one, and that one being might exist in three beings.[79]

Two observations need to be made concerning these words of Campbell and the scriptural evidence he sees concerning the three persons of the Trinity. First, Campbell is here directly responding to Stone's criticisms of Campbell's Trinitarianism as presented in his response to Timothy. Much of Stone's criticism of Campbell and other Trinitarians concerns the logic of what beings may experience; whether they can be both one and three; whether or not the Son can be the Father; whether one eternal God can have relation with himself; whether Jesus can be the one true God and coincidentally speak of following not his own will but the will of the one true God; whether Jesus, about whom the Bible says that he was rich but became poor, can be the one true God who is unchangeable. Campbell asserts in his second article that reason used in this way actually proves nothing about beings that are not bound by time and space and that human logic simply does not apply to spirits.[80] Although Campbell attempts to distance himself from a particular Trinitarian position and points out that both Trinitarianism and Socinianism are untouched by arguments concerning what is reasonable, he at least indirectly defends the reasonableness of his own position, what I take to be a fully Trinitarian perspective.

Second, in the course of his argument, Campbell makes the point that, "The bible teaches us something concerning three beings (I shall call them) the Father, the Word, and the Holy Spirit. It teaches us that there is but one God." Here Campbell again leaves himself open to the criticism that he inconsistently applies his refusal to speculate about the Trinity, since the parenthetical interjection, "I shall call them" does nothing to forestall the fact that he goes beyond the Bible's language in speaking of three "beings." But, further, in stating that the Bible "teaches us something" about the three beings, Campbell actually establishes the precedent of theologizing, taking the incremental step from the biblical foundation to speaking of "beings." He willingly does so in order to make what he considers an instructive comment *that in his opinion fits with what he takes the biblical theology of the three to be.*[81]

Here, rather than criticize Campbell for theologizing beyond the biblical language or for being inconsistent, as would be more in line with the traditional Restorationist perspective on speculative language, I want to point out that what he does is helpful, that there is movement in the New Testament in the direction Campbell takes when he describes the Father, Word, and Holy Spirit as "beings." In my opinion, his mistake is not in using unbiblical language but in not allowing the tendencies of the biblical language to take him even further in the direction of an overtly stated Trinitarianism. Such would, in my view, not be an aberration from biblical Christianity, but would constitute a fruitful, legitimate building of the church's doctrine on what is more than just hinted at in the Bible's presentation of the Trinity. Campbell's concern not to add to Christian disunity, not to speculate, and not to create another system or "ism" prevents him from saying more clearly what he should say (and perhaps from seeing more clearly what he should see), that he believes the Bible's witness to God is one that is fully Trinitarian.

There is one final note that should be added regarding this dialogue between Campbell and Stone, and that is simply that, like his father, Alexander Campbell is an implicit defender of the inclusion of the *filioque* clause as a description of the relation of the Holy Spirit to both Father and Son. Although he gives no specific scriptural reference to defend his statement, Campbell comments, "the Holy Spirit is the Spirit of God, the Spirit of Christ, which was sent by the concurrence of the Father and Son to attest and establish the truth, and remain a comforter, an advocate on earth, when Jesus entered the heavens."[82] This puts Alexander Campbell in line with the classical Trinitarian position adopted in the western church, and it is interesting that here Campbell allows himself for a moment to couch his remarks in terms of concepts that are closely connected to the classical debates concerning the Trinity, even if he wishes also to assert a direct connection between his position and explicit biblical propositions.

Reply to Broaddus

Five years after the 1827 *The Christian Baptist* correspondences, a union was forged between Barton Stone's "Christians" and the "Disciples" of Thomas and Alexander Campbell and Walter Scott. One result was that those from outside the RM who knew Stone's position on the Trinity occasionally questioned the Trinitarian orthodoxy of the former Disciples.

A public example of this kind of query occurred in the December 14, 1832, *Richmond Herald* when Andrew Broaddus, a prominent Baptist minister affiliated with the Dover Association of Baptists, negatively commented about the "Reformers," i.e., Campbell's Disciples, and their connection to "Unitarians and Arians of the West who deny the divinity of our Redeemer," referring to Stone and his followers. Broaddus and others with reservations about the union of the Disciples and Christians had a couple of months earlier caused the Dover Association to withdraw from fellowshipping with the Disciples, a decision set forth in what Campbell referred to as the "Dover Decree" or "Ordinance" from October 1832. Campbell criticized this decision by the Dover Association as a move that fostered division, leading Broaddus to claim Campbell's assessment of the decision was an "Unfair Representation" of the Dover Decree.[83]

In Alexander Campbell's response to Andrew Broaddus in the January 1833 edition of *The Millennial Harbinger*, he makes several affirmations about his own Trinitarian position. In addition, and more significantly, the April 1833 edition of *The Millennial Harbinger* carried both a new query by Henry Grew concerning Campbell's January response to Broaddus, and it carried answers to Grew's questions about Campbell's Trinitarian opinions. Both sets of correspondence offer important insights into Alexander Campbell's Trinitarian perspective.

Campbell's January 1833 response to Broaddus's December 14, 1832 piece in the *Richmond Herald* begins with an overt denial by Campbell that the Disciples have "become one people" with Unitarians and Arians, as Broaddus claims. Campbell says this claim is filled with slander, because joining into fellowship with the Christians meant the Disciples were accepting individual believers who had decided they could agree with the Disciples' doctrinal positions, not accepting the doctrinal positions of any factions to which Stone's Christians might have previously belonged. This union was no acceptance of Unitarians, or Arians, or any other denominated grouping, as such; it was an entrance into communion by Christians who were to be considered free from such labels.

In addition, it should be noted that Campbell's claim to have been slandered by Broaddus's accusation indicates his assessment of Unitarians and Arians. Clearly, Campbell considered the accusation a denigrating remark, whereby the Disciples were being identified with two groups whose Trinitarian positions were unacceptable for Campbell. Whatever Campbell's own Trinitarian position, he viewed Unitarians and Arians in the same light as did orthodox Trinitarians.

In answering Broaddus, Campbell elaborates on his own position, specifically stating where he would draw lines of fellowship regarding Trinitarian questions, which is interesting in that Campbell typically claims Trinitarian speculation may be the chief place where lines of fellowship are inappropriately drawn. In Campbell's view, historical Trinitarian speculation is to be viewed not only in contrast to biblical doctrine, but also as responsible for widespread division within Christianity. Apparently, for Campbell, then, the conditions he now names for fellowship are in his eyes *biblically* derived and grounded, rather than finding their source in human theologizing. One must wonder, of course, at the perspicuity present in Campbell's demarcation between human speculation/theologizing and scripturally based assertion. One person's human speculation is another person's extrapolation from, or even direct interpretation of, that which is stated in the Bible, as previously discussed. Nonetheless, with reference to

Trinitarian doctrine, Campbell asserts or implies that Christian fellowship may be withheld in the following matters: (1) the denial of the divine personhood of Jesus; (2) a denial of Jesus as the only begotten of God; (3) the refusal to worship and adore Jesus the Messiah with all of one's heart, soul, mind and strength; (4) the refusal to accept Jesus as Emmanuel, God with us, manifest in the flesh; (5) the refusal to give equal honor to the Son as to the Father; and (6) the failure to regard Jesus in the same high place in which he is held by the prophets, evangelists, and apostles.

Campbell's answer to Broaddus clearly shows he did not believe Stone and his people had violated Campbell's own criteria for fellowship, asserting that he sees no grounds on which to think Stone's Christians heretical. And, given Campbell's apparent assessment that the six items required for fellowship listed above are scripturally grounded, he must be identifying Stone's position with what he sees as biblically acceptable doctrine. Was he correct? While an answer to this question requires the full analysis in Chapter Three, it may be said that Campbell's desire for Christian unity may have led him to accept into fellowship those who held a Trinitarian position that was closer to an Arian view than Campbell himself was willing to admit.

Campbell apparently did not believe he was participating in speculation with his own principles for Christian fellowship, but was simply echoing biblical theology. In his mind, there was no inconsistency between his refusal to participate in speculative theology and his discussion about what most would consider some of the classic issues of Trinitarian theology. He even compares Broaddus to others (he specifically names the Catholic priesthood) who justify their faith or practice in ways other than by "scriptural argument," seemingly considering himself free from carrying out the same kind of argumentation.[84] However, as mentioned above, what exactly demarcates speculation and delving into metaphysics from scripturally based argumentation? How far does one need to stray from language that is specifically biblical before being accused of speculating? Campbell implies that with reference to the divine personhood of Jesus; to Jesus as the only begotten of God; to Jesus as Emmanuel; to Jesus as God with us; to Jesus manifest in the flesh; to the equal honor that is given to the Son, just as it is to the Father; and to the same high place in which Jesus is held by the prophets, evangelists, and apostles that Stone is not just orthodox, but is also in line with scriptural teaching. And, yet, expressions and concepts like "divine personhood," "only begotten," "equal honor," and "same high place in which He is held" are concepts about which those interested in Trinitarian doctrine often theologize and speculate. It is difficult, therefore, to agree with Campbell that he is successful in avoiding human Trinitarian speculation. Is he not actually stepping over a very thin line that he unsuccessfully attempts to draw?

Further, and more to the point, is there not something valuable, something helpful, something that appropriately fits within the context of human/divine interaction for Christians to wrestle with speculative questions about God, in a manner reflecting the spirit and ethos of scriptural revelation and humankind's search for understanding, even if such discussion utilizes terms and concepts that extend beyond specifically biblical language? Campbell decries speculation, and at various places attempts to either defend himself against charges that he is speculating or apologizes for doing so. But is human speculation necessarily and automatically so far removed from that revealed about God in Scripture that all theologizing and supplemental framing of biblical concepts and depictions need to be rejected? Campbell would, of course, argue that the problem with such speculative language has been, and will always be, that it wrongly is used in place of scriptural doctrine as the criterion for decisions about orthodoxy and fellowship. But is it not the case that divisions within the body of Christ seemingly deriving from determinations based in mere human speculation on theological matters more often find their genesis in sectarian and judgmental attitudes than they do in theologizing, itself?[85]

It is interesting that when listing the attributes and beliefs of those he accepts into fellowship, Campbell asserts that "they are opposed, indeed, to both Trinitarian, Arian, and Unitarian speculations on the *divine essence*...." Assumedly, he is referring to traditional discussions of οὐσία, ὑποστάσις, ὁμοούσιος, *persona, substantia,* etc., wishing to distance himself and other Disciples and Christians from such technical and speculative matters. But just how different are the discussions Campbell is willing to have about the divinity of Christ's personhood, his nature as "begotten," or the manner in which Jesus is the manifestation of God in the flesh?[86] On what grounds are some discussions allowed, when discussion about the divine essence is not? Does Scripture really present a clearly stated position on Christ's personhood, or on His nature as begotten, or on His fleshly manifestation of God vis à vis what is offered in the Bible concerning Christ's divine essence? It is hard to see that Campbell could justifiably answer in the affirmative.

What Campbell presents as his list of six points concerning Trinitarian doctrine ultimately conjoin into a position that looks quite traditionally orthodox. The divinity, high character, and nature that Jesus possesses as God means worshipful responders "all accord in rendering the same honor in thought, word, and deed to the Son, as they do to the Father who sent him."[87] With respect to his own Trinitarian position, Campbell fails to be completely silent, uses language and focuses on topics similar to traditional Trinitarian discussion, and is more closely aligned with those who are traditionally orthodox than he is separated from them because of his distaste for theological speculation.

Correspondence with Henry Grew

Because Alexander Campbell's response to Andrew Broaddus was published in *The Millennial Harbinger*, the hints found there about his own Trinitarian position could now become a point of public discussion in a way that had not taken place since Campbell's responses to "Timothy" six years earlier. It was not surprising, then, that in the April 1833 edition of *The Millennial Harbinger* editor Campbell printed a letter from Henry Grew, "Trinitarianism, Arianism, & Socinianism." Grew queries of Campbell:

> There are several of your readers, besides myself, in this vicinity, who respectfully solicit, for the truth's sake, and our fellowship in the same, a brief, but definite explanation of your remarks in the last Harbinger, p. 9, on the nature of our blessed Lord. Whether it is to be attributed to obtuseness of understanding on our part, or to indefiniteness of statement on yours, the fact is, beloved, that from the closest attention we are capable of giving to all you have written on this subject, we do not yet understand you. We are equally opposed with you to "Trinitarian, Arian, and Unitarian speculations on the *divine essence*." From the systems of fallible and erring men, we trust the Son has made

us free. Our desire is, simply to understand what the Spirit of truth teaches on this and every other subject. Most cordially do we unite with you in acknowledging the Messiah as "a divine person, the only begotten of God." Most devoutly would we love, "worship and adore him" AS *the only begotten of the Father, full of favor and truth*." But we tremble at the word of HIM who will not give his glory to another, and we obey that word which teaches us to love and worship the Son "*to the glory of God the Father.*"[88]

From here Grew proceeds to ask Campbell five pointed questions, which make it clear that Grew is entering the conversation from exactly the opposite side as Andrew Broaddus.[89] Grew is concerned that Campbell insufficiently indicates that there is a difference between the kind of glory that should be given to the Father and the only begotten of the Father, asking:

> Do you, or do you not, understand the terms first, only begotten Son, beginning of the creation of God, first born of every creature, "in the full import and meaning of (these) words," as we do, viz: as teaching, that the Son, in his highest personal nature, is a distinct being from the Father, and had a "beginning" of existence?

Those familiar with Stone's position, and, for that matter, with Arianism, will note the conformity of Grew's questions with the Trinitarian position of the founder of the Christians and the manner in which Grew's perspective moves away from traditional Trinitarian doctrine. Grew's other points are along the same lines, and he wonders in print if Campbell recognizes the full and literal import of both Jesus' words, "My Father is greater than I," and the teaching of Paul in 1 Corinthians 8:6 that Jesus is the Lord *by* whom are all things and *by* whom the Father saves, vis à vis the Father's position as the one *of* whom are all things and to whom worship is offered independently of the Son. Is the Son not the one who is worshipped *to the glory of the Father?*[90]

To Grew's questions, Campbell responds in a manner telling for our purposes.[91] First, Campbell notes that Grew's questions require that

Campbell enter into speculative theology, which Campbell, of course, is hesitant to do. Campbell even treats Grew's questions as if they require an interruption in his day that takes him away from truly important questions.[92] This attitude on Campbell's part is separated from the attitude of most others in approaching the subject of the Trinity, and the SCM would have benefitted from Campbell approaching such conversations differently. As it is, Campbell's entire attitude and approach to Trinitarian theology—of which this is a prime example—culminates in a doctrinal void.

Following his opening caveat, Campbell offers what he calls "preliminary reflections."[93] What is interesting here, even illuminating, is that in addition to offering his typical opinion about speculative matters and observing that humankind suffers from finitude and being bound by language that is simply inadequate for expressing the divine, Campbell states quite clearly that he, in fact, does not disagree with what he views as the Trinitarian position found in the Westminster Confession, but to the language in which the Confession is couched. He says:

> My principal objection to the popular doctrine of "the Trinity" is not that it is either irrational, or unscriptural, to infer that there are three Divine persons in one Divine nature. That these three equally have one thought, purpose, will, and operation, and so one God;—or, to use the words of the Westminster Confession, "In the Unity of the Godhead there be three persons, of one substance, power, and eternity;" I say, I object not to this doctrine because it is contrary to reason, or revelation, but because of the metaphysical technicalities, the unintelligible jargon, the unmeaning language of the orthodox creeds on the subject, and the interminable war of words without ideas to which this word *Trinity* has given birth.[94]

For Campbell, neither human reason nor divine revelation run contrary to the concepts inherent within traditional Trinitarian doctrine, meaning that the traditional position is conceptually acceptable to Campbell as being in line with divine realities and with the revelation God has offered both in Jesus and Scripture. In this sense, Campbell can assert his own fidelity to classical Trinitarian doctrine. It is when human speculation and language turns to the "divine modus of existence and the divine essence," leaving behind the language and clarity of Scripture and trying to describe and specify how three can be one and one three, that Campbell protests against the Trinitarian arguments. He says:

> Were anyone to ask me, Can there be three distinct persons, or even beings, in one God? I would say, Reason informs me not, and revelation does not assert it. But if asked, Can there be one, and one three in the same sense? I reply, Both reason and revelation say No. . . . Language fails and thought can not reach the relation in which the Father and the Son have existed, now exist, and shall forever exist.[95]

Surprising, then, is the fact that immediately after making the above statement Campbell, says:

> *But that there is, and was, and evermore will be, society in God himself, a plurality as well as unity in the Divine nature,* are inferences which do obtrude themselves on my mind in reflecting upon the divine communications to our race. I will add, that common sense, reason, and revelation give one and the same testimony, in my ear, upon this subject.[96]

If I have correctly understood Campbell, I am left wondering at what appears, again, to be an odd inconsistency. How is it that, on the one hand, language and thought are inadequate for delving into the relations of the Trinity, so that nothing really can be said about three being one and one three, while at the same time confident assertions can be made, based in *inference,* about there being "*society in God himself, a plurality as well as unity in the Divine nature*"? How can he properly "infer that there are three Divine persons in one Divine nature"? Perhaps Campbell's above-mentioned caveat about being forced to enter into speculation justifies the inconsistency, but I still find it interesting that, when pressed, Campbell does apply himself to Trinitarian issues, even indicating that *inferences* about the Trinity are in some cases justified, despite the fact that such inference clearly goes beyond the plain language of Scripture.

This apparent inconsistency notwithstanding, Campbell spends several paragraphs arguing for the acceptability of there being plurality and society within God. First, to believe such, he tells Grew, is no different from believing in the incomprehensible self-existent One—Yahweh—who is God. That there is plurality and society in God may confound the mind, but, Campbell maintains, the profound incomprehensibility in the mystery of God's plurality is for him more a joy and delight than a conundrum, and this mystery he simply believes in a way parallel to believing that God is.[97]

Campbell proceeds to describe the inferential process whereby he concludes that there is plurality within Yahweh, taking as his first clue the societal, relational nature of humankind made in God's image, followed by Scripture's affirmation in Genesis 1:27 that a plurality was present at creation, followed by the direct claims of John 1:1 and the eternality of the Word. He says:

> And while this name [Yahweh] is before us, let me ask the wavering to reflect, how man could be created social, and in the image of God; man, having in his nature plurality, incomplete in one person; for man is not without the woman, nor the woman without the man, in nature or religion. How could man be created in the image of God, incomplete in one person, social and necessarily plural; and that God, in whose image and likeness he was created, could be a solitary eternal unit, without society and plurality in himself! This I can not comprehend, when I believe that God said, "Let *us* make man in *our* image, in *our* likeness, and let him have dominion;" and "In the beginning was the Word, and the Word was with God, and the Word was God."[98]

That Campbell has in such a short paragraph run together his arguments for God's plurality, without any real explanation, fits with what he first described to Grew as his "off-hand and desultory thoughts of an hour snatched from other pressing subjects of examination."[99] His statements are too brief; absent from them is the careful reasoning from biblical exegesis to doctrinal opinion one may have expected from Alexander Campbell. There is some sense of flow here, but the reader is left to supply the support for the connections and applications of the texts that Campbell is making. Fortunately, he doesn't leave things standing just here.

In a series of paragraphs Campbell states—respectively—his objections to the Trinitarian, Arian, and Socinian positions. Of these, he gives the least attention to the Trinitarian position, arguing in concert with his points made to Timothy six years earlier that some classical Trinitarians give insufficient glory to the Word of God when they merely describe the Lord Messiah as the eternal *Son*.[100] But Campbell successively argues quite pointedly against both the Arian and Socinian positions, in the process making apparent use of a version of the classical objection to the Arian position first set forth by Athanasius (I say apparent because Campbell offers no reference to a source for this portion of his argument) that the role of the *created* Son would have to be limited to what created beings are capable of doing, and this does not include the blotting out and washing away of sin. For the Arian, the Son is a type of "sub-deity," . . . a "first and high-born One, of unrivalled glory amongst the creatures of God," but God "*gives him nothing to do, which the son of Joseph could not have done as well!!!*" This, Campbell claims, is simply folly.[101] He asks, "Could not Paul himself, do as much for the redemption of the world, as the Arian Son of God?"[102]

With respect to Socinianism Campbell makes essentially the same argument, saying, of the Son that he is the:

> wonderful child [prophesied by Isaiah] on whose shoulders the government of the universe was to remain, whose name was written "Wonderful Counsellor—the Mighty God—the Father of Eternity—the Prince of Peace—Immanuel": [that] when the prediction is accomplished, Mary travails, and the carpenter's son is born—a Son of God, it is true, as Adam was!!![103]

For Campbell, the personal dignity and standing of the eternal Word require that any humanly formulated proposition about the position of the Son must be consistent with the status given him in the "types, figures, prophecies, and promises," including "all the splendors of Divinity. . . ."[104] This standard, in Campbell's view, the Socinian position fails to meet.

Finally, in closing out what he is still calling his *preliminary remarks* before directly answering Grew's questions, Campbell briefly applies a form of an argument from relationality that shares very superficial similarities with Augustine's "missions" and his analogies from human nature. There is in both human and divine nature the notions of I, thou, and he, which coincide with there being Father, Son and Spirit, especially evident in the "sendings" that occur when the Father sends the Son, when the Father and Son send the Spirit, and when "Jehovah and his Spirit" send the Son.[105] At this point, Campbell is being so brief that his comments are barely more than veiled allusions to the traditional arguments from analogy and relationality, with which he is clearly familiar, but it is interesting that he allows himself to construct an argument that includes even vague referencing of classical Trinitarian explications.[106]

Campbell closes with five direct answers to the specific questions Grew had posed, and here Alexander begins to sound like the familiar biblically centered exegete insistent on using only scriptural language. In "QUERY 1, ANSWERED" and "QUERY 2, ANSWERED," Campbell replies to Grew's questions concerning the interpretation of 1 Corinthians 8:6 by asserting that Grew misses the original intention when Paul writes of "one God the Father out of whom all things exist" and "one Lord Jesus Christ through whom all things exist." Grew emphasizes what he sees as the distinction between the Father and Jesus Christ based in the differences in their relations to creation, indicated by Paul's use of the different prepositions ἐξ and διά and by Paul's calling of one "God" and the other "Lord." Campbell simply replies that Paul was not trying to create distinction between the two but was trying to contrast the One God of Christianity and the many gods of paganism. Paul was not trying to include or exclude the Son in referring to the "one God," but was trying to exclude the objects of paganism and idolatry as genuine forms of religious devotion, so that for Campbell Grew's question is irrelevant and based in a misperception of Paul's intent. For Campbell, the Father is "the one absolute Lord" while Jesus has also been made by the Father to be "our only Lord."[107]

To Grew's third question concerning the literal meaning of the expressions "only begotten," "beginning of the creation," and "first born of every creature," Campbell first indicates his preference for using *person* instead of *being*, and then replies that Scripture nowhere teaches that the Son in his "highest personal nature" had a "beginning of being or existence."[108] Here

Campbell references the prologue of the Gospel of John, quoting both John 1:1 and John 1:14 to make the point that, "I venerate 'the word made flesh,' as God manifest in the flesh."[109] At this point, it is difficult to miss the clear distinction Campbell is making between his own view and any position that resembles Arianism, including any perspective that would hesitate to say that Jesus was less than God or should be differentiated from the one God.

Grew's fourth question concerned John 14:28 and Jesus' claim that "My Father is greater than I." Would Campbell take this in a limited or unlimited sense; could such a statement be accepted without reservation? In the process of answering, Campbell, specifically separates himself from the Trinitarians whom he says actually concede Grew his point by speaking only of the eternal Son and indicates that he takes John 14:28 in "an economical or restricted sense" so that Jesus here speaks "as respecting his state of humiliation and its consequences."[110]

Grew's final question centered on the distinction that he evidently thinks must be made between the worship directed toward the Father and that directed to the Son. Although Campbell does conclude by saying that "They are one in the admiration of my understanding—they are one in the adoration of my heart," the real force of his answer concerns the unacceptability of creating distinctions in quality or quantity of worship. Campbell indicates that there is an absurdity about trying to draw distinctions in worship, as if it can be mathematically dissected and quantified. For Campbell, no such distinctions are appropriate, and he certainly does not make them as he approaches his Father and Lord in worship. Campbell concludes:

> Thus, Brother Grew, if compelled to philosophize, I would answer your questions. I own that much depends upon our views of the personal dignity and standing of the Lord Messiah. Indeed, such was the glory which he had with the Father before the world was, and such is the glory which he now enjoys as Lord of all in our nature, that I think we are much more likely to fail in forming too low, than too high, conceptions of his essential dignity. The Father has so glorified him as our head, and has so signified to us his delight in him, that, of all the texts in the Bible, there is none we could misapply in reference to Jesus

more than that which says, "Jehovah will not give his glory to another." He has laid no restrictions upon the admiration and adoration of the human or angelic hosts in reference to his only begotten Son; nay, all angels and men are commanded to worship him. No idolatry in worshiping the King of glory!! I would not for the universe weaken the force of a single expression, or subtract from the boldest metaphor aught of its riches, designed to set forth the peerless claims of our Redeemer to the unqualified adoration of my soul.[111]

Correspondence with Boston Unitarians

In the April 1846 edition of *The Millennial Harbinger* Alexander Campbell, beginning on p. 216, printed a notice that previously appeared in the *Christian Palladium* concerning a proposed "open correspondence" between Boston Unitarians and the Christians of Pennsylvania. The Pennsylvania Christian Convention for 1845 had passed a resolution encouraging dialogue between themselves and the Unitarians, and J. J. Harvey was given the task of initiating such contact. He did so in the April 1845 edition of the *Christian Palladium*, and also included Campbell as an addressee, along with Oroville Dewey of the Unitarians. Harvey also printed the resulting correspondence between himself and Dewey, along with the text of a resolution from the August 1845 session of the Pennsylvania Christian Convention encouraging further unionizing efforts between the Unitarians and the Christians. This was followed in the *Christian Palladium* with final comments by J. J. Harvey in which he responds to what he calls "fears in our behalf, as touching the above proceedings" coming from "inexperienced or timid brethren."[112] Throughout his final comments, Harvey expresses satisfaction that the Christians have taken steps to promote unity between themselves and others who follow Christ, and he indicates that for them to initiate relationship with the Unitarians fits perfectly with the ethos of the SCM.[113]

To this correspondence and to the resolution of the Pennsylvania Christian Convention, Alexander Campbell responds in a series of five articles, beginning in the April 1846 *Millennial Harbinger*, expressing his dismay at the decision of the Pennsylvania Christian Convention and at

J. J. Harvey's correspondence with Oroville Dewey. The result is a rather lengthy (for Campbell) discussion of Trinitarian doctrine that clarifies Alexander Campbell's traditional Trinitarianism.[114]

In the first article of April 1846, Campbell gives little specific attention to Trinitarian issues. He is more concerned that Harvey is willing to unite the Christians with a Unitarian sect, in principle ignoring the importance of being only Christians and not Socinians, Unitarians, or Trinitarians. Further, he is concerned that an offer for unity is being extended to the Unitarians not on the basis of what either party thinks of Christ, but, rather, on the basis of a common definition of what it means to be Christian. Campbell responds with invective:

> But is a definition of a Christian the basis of Christian union!! Is not an agreement in the doctrine concerning Christ, or a *declaration of our faith in the person; mission, and character of Jesus Christ*, essential to Christian union—indeed, to an admission into any Christian community! I cannot imagine a more radical mistake than to substitute, at the very threshold of an overture for Christian union, a declaration of our faith in what constitutes a Christian for a declaration of our faith in Jesus Christ himself.... The very soul, body, and spirit of the gospel—the marrow and fatness of Christianity—is in the proper answer to the question, *What think you of Christ?* Who is He? What is He?[115]

Although he does not specifically express it here, Campbell is apparently concerned about the answer Unitarians would give to such questions about the Son. He hints at this on p. 224 when he says that, "A centaur, or a sphinx, or any other chimera is quite as rational and as natural an imagination as a remedial system without a sacrificial atonement, or a Redeemer without a divine nature." The issue of Christ's divine nature will figure prominently throughout Campbell's five-article response about uniting with the Unitarians.

In the July 1846 second installment, Campbell responds to a pamphlet recently printed by the American Unitarian Association and written by Alvan Lamson. The pamphlet, of which Campbell reprints a sizable portion, attempts to give a simplified answer to the question about what Unitarianism is. Campbell responds to the pamphlet with consternation. In his view, they ultimately have no clearly agreed upon position concerning the person of Christ, they leave no room for the plurality of persons in the divine nature and, in fact, "they have no divine *nature* at all, for with them *God is one person*. . . . they have no divine nature, and consequently no participants of it. Thus, then, God is, with them, a mere person—one being."[116] He continues:

> In *our* Christian religion we have a *"divine nature,"* and we have *three persons*—the Father, the Word and the Holy Spirit. Our Unitarian friends at Boston have no divine nature, but one *personal God*. Their Messiah has, they say, only a "metaphysical rank." As to his pre-existence, they are non-committal, or wholly negative. . . . They imagine that God is a mere person, according to their notions of human personality. Their God, while spoken of sometimes in magniloquent, indeed, in sublime, and, sometimes, in very just terms, is confined to personal properties. Alas! for poor human nature when such men have cast such a mould for him who is everywhere and no where; who inhabiteth eternity; and is yet the Ancient of days; who fills heaven, earth, and hell; and yet dwells in the heart of every lover of the divine Saviour. When any one admits that God is infinite, eternal, that he always was, and is, and evermore shall be, he has admitted views still more supernatural and grand, than the manifestation of the whole divine nature, in the person of the Father, in the person of the Son, and in the person of the Holy Spirit. But who, of good sense, argues that these three persons—one being![117]

Campbell here argues that the singular personhood for God asserted by Unitarians limits God to certain conditions of *human* personhood, so that the personal property of being limited to singularity is inappropriately applied to One who can simultaneously dwell anywhere, who is infinite and eternal and who, therefore, transcends the single personhood or singular being of any one of the three *as any of these are conceived by the Unitarians*. Campbell says, "That God is one and plural, is just as evident as that he can be every where and no where." Unitarians would gladly admit that God can be everywhere and nowhere; why can they not just as easily admit that he is no more incapable of being one and plural than that he is omnipresent?

For our purposes, Campbell's argument is quite interesting. First, Alexander Campbell is arguing here, and in the other installments of this series of articles, about a matter that he has many times referred to as speculative, and one on which Christians should not be divided. But here there is a sense that J. J. Harvey actually "out Campbells Campbell" by arguing that unity between the Christians and Unitarians should transcend in importance their differences on the Trinity. Campbell, for his part, is clearly not willing to compromise on what he regards in this article as a key point of Christian doctrine. Was, then, the traditional doctrine of the Trinity important enough to Alexander Campbell that those who thought about it in what Campbell considered biblical ways should at times refuse fellowship with those who thought differently in some specific ways? Without a doubt; Trinitarian doctrine ultimately is not for Alexander Campbell merely a matter of speculation but is of cardinal doctrinal importance, even if the language typically associated with Trinitarian theology is unacceptably speculative.

Second, Campbell's point that the Unitarians think of God with singular personhood and as having no divine nature that could simultaneously be the possession of three divine persons argues in one sense simply that the position of the Unitarians does not cohere to what is essentially classic Trinitarian orthodoxy. Of course, Campbell does not bring creedal affirmations into his argument,[118] but what he argues is in fact a defense of the Cappadocian position of one nature and three persons. I am sure Campbell was not ignorant of the fact that he is by implication asserting the *biblical acceptability* of the classically orthodox position, nor would he claim this is *"our"* position if he thought for a moment it could not be justified on biblical grounds. Alexander Campbell may be anticreedal, antisectarian, and opposed to language that is not biblical, but clearly this does not necessitate that his actual position be in opposition to the traditional, creedal one.

Third, despite his position about speculative, nonbiblical language, Campbell clearly is comfortable with expressing a position about the Trinity in creedal language, if he thinks such language derives from, or at least coheres with, the Bible. Not only does Campbell assert a position that coheres closely with the Cappadocian Fathers or creedal affirmations, but he makes no effort to avoid use of the historical language of the Fathers, specifically applying in his argument words such as *nature* and *person*. He uses such language in both the second and third articles in this series.

Fourth, Campbell asserts that the Unitarians are inappropriately limited in insisting on God's singularity when they think of His personhood in line with human personhood. This is, of course, one of the arguments Campbell had made to Barton Stone—that Stone's vision of God was simply limited in that he could not conceive of God possessing a nature that transcended the limitations of personhood as typically construed. For Campbell, whether one is fully identified as Unitarian or remains an unaffiliated quasi-Arian like Stone, anyone thinking that the singular nature of God's personhood would prevent him from having one nature that could exist inclusive of three persons is making a significant doctrinal error.

In the series' third article, from August 1846, Campbell presses home three points. First, he reiterates the point from his July article, that by stressing God's *personal unity* Unitarians take a position that denies to the one God any nature or essence, in specific contrast to Genesis 1:26 (where humans, who clearly possess human nature are said to have been created in God's image, implying that God, too, must have a nature), to Galatians 4:8 (where it is stated the Galatians were in their pre-Christian lives enslaved to those that by nature are not gods, implying there is One who in his nature is God), and to 2 Peter 1:3–4 (where Christians are said to have opportunity to share in the divine nature).[119] For Paul and Peter, then, there was a divine nature in which Christ fully shared, even as he possessed a personhood separate from the Father's, whereas the Unitarians assert no such divine nature but only a personhood that, while they take it to be divine, is actually sub-divine. Campbell says:

> Their highest conceptions of Divinity has, therefore, for its beau ideal, *a man!*—an angel, without a nature!
>
> The person of their God, like an angelic person, or a human person, is one being of certain fixed personal attributes, without any other essence than what is contained in *one person*. . . . Ah

me! what philosophers! what students of the Bible! what students of nature are they who deny nature to God, as an essence beyond a mere personal form and being!¹²⁰

Second, in making his point concerning how Unitarians speak of God's personhood in human terms, Campbell briefly mentions that such a conception of God's personhood, limiting the divinity of the Son, compromises the saving power of Christ. There is in the Unitarianism system no "remedial dispensation" or "redeeming quality" because they teach only a "human saviour," a "created saviour" who offers "no salvation for man."¹²¹ Like his use of Cappadocian language in referring to one nature and three persons, Campbell—no doubt with full awareness—makes use of the Athanasian soteriological argument concerning the need for a *fully divine* Savior to extract sin from humanity. Again, Campbell is unafraid to assert the classical position or to use a classical argument when it is appropriate and needed to counter a position he believes is heretical.

Third, Campbell argues that despite the clear evidence of Scripture that the divine nature exists, there is no existence known to anyone anywhere of a nature represented by only one person. Therefore, if the Unitarians assert singular personhood for God, they must deny his divine nature because a singular person with an identifiable nature does not exist. Instead, there are three divine *persons* revealed in the Bible, which matches with the biblical conception of the divine *nature*.¹²²

In Campbell's fourth reply to the Unitarians in November 1846, he mainly argues from a λόγος Christology, as he had done years before in *The Christian Baptist*.¹²³ He logically asserts that the person of Jesus pre-existed in the Word, so that it was the Word that became flesh. But clearly, prior to becoming human the λόγος was something other than human, possessing something other than a human nature. Since only divine, angelic, and human natures exist, and since the λόγος is neither an angel nor human in his pre-existence, he must be of divine nature and, therefore, must be "God in the flesh" when he becomes a human being.¹²⁴ Here Campbell is again adamant that he would not accept the classical ideas of eternal generation, eternal filiation or eternal procession,¹²⁵ but the idea of the pre-existent

Word who "*was* God in another form—the brightness of his glory and the *express image* of his person" substantiates the full divinity of the Son.[126]

At the end of the fourth installment, Campbell announces that he will use the fifth installment in December 1846 to make a "proper examination of the titles, honors, and achievements of him who 'in the beginning was the *Word* that was *with God,* and that *was God.*'"[127] Instead, Campbell's fifth article in the series constitutes a response to a lengthy reply to his articles that he had received from J. J. Harvey. Harvey writes to Campbell:

> Do you mean to make opinion the ground either of union or an objection to the proposed union? So it would seem. I have not said any thing about Trinity or Unity in this discussion, but you have introduced both, and *appear* to favor the one and discard the other, and object to the proposed union among Christians, because the Unitarians think favorably of, and are willing to encourage it, for the reason (as it seems to me,) simply because they are Unitarians. . . . In order to express my views of Christian union, I deemed it proper to say who I esteemed a *Christian*. But I did not make that definition '*a basis of union,*' as you strangely infer. Such an inference "appears to me extremely imaginative and inapposite."[128]

Campbell responds by essentially asserting that his own view of the necessity of claiming Christ in concert with orthodox Trinitarian doctrine is in line with doctrinal truth, rather than merely being an opinion. Union, he says, "Must be *union in truth—union in faith, hope, and love* and not union in opinion—not union in outward forms and ceremonies."[129] He continues by asserting that Christian union must take place between *Christians* and that a Christian is one who "*believes that Jesus is the Messiah, the Son of the living God, and submits to his government. This is the central truth of the Christian system.*"[130] However, Campbell also takes the position that despite their confessing Jesus as the Christ, various *opinions* held by Christians can work to destroy the effects of the good confession they make about Christ. This he clearly believes is the case with the Unitarians:

> Those professors that annihilate the sufferings of Christ as atoning sacrifice, and reduce him to a mere man, or a mere angel, or some other kind of creature than the Word *that was God and became incarnate,* are propagating views more fatal to God's corner stone, than the opinion that circumcision and the law of carnal ordinances ought to be superadded to the gospel to the Gentiles as a proper introduction to the Christian church.
>
> Any theory that degrades my Redeemer to the rank of any mere creature, and his death to that of distinguished martyr, expresses opinions more subversive of the Christian faith than those which Paul notices as making Christ of none effect,—more injurious than any of the doctrinal opinions with which the Lord upbraids any one of the Asiatic churches,—equal, at least, in their disastrous tendencies to the opinions of those speculators on Christian doctrine whom John the Apostle inhibits from the rites of Christian hospitality. . . . The great question—What think you of the Messiah?—is of all others the most fundamental; because our views of sin, righteousness, holiness, and redemption, as well as our views of God and of ourselves are affected by them. Just as every one thinks of Christ, he will think of God, of himself, of sin, of justification, of condemnation—of the whole remedial dispensation, indeed, of the gospel of God. I am sorry that in your letter there is no offering to his praise, and honor, and glory, and that you have failed to distinguish between faith and opinion, so far as pertains to the *person,* and *office,* and *character* of the Lord Messiah. He being the only foundation on which God's temple stands, any error here is radical in the superlative degree.[131]

Campbell's words here are especially striking. He implies that the Unitarian position is of more detriment to Christian truth than that of the Judaizers faced by Paul; he says it is further from truth and more damaging than the heresies of the seven churches addressed in Revelation 2 and 3. Not only has he sided with traditional orthodoxy with reference to Trinitarian doctrine, but Campbell moves toward asserting the *theological priority* of the Trinitarian position! By 1846 Campbell is asserting the very point that this book intends to make, that his followers should not only be overtly Trinitarian, but that orthodox Trinitarian doctrine should take a governing position within SC theology. And, lest it be doubted where he himself stands, Campbell in the final paragraph of the 1846 series of articles on Unitarianism says:

> I cheerfully admit, and I rejoice in the admission, that an innumerable multitude of persons scattered up and down, do believe in the Lord Jesus Christ, not as Nicodemus did, before he was born again, and as you [J.J. Harvey] say some Unitarians do—"a teacher sent from God," or as you perhaps more clearly expressed it—"God's constituted teacher."—So was Moses, so was Paul, and so was Peter. Was Jesus of Nazareth no more than "God's constituted teacher?!!" Multitudes, I say, have a greater, a larger, and more divine faith in Jesus of Nazareth than this. They regard him as *"Emmanuel,"* as *"God with us*—the only begotten Son of God," as "he who was *in the beginning with God,* and who was God," who *was before all things,"* "*by* whom and *for* whom *all things were created and made."* The Alpha and Omega, the Beginning and the Ending, the First and the Last, whose name is Jehovah our Righteousness, the "I am" that was before Abraham. *"Who had all glory with the Father before the world was"*—who was both the Root and Offspring of David. The Lord God of Shem, "David's son, and the Lord of David." 'Jehovah said to my Jehovah, sit at my right hand.'[132]

While Campbell reiterates on this same page that he stands neither with the Unitarians nor the Trinitarians, it is clear that his position is essentially in concert with a traditionally Trinitarian position.

The Christian System

Finally, I will refer to a portion of the 1839 edition of Alexander Campbell's *The Christian System,* a work that essentially functions as Campbell's summary theology. Here there is nothing new beyond what has been previously expressed in his articles, but the place of this volume in the history of Campbell's thought deserves an examination of how he here addresses the Trinity. One of the things to be noted is just how much his position, and the way in which he states it, feels like an attempt to state a Trinitarian position in summary, systematic fashion. On pages 7–8, under numbered paragraph 4, Campbell speaks of what he calls God's "divine nature in the abstract, or of the divinity, or godhead," which he says in the note on page 9 he takes from Acts 16:29, Romans 1:20, Colossians 2:9, and 2 Peter 1:3–4. He says further that:

> The divine nature may be communicated or imparted in some sense; and indeed, while it is essentially and necessarily singular, it is certainly plural in its personal manifestations. Hence we have the Father, Son, and Holy Spirit equally divine, though personally distinct from each other. We have, in fact, but one God, one Lord, one Holy Spirit; yet these are equally possessed of one and the same divine nature.[133]

What is striking—and what we have seen before—is that Campbell here uses what are essentially the classical conceptions, speaking of a singular divine nature in the same manner that ancient formulas speak of οὐσία. The personal manifestations or personal distinctions are treated as is *hypostasis,* each possessing equal divinity and each "possessed of one and the same divine nature." So, although Campbell will not claim for himself adherence to the ancient creedal formulas, he is not afraid to use language that parallels the ancient creedal language, and the difference between his summation of God's divinity, it seems to me, is hardly different from the creed of Constantinople in terms of essential content.

Under numbered paragraph 5 on page 8 Campbell makes a point that he has made before, that those who reason that the divine nature's singularity must rule out a plurality of persons in that nature—because it is singular—reason incorrectly, binding a *mathematical* point about singularity upon the *divine* nature—a conclusion they reach due to a failure of reason and imagination. It is impossible, he concludes, to be dogmatic about "what is, or is not compatible with the unity, spirituality, and immutability of God."[134]

Under his major section on the Son of God beginning on page 9, Campbell makes two points that tend in the same direction. First, he speaks of the "supreme deity" of the Word of God, which existed "before the *relation* of Father, Son, and Holy Spirit began to be, [in which] his rank in the divine nature was that of the *Word of God*."¹³⁵ This is the same point Campbell had made in his *The Christian Baptist* article of May 7, 1827 in which he speaks of the divine λόγος as eternal but views the relation of Father and Son as coming about only with the incarnation—a "temporal relation."¹³⁶ Second, Campbell is clear that in Jesus "God was manifest in the flesh," not just the λόγος in the flesh, and that Jesus was, indeed, "Emmanuel, God with us." He further refers to Jesus as "the one Lord," but there is clearly in his mind no separation here between the one God and the one Lord in 1 Corinthians 8:6, aside from their personal distinctions. God and Lord clearly for Campbell refer to the same exact divinity.

Referring to the Spirit of God, Campbell says there is a separate and distinct existence for the Spirit of God vis à vis God, but says that "in the sublime and ineffable relation of the deity, or godhead, [the Spirit] stands next to the Incarnate Word."¹³⁷

Most remarkable in Campbell's depiction of Trinitarian theology in *The Christian System* is how he speaks of the necessary belief in "those relations in the Deity." "Destroy these," he says, "blend and confound these, and nature, providence, and grace are blended, confounded, and destroyed." And as Campbell continues, it is clear that it is the divine Trinity seen in God's economic efforts directed at humankind which are necessary for humankind's redemption. He concludes:

> The divine doctrine of the holy and incomprehensible relations in the Divinity is so inwrought and incorporated with all the parts of the sacred book—so identified with all the dispensations of religion—and so essential to the mediatorship of Christ, that it is impossible to make any real and divine proficiency in the true knowledge of God, of man, of reconciliation, or remission of sins, of eternal life, or in the piety and divine life of Christ's religion, without a clear and distinct perception of it, as well as a firm and unshaken faith and confidence in it.¹³⁸

Throughout his career and life-long commitment to Scripture, Campbell refused to bind on Christian believers the Trinitarian language of creedal formulations, but he speaks here of what is essentially classical Trinitarianism as essential to authentic, efficacious Christian faith. This he does just a few pages into a discussion of God, in a work that he intends to serve as a summary of his personal beliefs, intending that his theological positions be not thought of by anyone as a "condition or foundation of church union and cooperation."[139]

Conclusion

It is quite within the spirit of Restorationism to inductively build one's case through the careful examination of texts, whether biblical texts, the texts of one's theological opponents, the texts of those who have proved influential and inspirational—or, in this case, the texts of early Restorationist writers being examined by today's students of historical theology in an attempt to analyze the positions of their theological forebears. A close examination of the specific Trinitarian writings of the Campbells is exactly what is needed in order to establish the tenor of their Trinitarian positions. The relative brevity of the two Campbells' writings on the subject allow for the kind of close treatment and explication that could not be done on an 800-page tome.

Although his father was in complete agreement, it was Alexander who more consistently presented a rationale for avoiding the speculation and theologizing he found so unacceptable in Trinitarian discussions. He hesitated to be openly Trinitarian because of: (1) the lack of an obvious, explicitly stated Trinitarian position within the New Testament, combined with an epistemology and hermeneutical approach that required explicitly stated biblical backing for any major premise within his doctrinal system; (2) his perception that disputes over the doctrine of the Trinity were one of the major contributors to ecclesiastical disunity, particularly in the previous two centuries of the church in Great Britain and the United States; (3) his aversion to Roman Catholic and creedal Christianity, which had consistently made the doctrine of the Trinity a major premise of nearly all creedal statements—both those framed by the early ecumenical councils and those arising as part of post-Reformation Protestantism.

Despite their preferences for theological description that is non-speculative and directly connected to biblical language, both Thomas and Alexander Campbell at times implemented the language of classical

Trinitarian debate in defending a position traditionally associated with orthodoxy. Close examination of their Trinitarian views shows them applying traditional Trinitarian language and argumentation, even when, in Alexander's case, specific criticism is being leveled by him at those who use speculative language and Trinitarian theological jargon. However, instead of accusing Campbell of suffering from inconsistency, it is better to describe him as trying to walk very close to a very thin line, without the ability to completely avoid transgressing onto the side on which he does not want to be. He wants to talk about the Trinity, but he wants to do so in wholly Scriptural categories, clearly separating his own efforts from what he considers speculation. However, neither the line between Bible and theology nor his own separation from speculative categories is as easily marked or negotiated as what he hopes.

With respect to their personal Trinitarian positions, an analysis of the Campbells' submissions on the Trinity supports the conclusion that Thomas and Alexander Campbell were self-consciously Trinitarian, despite the consistent devaluing of the views of "the Trinitarians" by Alexander. This is clearly the case with Thomas, even if he exhibits some tendency toward a slight subordinationism, and it is true of Alexander, even if he wishes to distance himself from any and all "isms" and from notions of Christ's eternal generation. Alexander uses language that in his view separates him from classical Trinitarianism and keeps him centered only in Scripture, but the essence of his Trinitarian view appears ultimately to be traditionally orthodox, so that even he admits that his view is in line with The Westminster Confession of Faith.

The examples of the Campbells demonstrates that twenty-first century SC theologians who recognize their indebtedness to the Campbells would not be in complete violation of their theological heritage were they to take an overtly stated, classically Trinitarian stance. Perhaps the fears that created the Campbells' hesitancies to reveal their personal Trinitarian positions, which also led their theological descendants to avoid Trinitarian theology, may be transcended by an overt, but gracious, nonsectarian Trinitarian perspective. The next three chapters will continue to analyze early SC Trinitarian thought, and Chapters Six and Seven will examine the benefits and possibilities of an overtly stated Restorationist Trinitarian theology.

Notes

[1] Thomas Campbell, *Declaration and Address of the Christian Association of Washington.*

[2] Published at Buffaloe (Bethany) Brooke County, Virginia, 1823–1830.

[3] Published at Bethany, Virginia, in five series with Alexander Campbell as editor 1830–1866.

[4] Alexander Campbell, *The Christian System.*

[5] Alexander Campbell, *Christian Baptism.*

[6] Walter Scott was also the editor of *The Evangelist* from 1832–1842. Cf., Walter Scott, *The Gospel Restored.*

[7] Published at Georgetown, Kentucky, November 1826–April 1845.

[8] Stone, *The Last Will and Testament of the Springfield Presbytery*, 19–23.

[9] Stone, *An Address to the Christian Churches in Kentucky, Tennessee, & Ohio.* All subsequent references to Stone's *An Address to the Christian Churches* will be to the second edition of 1821 unless otherwise indicated.

[10] As noted in Chapter One, Walter Scott made no substantial contribution to SC Trinitarian thought and thus does not require further examination in this book.

[11] Those designated as Latitudinarians here are to be thought of separately from the early High Church version that remained staunchly Anglican, even while advocating philosophical reform. See further discussion on this topic in Chapter Four.

[12] Much more will be said of the effect of Dissent and Independency on the theological and ecclesiological outlook of Thomas Campbell and those who followed him in Chapter Four.

[13] Alexander Campbell, *Memoirs of Elder Thomas Campbell,* 9–10.

[14] See Articles I, II, V, and VIII in the *Thirty-Nine Articles* of Anglicanism.

[15] Cf. Eva Jean Wrather, *Alexander Campbell: Adventurer in Freedom,* 15 and Lester McAllister, *Thomas Campbell: Man of the Book,* 29–30. One may note the significant discrepancy between Wrather and McAllister regarding the years of Thomas Campbell's education and ordination. Richard Phillips argues persuasively for Wrather's accuracy in "Thomas Campbell: A Reappraisal Based on Backgrounds," 77.

[16] More about Thomas Campbell's heritage among the Irish Anti-burgher Presbyterians and the specifics of his latitudinarianism he espoused will be discussed in Chapter Four.

[17] See Phillips, "Thomas Campbell: A Reappraisal Based on Backgrounds," 85–93. Phillips gives an excellent account of which specific preachers and teachers of reform Thomas Campbell contacted and heard preach, although he emphasizes the influence of a reforming Church of Ireland on Thomas. That Phillips sees this Anglican background as crucial fits with what I believe is the significant and lasting influence of Campbell's classically Trinitarian background in the Anglican church, which was affirmed by his later stint with the Presbyterians.

[18] Alexander Campbell, *Memoirs of Elder Thomas Campbell,* 10–11.

[19] Ibid., 8, 10.

[20] Given his predilection for a Latitudinarian orientation in things theological and ecclesiastical, it is noteworthy that he actually maintained his Trinitarian perspective, no doubt with intentionality, in contrast to what he witnessed in other Latitudinarians.

[21] Alexander Campbell, *Memoirs of the Elder Thomas Campbell,* 11.

[22] Ibid., 13.

²³ Lester McAllister, *Thomas Campbell: Man of the Book*, 72–77.
²⁴ Alexander Campbell, *Memoirs of Elder Thomas Campbell*, 229.
²⁵ Ibid., 231–32.
²⁶ The word "Godhead" is found three times in the King James Bible (Acts 17:29, to; θεῖον; Rom. 1:20, θειότης; and Col. 2:9, τῆς θεότητος), which Alexander Campbell seems to take as a reference equivalent to "Trinity."
²⁷ McAllister, *Thomas Campbell: Man of the Book*, 178.
²⁸ Thomas Campbell, *Circular Letter*, 1:539–555.
²⁹ Although delivered in 1816, The Sermon on the Law was not published in its entirety until it appeared in the *Millennial Harbinger* in 1846. Alexander Campbell, "Sermon on the Law," 493–521.
³⁰ Robert Richardson, *Memoirs of Alexander Campbell* 1:479.
³¹ Ibid., 480.
³² Ibid., 482.
³³ Ibid., 480–481.
³⁴ Cf. John D. Zizioulas, *Being As Communion*, 27–65; and Miroslav Volf, *After His Likeness*, 73–83.
³⁵ Thomas Campbell, *Circular Letter*, 550.
³⁶ Ibid., 546.
³⁷ Ibid., 550.
³⁸ This technical language is seen also with respect to his use of rationality and reason, and it is clear that he has Locke as part of his intellectual landscape when he speaks of rational creatures, understanding, and truths and facts.
³⁹ Thomas Campbell, *Prospectus of a Religious Reformation*, 8. At the end of the electronic version available through Abilene Christian University's Center for Restoration Studies, Ernie Stefanik details the reasons for deciding on an 1829 dating, making clear that 1839 is also a possibility. See https://webfiles.acu.edu/departments/Library/HR/restmov_nov11/www.mun.ca/rels/restmov/texts/tcampbell/etc/PORR.HTM (as of February 12, 2014).
⁴⁰ Because he seems to be delineating different soteriological roles for the members of the Trinity, I take Thomas Campbell here to be using "God" as equivalent to "Father," rather than as a summary term of Trinitarian divinity.
⁴¹ See Thomas Campbell, "The Direct and Immediate Intention of the Christian Institution," Essays 1, 2, and 3.
⁴² Thomas Campbell, Essay 1:42
⁴³ Ibid. Cf. Thomas Campbell, "Christian Society," 400.
⁴⁴ Thomas Campbell, Essay 1:43.
⁴⁵ Thomas Campbell, Essay 2:93.
⁴⁶ Thomas Campbell, Essay 3:215–16.
⁴⁷ Ibid., 218.
⁴⁸ Ibid.
⁴⁹ Ibid., 220.
⁵⁰ Alexander Campbell, *Memoirs of Elder Thomas Campbell*, 231.
⁵¹ Ibid., 232.
⁵² See John Zizioulas, *Being as Communion: Studies in Personhood and the Church* (New York: St. Vladimir's Seminary Press, 1985) and Miroslav Volf, *After His Likeness*:

The Church as the Image of the Trinity (Grand Rapids, Michigan: William B. Eerdmans Company, 1998).

[53] Alexander Campbell, *Memoirs of Elder Thomas Campbell*, 232.
[54] Alexander Campbell, "To Timothy," 333.
[55] Ibid., 333–35.
[56] Alexander Campbell, "To Timothy," 333.
[57] Ibid.
[58] Ibid.
[59] Ibid.
[60] Ibid., 334.
[61] Ibid., 333–34.
[62] Ibid., 334.
[63] Ibid.
[64] Ibid.
[65] Ibid., 334. Campbell seems unconcerned about calling God "Father" when there is no Son, so that, in eternity the person of the Father stands in contrast to the Word.
[66] Alexander Campbell, *The Christian System*, 10.
[67] Alexander Campbell, "To Timothy," 334.
[68] Ibid.
[69] Ibid.
[70] Ibid. In his response to Timothy, Campbell does apply "eternal" as an attributive adjective to both "glory" (333) and "dignity" (334), but in both cases he is referencing these as characteristics of the "Saviour," a term Campbell uses to encompass the One who *as* the pre-existent λόγος becomes the incarnate Son of God. Hence, "eternal" is still used by Campbell only for the pre-existent One, and not with specific reference to the Son of God Incarnate, alone.
[71] Ibid.
[72] Ibid., 334–35.
[73] Ibid., 334.
[74] Ibid., 334. The distinction Alexander Campbell makes between the "spiritual" relationship between God and the eternal Word and the "created," "homogenial" relationship of father and son disallows him from describing the Only Begotten Son and Son of God as being eternally related to the Father. Does this adequately take into consideration the claims Jesus himself makes *as Son* about His relationship with His Father? Further, is Campbell's criticism of the Calvinist position fully justifiable; does his description of the Reformed position adequately fit Calvin's view? He says on page 333, "If he were only the Son of God from all eternity, he is entitled to very little, if any more glory, than what the Arians give him." But do Calvinists maintain that the Savior is *only* the Son of God from all eternity and not also the λόγος from all eternity? Cf. John Calvin, *Institutes of the Christian Religion*, 1:6–25; B. B. Warfield, "Calvin's Doctrine of the Trinity," 553–652; Roger T. Beckwith, "The Calvinist Doctrine of the Trinity," 308–15. Calvin's doctrine of the *autotheos* certainly seems to say of the second person that he is more than just an *eternal Son*, if Campbell takes the idea of his eternal status as Son to mean that his full divinity is somehow diminished by such a description.
[75] See Alexander Campbell, "To the Christian Messenger," 380.
[76] Ibid., 379–80.

⁷⁷ Ibid., 380. It is interesting that Campbell would thus describe his first contribution to this series of articles as he obviously had more in mind than an exegetically straightforward explanation of John 1:1. As suggested above, Campbell consistently indicates he simply wishes to expound Scripture, but that very act necessarily includes some extrapolation where Scripture naturally leads beyond its own simple statements. In this case, examining "the ideas attached to the *term*" λόγος flows into a discussion of "the relation existing between him that '*was made flesh,*' and sent into the world, and him who sent him." Clearly even Alexander Campbell himself cannot easily adhere to the goal of avoiding theological construction and only restating scriptural propositions, partially because *Scripture does itself take its readers toward considering such issues.* What then is "speculation," and what is legitimate theologizing closely connected to Scripture? Further, if Campbell at some level felt himself justified in theologizing to at least this extent, if he thought there was some value for his readers in his doing so, is it not legitimate for Restorationists today to ask if there may not be value in their own Trinitarian theologizing? The claim made here is that there is.

⁷⁸ Ibid.
⁷⁹ Ibid.
⁸⁰ Ibid.
⁸¹ Cf. Campbell's comments on using the word "person" instead of "being" in Alexander Campbell, "To Brother Henry Grew," 158.
⁸² Campbell, "To the Christian Messenger," 381.
⁸³ See Alexander Campbell, "Mr. Broaddus," 8.
⁸⁴ Ibid., 10.
⁸⁵ Campbell's fears about speculative Trinitarianism and other theological matters, which grew out of concern for Christian unity and scriptural fidelity, ultimately led to the denigration of systematic theology on the part of Restorationists, as was mentioned in the Chapter 1. Hence, theological discussions that otherwise could have positively influenced Restorationist thought and practice have been to a large extent ignored or intentionally avoided.
⁸⁶ See Alexander Campbell, "Mr. Broaddus," 9.
⁸⁷ Ibid., 9.
⁸⁸ Henry Grew, "Trinitarianism, Arianism, & Socinianism," 153.
⁸⁹ Henry Grew (1781–1862) was originally a Baptist pastor, teacher, and writer whose studies led him to non-Trinitarian conclusions. There appears to be no connection between Grew and either the Disciples or Christians, other than his correspondence with Campbell after having seen Campbell's response to Andrew Broaddus, Grew's fellow Baptist.
⁹⁰ Henry Grew, "Trinitarianism, Arianism, & Socinianism," 153–54.
⁹¹ Alexander Campbell, "To Brother Henry Grew," 154–60.
⁹² Ibid., 154. Campbell says that in answering Grew's questions he will, "attempt to give them as practical an aspect as the off-hand and desultory thoughts of an hour snatched from other pressing subjects of examination will afford." This does not sound like one who is thrilled to be discussing the Trinity.
⁹³ Ibid.
⁹⁴ Ibid., 155.
⁹⁵ Ibid.
⁹⁶ Ibid.

[97] Ibid., 155–56. Cf. same source, 158, where Campbell says, "I find no difficulty in believing that there was, and is, and evermore shall be, society, plurality—a literal *I*, and *thou*, and *he*—a *we*, and *our*, and *us*, in *one divine nature*. This to me is as easy as the idea of SELF-EXISTENT."

[98] Ibid., 156.

[99] Ibid., 154 and 155.

[100] Ibid., 155–156. See Alexander Campbell, "To Timothy," 334 and the discussion of that letter above. Campbell introduces this portion of his response to Grew by saying,

While, then, I do most cordially repudiate the whole scholastic phraseology of the Trinitarian, Arian, and Socinian speculations, I do not, with some Trinitarians, regard my Lord Messiah as having always been an eternal Son; nor can I, with the Arian, view him as some super-angelic creature, filling an immense chasm between Jehovah and the supernal hosts; and still less can I degrade him, with the Socinian, to the rank of a mere man, the son of Joseph. Common sense, reason, and revelation, put their veto on such hypotheses. No my Lord and Saviour is no creature, nor the son of a creature. In the beginning he was THE WORD OF GOD, is now the Son of God and will, when government is no longer necessary, be again recognized as the Word of God, "a name which no man knows, but he himself."

Again, Campbell cannot keep himself from expressing his view on Trinitarian matters, despite his *cordial repudiation*, a fact for which I would commend him rather than charge him with being speculative. But interesting, here, too, is how he shows himself, again, with consistency, to refer to common sense, reason, and revelation in making Trinitarian assertions. In doing so Campbell reveals his propensity to echo John Locke, despite what I would see as a clear difference between where the two eventually arrive with reference to the Trinity. Like his 1827 correspondence with Timothy, Campbell stresses the full divinity of the Word, wanting to make it clear that for him the second person of the Trinity is not just an eternal Son, but is the eternal Word of God. Cf. William Babcock, "A Changing of the Christian God," 142–44 on John Locke's view of the Trinity. I take Campbell to be much closer to a classically Trinitarian position than Locke is thought by many to be.

[101] Alexander Campbell, "To Brother Henry Grew," 157.

[102] Ibid., 158.

[103] Ibid.

[104] Ibid.

[105] Ibid., 159.

[106] I am thinking here of Augustine's discussions in *De Trinitate* concerning the sendings/missions, e.g., Book 2, Chapter 3 or Book 4, Chapter 5, and his analogies between Trinity and human psychology in Book 9. But Campbell's comments are too brief to establish a relationship, much less a dependency on Augustine. Campbell was, one can surmise, familiar with Augustine's work, but he clearly has no interest in working through Augustine's argument in order to formulate his own position.

[107] Ibid.

[108] Ibid.

[109] Ibid.

[110] Ibid., 160.

[111] Ibid.

[112] See Alexander Campbell, "Union Among Christians," 216–20.

[113] Ibid., 219–20.
[114] See Ibid., 216–25; Alexander Campbell, "Unitarianism, Or, Remarks on Christian Union, No. II," 388–94; "Unitarianism as Connected With Christian Union—No. III," 450–54; "Unitarianism as Connected With Christian Union—No. IV," 634–38; "Christian Union—No. V," 686–95.
[115] Ibid., 222.
[116] Alexander Campbell, "Unitarianism, Or, Remarks on Christian Union, No. II," 392.
[117] Ibid., 393–94.
[118] In the third article in this series, page 451, Campbell is very clear that he rejects creedal Trinitarianism, saying, "I am no advocate of scholastic Trinitarianism, and never have been; for its vocabulary is not only as unscriptural as that of the Unitarians, but as metaphysically and as learnedly obscure and unintelligible."
[119] Alexander Campbell, "Unitarianism as Connected With Christian Union—No. III," 452–53.
[120] Ibid., 450–51.
[121] Ibid., 452.
[122] Ibid., 453.
[123] See Alexander Campbell, "To Timothy," 333ff.
[124] Alexander Campbell, "Unitarianism as Connected With Christian Union—No. IV," 634–35.
[125] Ibid., 636.
[126] Ibid. Campbell also references here the argument from divine plurality that is traditionally made from the Hebrew plural pronoun of Genesis 1:26, and he applies the traditional analogy of the trinity of body, soul, and spirit within human beings as being similar to the Three within God, in whose image human beings are made. Again, Campbell is not afraid to use the traditional arguments of orthodoxy when they suit him.
[127] Ibid., 638.
[128] Alexander Campbell, "Christian Union—No. V," 687.
[129] Ibid., 690.
[130] Ibid.
[131] Ibid., 692–93.
[132] Ibid., 694. Cf. Alexander Campbell, "A. Campbell to Elder A. Broaddus—*No. III*," where Campbell writes, "For myself, I acknowledge that my sectarian partialities, as well as my more mature convictions, are all on the side of the general views of the Protestant reformers in those questions which involves the *person, office,* and *work* of the Messiah."
[133] Alexander Campbell, *The Christian System,* 8.
[134] Ibid., 9. Compare above where Campbell answers Barton Stone with the same argument.
[135] Ibid., 10.
[136] Ibid., 10.
[137] Ibid., 11.
[138] Ibid., 12.
[139] Ibid., xvii–xviii.

The Trinity in the Writings of Barton Stone: STONE'S QUASI-ARIANISM

Aside from discussion at the beginning of the Movement concerning why the doctrine of the Trinity should be relegated to a place of less significance than other Christian teachings, it is likely that no other specific issue within SC Trinitarianism has been as widely discussed among historical theologians as the Trinitarian perspective of Barton Warren Stone. Although Stone's Trinitarianism received little attention until the last quarter of the twentieth century, the general increased interest in Trinitarian theology, combined with the publication in 2000 of Newell Williams' biography of Stone, has raised awareness of Stone's non-Trinitarian perspective.[1]

Barton Stone has in general received less attention within the history of SC thought than Thomas and Alexander Campbell, with the latter clearly being considered the major contributor to whatever may be identified as *the* SC theological ethos. With respect to Trinitarian doctrine, Alexander Campbell's understated (even "intentionally avoided") orthodox Trinitarianism has dominated SC perspectives, and average Christians and many in ministerial positions in SC churches are likely to be ignorant of Stone's thoughts on the Trinity.

Barton Stone's Historical Path Toward Quasi-Arianism

Details of Barton Stone's life—some of which are significant for assessing his Trinitarian position—are well-known due largely to his own autobiography and the work of a few historians who have supplied additional details.[2] Stone was born on December 24, 1772, near Port Tobacco, Maryland, apparently to an upper-class, Anglican family. After the death of his father, his mother in 1779 moved the family to Pittsylvania County, Virginia, where Barton began to attend school and eventually came under the tutelage of Englishman Robert Somerhays. Following the Revolutionary War, Stone became aware of religious affiliations other than the Anglican church, particularly the Methodists and Baptists. However, his greatest interest was in furthering himself through a liberal education and a career in law, and so he entered David Caldwell's classical academy in Guildford County, North Carolina, in January 1790.

Caldwell was a Presbyterian minister of the New Light tradition, meaning he was prone to accept the features of Christianity of the Great Awakening, including an emphasis on religious experience. These ideas he freely brought into the lives of his students, although Stone, as a studious Anglican, initially saw it as little more than a distraction from his studies. Eventually, Stone gave in to invitations from his roommate to hear James McGready preach. After hearing McGready, Stone resolved to seek religion whatever the cost, although he was not convinced of the validity of his own conversion. After months of wrestling, Stone eventually became convinced of his salvation, and he completed the majority of the last two years at Caldwell's Academy with a new fervor for both his education and his faith.[3]

By the time Barton Stone finished his liberal education at Caldwell's Academy in winter 1793, he had decided to seek a vocation in Christian ministry in order to preach the gospel, and he entered into study for ordination to the Presbyterian ministry. In preparation for the ordination examination, Stone and classmate Samuel Holmes were assigned to study the being and attributes of God and the doctrine of the Trinity, and they were asked by the Orange Presbytery to read a text by Herman Witsius, a Dutch Reformed theologian. Stone's biggest struggle in his reading was what he saw as the *unreasonable* presentation by Witsius of the Trinity, including his suggestion that in the doctrine of the Trinity there was a mystery that was to be accepted by every Christian as part of one's renouncement of human wisdom.[4]

Fortunately for Stone, the Presbyterians who had some control over his ordination process were for the most part little bothered by his hesitancies about Witsius. In fact, Henry Patillo, who was in charge of the ordination examination for Stone and Holmes, was an advocate of the writings of Isaac Watts on the Trinity, and Stone and Holmes read and accepted Watts's *The Christian Doctrine of the Trinity*, which put them in a ready position for their exam. They both passed, even though it would be several years before Stone would actually be ordained.[5]

Newell Williams records Stone's continued consternation concerning the Trinity in the years prior to his ordination by the Transylvania Presbytery of Kentucky.[6] Although he labored to believe Trinitarian doctrine as found in The Westminster Confession of Faith, he could not bring himself to become a conscientious subscriber. Stone was able to accept ordination in 1798 only because of an allowance made for those who believed in the essentials of the Confession, as was set forth in the Adopting Act of 1729. That allowance was in 1798 being applied by Presbyterian "New Lights" who were willing to ignore the fact that the Adopting Act had been overturned in 1758. Following discussion with James Blythe and Robert Marshall, both members of the Transylvania Presbytery, Stone agreed to be ordained, permitting that he could simply say he agreed with the Confession "as far as I see it consistent with the Word of God." This was sufficient for the New Lights conducting Stone's ordination.[7]

However, this was neither the end of Stone's wrestling with Trinitarian issues nor the last time he would publicly be confronted because of his views.[8] Between 1798 and 1803, Stone was gradually moving away from the orthodox Presbyterian faith, especially with reference to the atonement, although he was still intensely involved with Presbyterian ministry. This culminated in 1803 with the departure of Stone and several others first from the local Presbytery and the Kentucky Synod and eventually from Presbyterianism altogether. In 1805 Stone published his *Atonement, The Substance of Two Letters Written to a Friend* as part of the clear disagreement he was experiencing with Presbyterianism regarding the efficacy and extent of Christ's atoning death.[9] In response, David Rice and John Campbell (no relation to Thomas and Alexander) challenged Stone concerning his position and how his views on the atonement seemed likely to lead him into Pelagianism, Arianism, Socinianism, deism, and atheism.[10] Specifically, Rice asserted that Stone was following this path because of an unwillingness to accept "unreasonable mysteries."[11] For John Campbell, Stone was virtually a deist, "a reasoner," who denies Christ's "equality with the Father; [who] should be ashamed to deliver such absurd doctrine."[12]

Although Stone responded in 1805 to Rice and Campbell by saying he believed the divinity in Christ was the same divinity that is in the Father, one must wonder what he thought the ramifications of his position would be in relation to the traditional Trinitarian orthodoxy of his critics. Stone says:

> I do not believe that the man Christ Jesus was equal to God; nor do I believe that the divinity in Christ was equal to God, for that divinity was God himself.—*In him dwelt all the fullness of Godhead bodily—the Father dwelt in him,* etc. Sameness and equality have a different meaning. Equality implies plurality, and one cannot be equal to itself. God is one, infinite, self-existent and independent being. Now if there is another equal to this one, then there are two equals in infinity, self-existence, power, and independence. The very notion destroys itself; for two infinities is the greatest absurdity; as one infinity fills infinity, and leaves no room for another. But Christ is equal to the Father *in name. His name shall be called the mighty God, the Everlasting Father, the Prince of Peace.* . . . By office he is equal to the Father.[13]

Here, Stone offers a glimpse into an idea that will later be fully developed in *An Address to the Christian Churches:* that the *divinity in Christ* cannot be equal to God because that divinity *is God himself,* and, according to Stone's reasoning, that which is the same as another cannot be equal to the other because the concept of being equal implies there are two items of comparison. Further, Christ's divinity is a feature of God's indwelling of the Son, and not of the Son's ontology. Further, still, there is only one true God; there cannot be two, and the Son, if he has separate personhood from the Father, cannot be that one only true God. In 1805, those aware of Stone's position were already asking questions of the now-renegade former Presbyterian: Is the equality Stone recognized between Christ and God an equality between the deity *in* the man Jesus and God, apart from Jesus the man, himself, so that the humanity in Jesus in no way participates in divinity? Is the equality here expressed only equality in name? Is Christ equal with God only according to his office, but not his personhood? To what extent does Christ share the infinity, aseity, and independence of God? Although such questions could sincerely be asked of his still developing position, at the very least it was clear Stone was moving or had moved beyond Presbyterian orthodoxy with respect to the Trinity.

It is not surprising that Newell Williams would assert that although Stone "was spiritually a Presbyterian, his mind was also deeply influenced by the popular rationalism of the early American republic."[14] From Caldwell's Academy, from James McGready and others, and from the general intellectual/philosophical climate of the times, Stone learned that God deals with rational creatures through rational ideas, so that doctrines and propositions contrary to reason were necessarily suspect. Thus, Stone found it difficult to believe that three persons in one God could be real, distinct persons, as that would contradict the teaching that there was only one God who also shared the features of personhood. Further, if the one true God could suffer and die, how could he be immutable and without passions? Although in 1805 Stone may have not been completely clear as to where he stood regarding the full deity of Christ, within a decade he would take an opportunity to make himself quite clear. A consideration of key works published by Stone show his position strongly headed in the direction of Arianism.

In 1814 Stone published his Trinitarian opinions for the first time in an orderly, intentional way in *An Address to the Christian Churches in Kentucky, Tennessee, and Ohio, on Several Important Doctrines Of Religion;* a second edition followed in 1821.[15] This summary of Stone's conclusions on both the Trinity and Jesus as the Son of God (including material on the atonement, along with several other doctrines) includes some preliminary observations followed by a carefully presented series of arguments challenging numerous features of the orthodox positions on the Trinity and Christology. For our purposes, it is important to set forth Stone's position in detail, identifying the 1821 second edition of *An Address to the Christian Churches* as the key document from which to ascertain Stone's position on the Trinity. Stone presented other lengthy discussions of the Trinity and the atonement, typically in response to the efforts by others to answer his arguments, and these will be treated as supplemental evidence for his position. He also occasionally published articles in *The Christian Messenger,* as we have already seen in the case of his dialogue with Alexander Campbell, and some of these will also be treated in detail.

Barton Stone's Key Work on the Trinity: *An Address to the Christian Churches*

Perhaps the first thing to note about Barton Stone's *An Address to the Christian Churches* is that there is a defensive, almost polemical tone to the work, including a way of dealing with the doctrine of the Trinity that is designed to acknowledge and answer other positions as much as it is intended to positively state a biblical doctrine. From the outset of the introduction to the second edition, Stone speaks of the criticism and "censorious strictures" that have come his way in response to the first edition, and he says the reason he is currently addressing these doctrines is to allow his readers to "better judge of the reasonableness of our objections to them, and whether our brethren have good cause for censuring us so harshly."[16] He says, "We have borne the opposition against us with tolerable patience"[17] and that "It is well known to you that there are many reports of a heretical nature in circulation against us as a people, and especially against us, your ministers, which I think are without any just grounds."[18] He further admits that he has "ventured to deny what is termed the orthodox explanation of some very popular doctrines" but points out that he has attempted to refute just the traditional explanations of the doctrines, not the doctrines themselves.[19] He gives as an example the doctrine of election, saying he does not deny that Christianity includes such a doctrine but that his explanation of it would be different than the traditional position.

"Section I. Of Trinity."

Following these introductory remarks—which are echoed in his style of argument, in that frequently an argument against the traditional position constitutes the focus of his comments—he launches into "SECTION I. OF TRINITY."

Stone begins his discussion of Trinitarian doctrine by stating what is a foundational principle for both the Judaic/Christian way of thinking and for *his* entire way of thinking about the Trinity: "That there is but one living and true God," and that this "is a plain doctrine of revelation." Further, quoting from 1 Corinthians 8:4–6, he makes it clear that based on these verses he sees a difference between the Father, who is called God, and Jesus Christ, who is called Lord, and that there exists between them a distinction consequent of the fact that there is only one true and living God.[20] Because there cannot be two or three Gods, and because "all agree that this *one only* God is *an infinite spirit without parts;* all must agree that this infinite spirit is not a compound of two or three spirits, beings, or Gods."[21] From the start, then, Stone has stated his opposition to the identification of the Son with the one only true God, taking as part of his argument the logical conclusion he sees as necessary: if there is in fact only one God the Father who cannot be separated into different persons, beings, or Gods, then Jesus cannot be a separate person who can at the same time be the person who is the Father. There are many additional arguments that Stone will make that claim places for the Son, for Jesus Christ the man, and for the Spirit that are in some ways less than the place claimed for the Father, but this first argument for Stone is, in my estimation, both prior to and foundational for the remainder of his argumentation.

From these opening remarks, Stone proceeds to make the claim that the word "Trinity" is not actually found in the Bible.[22] This point seems a bit out of place in his argument, disrupting the flow, and, in fact, this is a rather clumsy insertion into the second edition of 1821 that was absent from the 1814 edition. It is interesting that Stone even makes the point, partially because it is well-known to most, but partially because it runs in the face of Isaac Watts's choice to consistently use the word "Trinity" in all of his Trinitarian writings. Since Stone refers to Watts as the one whose Trinitarian position he emulates, his denigration of the word "Trinity" cannot help but insinuate something about Watts's frequent use of the term, indicating there are at least some differences between Stone's way of construing Trinitarian doctrine and those of Isaac Watts.[23]

Stone makes it clear, as he had years before in his reaction to the work of Witsius, that he rejects the notion that the difficult and seemingly illogical nature of the classical Trinitarian view cannot be defended by claiming it is too mysterious for comprehension.[24] He says "many of these expressions we have rejected," leaving the impression that, as a rational man living in a time influenced by Enlightenment, there is no room for unclear expressions of religious truth. Although he does not here make Locke's claim that he will not accept propositions about God that are contrary to reason, it is easy to hear in the background echoes of the general intellectual climate that would push Stone in the direction of reasonableness and away from mystery.

Following what are almost digressions in referring to the word Trinity and to the mysterious nature of the concept, Stone spends several paragraphs addressing his main point, that within the one only true God there cannot be three persons, or three distinct spirits, beings or Gods, "each possessed of the personal properties of intelligence, will, and power; for this would not only contradict the scriptures, but also those sections of their [the Trinitarians] creeds . . . which declare that there is but one only living and true God, without parts."[25] In Stone's eyes, acceptance of such a reality would so violate the definition of *personhood*, that the three who comprise the one true God would necessarily have to be considered as something other than persons; but what this "something other" would be is not found in Scripture nor does such a conception of personhood fit with what reason knows about persons. Some have tried to explain the individuality of the three by describing them as God's power, wisdom, and love, personified, but such attributes or perfections in God could easily be multiplied beyond three; at what large number would such a connection between attributes and personhood stop? Certainly not just at three. On the same grounds, neither should the Three be considered representatives of such offices as Creator, Redeemer, and Sanctifier.[26] Instead, to explain how three Persons can exist within the one Person of the one only true God, theologians must resort to the language of mystery, where they will wander through the "unknown fields of eternity, infinity and incomprehensibility."[27]

As part of his argument, Stone examines places in Scripture he says others use to support the three-in-one idea, turning first to an interpretation of 1 John 5:7. His identification of this particular verse is interesting in that the part with which he is most concerned (part of verse 8 in the KJV) has virtually no support among the best New Testament manuscripts available and has been excised from recent translations of the New Testament. Stone himself draws attention to the tenuous authenticity of the words, "in heaven: the Father, the Word and the Holy Spirit, and these three are one. And there are three that testify on the earth," pointing out that these words had been dropped by Griesbach in his Greek text and that Philip Doddridge questioned their authenticity.[28] Nonetheless, he argues the point that the context, particularly verses 10-12, indicates the "oneness" of the Three is actually a unification of mindful agreement in bearing witness to the Son and his efficacious role in salvation, rather than his place within the Trinity. Therefore, this is not a statement indicating that the Three are ontologically one.[29] Further, he cites John 10:30 and John 17:21-22 as texts used by Trinitarians to assert the ontological oneness of Father and Son, when actually only intellectual or purposeful agreement are intended by Christ in such texts, as in the common agreement that two minds may share with respect to a perspective or opinion. He concludes: "The fact is, all believers are one in spirit, purpose, and mind—and this is the oneness which our Lord prayed they might have [in John 17:21-22]—this was the oneness of Paul and Apollos.—This appears to me to be the oneness of the Father and the Son."[30] Further, in John 14:38 Jesus makes the claim that "My Father is greater than I." Not only does such a proposition clearly state the inequality of the Father and Son, but the language is in fact comparative, which is just the kind of language the Bible could not use about the relationship between the two were they identical, because there could then be no grounds for comparison. Again, note that Stone's procedure for establishing what he believes is less a positive statement of a biblical position than a refutation of the arguments traditionally used to support classical Trinitarian doctrine.

Stone now turns to address the grammatical/morphological evidence used by some to argue for a plurality of persons within God, specifically referencing the plurals *Elohim* and *Adonim* from the Hebrew Bible and the way in which these terms are used in the plural to refer to the one true God. Citing Robertson's Hebrew grammar, Stone argues that the use of a plural designation can indicate greatness and excellency, rather than a plurality of persons, and he cites places in the Hebrew Bible where *Elohim* is used of persons or things which obviously are not plural in nature: Moses in Exodus 7:1; the molten calf in Exodus 32:4, 8; a reference to individual idols in Judges 16:22, 24, 1 Kings 11:32, 2 Kings 1:2, and 2 Kings 19:37. The plural word *Adonim,* master, is found in Genesis 24:9, 10, and 51 in reference to the greatness of Abraham, and *Adonim* is used to describe Potiphar in Genesis 39:2, 3, 7, 8, 16, 20. The captain of the guard is *Adonim* in Genesis 40:7, and Joseph is *Adonim* in Genesis 42:30, 33. In all these cases, the singular is used for the plural to show reverence.[31] Having made his point, Stone says:

> It would be unnecessary to multiply quotations. These surely are sufficient to prove to any unprejudiced mind, that the plural word, put for a singular, does not imply a plurality of persons ... That the scriptures speak of the Father, Son and Holy Spirit, is believed and admitted by christians of every name; and that these three are *one* in some sense, I think, none will deny. My view of this oneness I have expressed a few pages back. If they are one in any other sense, I shall rejoice to know it.[32]

Stone finishes his first section on the Trinity by stating the prejudices that would keep otherwise fair minds from accepting his views, claiming some hear only the labels others use to denigrate his position, while others reject his perspective only because it is so simple. They prefer the language of mystery and are accustomed to thinking of Trinitarian doctrine in just these mysterious, incomprehensible terms. For his part, Stone considers such mysteries both above and contrary to reason, and he would only accept them if he could be satisfied that in Scripture they had been revealed. As it is, he will reject the mysterious language of orthodox Trinitarianism as unscriptural, but he will accept into fellowship those who continue to accept the language of the creedal statements, refusing to, like them, make the acceptance—or the rejection—of this creedal Trinitarian language a test of orthodoxy.[33]

"Section II. Of the Son of God."

Stone begins the second section of *An Address to the Christian Churches* by denying the claim that he refuses to accept the divinity of the Son of

God. He does not, he writes, deny the divinity of the Son, but he denies the traditional orthodox position regarding his divinity. Stone first catalogues what he thinks are the three standard opinions about the deity of the Son: (1) he is the eternal Son; the eternally begotten Son (traditional Trinitarianism and traditional Christology); (2) he never existed as a Son before being born of Mary; and (3) he is the first begotten of the Father, the firstborn of every creature, brought forth before all worlds, then united to a body, so that all the fullness of God dwells in him. The last of these perspectives he claims for himself, saying he will briefly explicate the previous two positions, then spend the balance of this section delineating his own position.[34] It is interesting that at this point Stone uses the word "creature"—an allusion to Colossians 1:15—as this is an indication of the Arian direction that he obviously is not hesitant to at some level claim for his own position, even though he specifically denies being a follower of Arius and claims to be ignorant of the Arian stance.[35]

Addressing the Orthodox Perspective. The first section in which Stone addresses the traditionally orthodox Trinitarian perspective is six pages long, and it begins with Stone stating the position he will now critique, which he takes from The Westminster Confession of Faith, Chapter 8, section 2. In these words, he says, "I find several opinions against which I object":

> The first opinion is that "The Son of God, the second person in the Trinity, being very and eternal God, of one substance, and equal with the Father, did, when the fullness of time was come, take upon him man's nature, with all the essential properties, and common infirmities thereof, yet without sin: being conceived by the power of the Holy Ghost in the womb of the Virgin Mary, and of her substance. So that two whole, perfect and distinct natures, the Godhead and the manhood were inseparably joined together in one person, without conversion, composition or confusion, which person is very God and very man, the only mediator between God and man."[36]

Stone begins his critique by saying that the idea that the Son was very and eternal God, and yet eternally begotten, is unacceptable on the grounds that the expressions "eternal son" and "eternally begotten" are not in the Bible. They are human inventions susceptible to being examined by human reason, and reason tells us that the same substance cannot beget itself or be begotten by itself. Therefore, the substance of the Son was never begotten nor born, because the claim of Trinitarians is that the Son shares the eternal, "unbegotten" substance of the Father. If the substance of the Son is eternal, then it was never begotten; if the Son were eternally begotten, then he had no substance, for the Father's substance is not begotten. And, if he had no substance, then he could not exist, and so is not real.[37] There are, then, on this point two sources for Stone's objections: one is that they do not express truths about the Son "in biblical language," and the other is that they result—in his mind—to logical absurdities. Both of these sources of critique are, of course, standard fare within SC churches even today, running very much in line with the hermeneutical style of Alexander Campbell. Stone and Campbell may not have agreed on the doctrine of the Trinity, and, therefore did not always agree on the ways in which logic was to be applied to biblical propositions, but they would agree on the basic premises that doctrine was to be formulated upon the exact language of the Bible, evaluated according to a strict application of reasonable logic.[38]

Stone continues to argue along similar lines for the next several pages of *An Address to the Christian Churches*, typically asserting either the logical absurdities or the absence of a biblical grounding of the traditional Trinitarian position:

- The language of begetting implies a preceding begetting agent; if the Father existed before the Son and his action of begetting existed before the Son, the Son is not eternally begotten because the Father preceded him.[39]
- If the Son is the very and eternal God, because there is only one God, then, the Son begat himself and was his own Father! How could the Son exist before He was begotten?[40] If He did exist before He was begotten, then he never was begotten at all. If He did not exist before He was begotten, then He was not begotten from eternity, is not eternal, and is not the one true eternal God.[41]

- If the Father begat a real, eternal being, who is the Son, so that it can be said that the Son is a real, eternal being, then there must be two real, eternal beings; or the real being of the Son must be denied.[42]
- If the same real eternal being that was God was sent by a real eternal being who is God, then one being (God) is sending and being sent, and is both active and passive in the sending, which is impossible.[43]
- If it cannot be a real, intelligent, eternally begotten being who was sent into the world, then it is perhaps a personal property or divine perfection, but this would either be a denial of the Son as a real proper person, for no property is a real, intelligent being, or it would be a denial that the one who is sent is the Son of God or God, both of whom are Persons.[44]
- Stone rhetorically asks, do people believe that the one and only true eternal God was born of Mary? He does not answer his question, but his implication concerns the absurdity of an answer in the affirmative.[45] He argues similarly by then essentially asking, do people believe that the eternal God truly suffered on the cross? That he was dead? That he was buried? These to Stone are all absurd notions unaligned with the biblical witness about the one only true God.[46]

Not to be missed at this point is the extension of Stone's argument from identifying the absurdities of classically delineated Trinitarian relationships to including the absurdities of classical Christology. The traditional position, he says, is:

> That the second person of trinity was united with our nature, that the two whole and entire natures, Godhead and manhood, were *inseparably* united, *never to be divided,* very God and very man in one person, who truly suffered, was crucified, dead and buried, to reconcile the Father to us. Hence we must conclude that the very God suffered, yea, *truly* suffered!—that the very and only one God was crucified! yea, was dead!—and buried too!!—and continued three days and nights under the power of

death!—for the two natures, Godhead and manhood, are *inseparably united never to be divided*—therefore as the human body was in Joseph's tomb, so must be the Godhead too!—All this was done and suffered by the very God, say our brethren in the forecited, articles, to reconcile the Father to us! Here is certainly the notion of two distinct Gods held forth—the one an unchangeable God; the other a changeable one—the one a living God; the other a dead, buried one—the one reconciling; the other reconciled! But as all acknowledge that there is but one only *living* God; therefore we must conclude that the one that was dead was not that one only living and true God. And as all acknowledge the one only living and true God is *without passions,* therefore he that suffered such exquisite *passion* on the cross, was not the only living and true God.[47]

It is interesting that Stone combines the idea that God is impassable and immutable, and so cannot suffer, with the idea that there must now be two Gods, for surely one God could not be capable of both impassability and suffering. Interesting, too, is his theological understanding that the one *living* God would be incapable of experiencing death, and so he could not be the One who hung on the cross, meaning "we must conclude that the one that was dead was not that one only living and true God."

Clearly the perception by Stone of what is possible in God's existence includes the same kind of dispassionate monotheism against which Jürgen Moltmann and many theologians today have juxtaposed their own Trinitarian views. His argument, then, is not only based in what is reasonable, or in what is allowable with reference to exact biblical language, but in theological understanding regarding God's attributes. The issue here is not just a question of what is possible in light of God's ontology, but of his personality and attitudes and what they allow for in God. What will the compassionate nature of God allow? What is he capable of enduring on behalf of humankind? To what extent does suffering love comprise the very personhood of God? For Stone, nothing of God's character would allow for suffering within His personhood. Clearly, if a fully Trinitarian stance is taken—at least one that coheres with the kind of God envisioned in much of contemporary Trinitarian theology—possibilities for viewing God in a way other than as the impassable monarch become possible. At this point much of Stone's argumentation would lose its force.

- If God cannot suffer, and the Son of God is the one true God, then the suffering that occurred on the cross could not be endured by God or the Son of God, meaning that the one crucified could only be a mere man. If this is the case, then how is God's love commended in him or His death efficacious?[48]
- Again referring to the two natures doctrine of Chalcedon, Stone simply wonders how the two inseparable natures can be found to be crying out, "My God, My God . . ."? How can he be God of the universe and in a tomb at the same time? How can the Son at the end of the world be subject to the Father?[49]

Stone ends this section by again drawing together the two main lines of argument he consistently applies in refuting classical Trinitarianism. He says:

> Though the notions that the Son, the second person of trinity, was eternally begotten—that the very God was united with human nature in the womb of Mary, and born of her—that Godhead suffered, died and was buried—that the very God suffered thus to reconcile the Father to us—though these notions appear absurd to our limited capacities, yet I would humbly admit them if the Scriptures ever made such declarations. But as I find no such declarations in the Bible, I can not admit them as articles of my faith. Some, better read in the divinity of the schools, than in that of Jesus and his disciples, may be ready to call this blasphemy. Of such I would ask, where did Jesus or his disciples ever teach or propose such doctrines? Search the Scriptures.

On the basis of reasonable absurdity, then, along with the lack of specific scriptural warrant for the premises of classical Trinitarian doctrine, Stone rejects orthodox, creedal Trinitarian theology, stating that he also refuses to accept or admit the possibility that such theological precepts are difficult to square with human reason only because they constitute the mysteries of the divine.[50] Instead, statements of faith—classical creedal formulas—constitute instruction that should be rejected in favor of a position that presents Jesus Christ as the divine Son of God, but who is nonetheless not to be identified with the one only true God who alone is eternal, "unbegotten," and supreme.

Addressing the Socinian Position. Stone's second division in the section on the "Son of God," is a brief refutation of what he takes to be the Socinian position—that the Son of God did not exist until he became a human being born of Mary. The essence of his argument is that Trinitarians and Socinians are in essence the same position, because Trinitarians deny that the Son was a real, intelligent, separate being from the Father who was sent into the world; he was a property or effulgence or perfection, but not a real separated person. This property, Trinitarians must believe, was united with a reasonable soul and body in Mary and did not have proper existence as a person before this. Only upon the joining together of the property or effulgence with a body did the Son actually exist as a person or being, which amounts to this perspective being similar to the Socinian view, where there was no separate Son of God until he was formed in Mary.

Unfortunately, what Stone actually does is to make a simple assertion favorably comparing what he thinks to be true of classical Trinitarianism—that Trinitarians illogically and unscripturally conclude that the Son was a separate being existing from eternity—with what he takes as true about a particular version of Socinianism, rather than to make an argument about Socinianism or Trinitarianism. Then, since what he says about Socinianism is really nothing more than further argument against Trinitarianism ("the Trinitarians are nothing more than Socinians"), he asserts that he will actually counter Socinianism by positively presenting his own position about the relationship between the Father and Son.[51]

Offering His Own Position. The third division of Stone's section on the Son of God begins with a plain statement of his own position:

> My own views of the Son of God are that he did not begin to exist 1820 years ago, nor did he exist from eternity; but was the first begotten of the Father before time or creation began—that

he was sent by the Father 1820 years ago into the world, and united with a body, prepared for him; and that in him dwelt all the fullness of Godhead bodily. These propositions I will endeavor to establish by arguments drawn from the oracles of truth.[52]

It should be noted that here Stone is quite specific in speaking of the Son of God's origin into a non-eternal—but before time and before creation—pre-existence, vis à vis his existence as the eternal divine λόγος as seen in the position of Alexander Campbell. The Son comes into existence ("was first begotten") at some unspecified point before the rest of creation and so is not eternal, and, therefore, must have a separate existence from the one only true eternal God; and, yet, the full divinity of God did, in fact, indwell him. He does not state here what exactly makes up the constitution of the Son of God is in his pre-existence, especially as he exists as the "first born of all creation." If Stone exactly follows Isaac Watts at this point, then he will argue not only for the "begottenness" of the Son, but also for the joining together—prior to anything else being created—of the begotten Son with a pre-existent human soul.

Following this opening summary of his position, Stone enumerates ten arguments to support his view concerning the Son of God. Many of his points are little more than restatements of what he has already presented concerning the logical problems that occur if Trinitarians are still to think that the Son is the one only true God. However, per his dependence on the perspective of Isaac Watts, the other major focus of the ten arguments is to establish the pre-existence of the Son but without wishing to establish his eternality.

- The Son is said to be the firstborn of all creation, but this cannot be according to his flesh, since millions were born into flesh before him. His being born or begotten, must, then, refer to and have occurred in some pre-existent time before the rest of creation came to be, when he came into existence but not in bodily form. Those who would argue that the status of the Son as *firstborn* is actually a reference to him being the first to rise from the dead miss the context of Colossians 1:15, which is clearly referring to a time anterior to creation. As with his previous arguments against the classical Trinitarian position, Stone reasons by an application of logic to scriptural propositions, in this case formulating a scenario that logically reconciles the propositions concerning the Son's status as firstborn with his existence before creation.[53]

- Since the one God—the Father—is the only efficient cause of all things, the Son is the instrumental cause. Therefore, there are not only two beings with different roles, but the Son existed before all the rest of creation without being God.[54]
- When the Son prays to the Father in John 17, he prays for glory to be returned to him, a glory that he at some point lost; that because God cannot change, the Son cannot be God; and that whatever he lost he lost before the world was, and so he obviously existed with the Father before the creation of the world. He is, therefore, pre-existent, but not the one only true God.[55]
- Argument 4 applies Proverbs 8:22–24 and John 17:5 in reaching the conclusion that the Son was pre-existent as one who was "*set up* from everlasting."[56]
- Applying 2 Corinthians 8:9 in Argument 5, Stone makes the point that Paul's claim that Christ became poor cannot refer to something that happened in his earthly existence, since he was from the outset poor in this world. His condescension must, then, have happened at a time prior to his earthly existence, establishing his pre-existence, but not his identity with the one only true God.[57]
- The premise of Argument 6 is that John 1:15, 17 make it clear that Jesus is pre-existent because he was before John the Baptist, dispensing grace and truth. Further, if the saints of old received grace and truth from God, they received it from the Son, indicating that he was before Abraham and Moses, and even before Adam.[58]
- Argument 7: That Christ ascended to where he was before He came to earth (John 6:62) and that Stephen in Acts 7 saw Christ at God's right hand indicate His pre-existence at God's right hand.[59]

- In Argument 8, Stone makes the claim that if the Son humbled himself in becoming a human being (Phil. 2:6), He changed from one superior state to another inferior one—but God cannot change. Further, the man Jesus was humble from the beginning of his earthly life, and so no change in status is reflected in his earthly life, meaning that His being humbled cannot refer to a change within His humanity. So, the Son of God who is pre-existent is neither just a man nor is He the one only true God. He is the glorious Son of God, who has experienced suffering and eternal praises.[60]
- From John 6:32 we know that there was one who pre-existed and who came down from heaven and joined a body, but we also know that he was not the one only true God, because he came to do the will of God.[61]

Although Stone now claims that he has accomplished the task that the ten arguments were intended to accomplish—he has established the pre-existence of the Son of God—a good number of his arguments also included a denial—based most often in syllogistic comparisons of biblical propositions with the claims of orthodox Trinitarianism—of the identification of the Son with the one only true God, a point that is obviously central in his perspective regarding the Son. He has consistently *negatively* argued against classical Trinitarian thought, then, as much as he has *positively* asserted the status of the Son in his relationship with God. In fact, we are still left wondering as to the exact relationship between the begotten Son and his humanity, in that the Son is begotten but not human in his pre-existence, and yet the claim of Colossians 1:15, according to Stone's understanding, is that the Son is the first born *of all creation*. If in his pre-existence he is the first born of all creation, then at some point prior to the rest of creation, there must become something about him that connects with creation. This is the move that Isaac Watts made in positing the coming together of the Son of God with a pre-existent human soul of Christ, but as of yet no hint of this is to be seen in Barton Stone's thoughts on the Son of God. The Son is begotten prior to the rest of creation, but he is not in Stone's view, at this point, directly connected to creation.

The next major move Stone makes is to "establish the doctrine of his divinity, as I find it revealed in the scriptures."[62] Obviously Stone's perspective will allow him to both accept the full divinity of the Son and to deny the identification of the Son with the Father, so that he may be described as divine without being the one only true God. The concept that permits this to be the case is that of God's indwelling of the Son.

Texts typically applied by Trinitarians to establish the *common identity* of Father and Son are used by Stone to indicate that the Father's divinity *indwells* the Son (John 14:8, 10; John 10:38). All the fullness of the Father indwells the Son, not because of their common substance or common nature, but simply because the Father's divinity has externally and at a point in time entered the Son. Such an indwelling, Stone argues, allows the Son to be *called* "mighty God," "everlasting Father," "the true God," and even "Jehovah," but this is entirely a function of the Father's indwelling and not a function of the Son's ontological nature.[63] He possesses all the glories and fullness of God without actually being the one only true God, instead attributing his powerful deeds to the Father, who has indwelled him. As the one who possesses the Father's glory, he is called in Scripture the *image of the invisible God* and *the brightness of His glory*, the *character of His substance*. Looking at Christ is like a person looking in a mirror at an exact image of something that is behind her, but it is still just the image that she sees, with the original of the image actually being out of view and unseen.[64]

Stone expresses the concern at this point that some are troubled, as he seems to be denying the full equality between Father and Son. Rather than deny such an accusation, he wonders at the charge, stating that, indeed, the concept of equality implies that whenever there is equality there are by necessity two entities that can be compared, but, as Stone has indicated so many times, God is the one infinite and true God, and there cannot be another equal to him. Of course, if Scripture were to claim equality between Father and Son, it would be a concept that he would have to accept. But Stone says neither John 5:18 nor Philippians 2:6–7, the two places in Scripture he knows are interpreted in this way, actually claims that the Father and Son are equal. In the case of John 5:18, Stone says, the Jews who accuse Jesus of making himself equal with the Father are simply mistaken, as the following verses obviously show. And in the case of Philippians 2:6–7,

Stone claims the one only true God did not empty himself, and that the passage is simply suggesting that the one who is indwelled by the Father did not think it robbery to be "as God."[65] Here Stone mentions for support Philip Doddridge and Daniel Whitby, criticizing Thomas Scott and John Pearson for their common understanding that ἴσα should be translated as "equal."[66] Ultimately, if it is to be accepted that Christ is equal to God, it could only be on the basis of the indwelling that he has received, and not on the basis of his ontological sameness with the one only true God.[67]

Continuing with what can rightly be called his polemic, Stone comments first on the accusations that consistently come his way because he claims for the Son an instrumental role in creation, and he then addresses the charges of idolatry directed at him because he says he worships one whom he does not believe is the one only true God. In neither case does he deny the essence of the charge but instead claims that his attitudes on both matters are correct. In the case of the worship he extends to the Son, he does so, he says, because the Father has indwelled the Son, and so he actually worships the Father in and through the Son when directing adoration to the Son of God.[68] When the Son is worshipped, He cannot be worshipped as a supreme God lest it be thought that there are two Gods at this same divine level.

Finally, Stone addresses the typical claim by Trinitarians that divine names and titles are frequently used in Scripture to refer to the Son, and that such names and titles would be blasphemous if they did not indicate his unity with the Father. Stone, for his part, says that he, too, uses such titles for the Son, just as do the Trinitarians. He says,

> The difference is this. They ascribe these attributes and names to the Son, as in him from eternity. Be we ascribe them to him because the Father dwells in him. . . . Let our brethren prove that the Son was eternal and independent; then we will acknowledge that he was eternally divine. The divinity in him we acknowledge was eternal, because all the fullness of Godhead was in him. But we cannot acknowledge two eternal, distinct beings, possessed of infinite power, wisdom, &c.[69]

Christ, then, may be referred to with divine names and titles and be ascribed with divine attributes, but not because these things accurately say something of his ontology; they are accurate only because, and to the extant that, the divinity of God indwells the Son.

Stone's Dominant Theme

This exposition of Barton Stone's *An Address to the Christian Churches* has established the specifics of his position on the divinity of the Son of God and the manner in which he arrives at this position. The thorough treatment of the above, although tedious, takes account of his complete argument. Stone typically applies syllogistic reasoning both to the classical Trinitarian position and to what he takes to be the revealed propositions of Scripture, showing the discrepancies he believes are present between the two. Throughout the document, and in numerous pertinent points, a dominant theme is consistently reiterated: that there can be only one true God, and that the Son, who is, nonetheless, pre-existent and indwelled with God's divinity, cannot be this same, one, only, true, eternal God without necessitating the existence of two such Gods. Stone accepts the divinity of the Son, but denies his eternal existence and his equality with the Father. He is the *begotten one,* in whom the Father dwells, pre-existent before all else in creation. But the glory and divinity and whatever other Godlike attributes Christ possesses, arise from the Father's indwelling of him as the image of God, not because the Son entirely possessed both a fully human and fully divine nature within his one person, as in the traditionally orthodox position. Whereas others have accepted apparent contradictions and paradoxes regarding the relationship between the Father and Son and claimed such difficulties point only to the mysteriousness of Trinitarian relationships, Stone insists that Christians should no longer accept a position that so clearly contradicts reason and simply has no basis in Scriptural revelation.

At least one matter of interest with respect to Stone's *An Address to the Christian Churches* still deserves clarification. On page 32 and again on page 34 of the second edition, there are signed declarations by seven witnesses and five witnesses, respectively, indicating that no later than the period of 1808–1811 Barton Stone had already been preaching and teaching concerning the "pre-existence *of the human soul of Jesus Christ*" (page 32) or "the pre-existence of the Son of God; or, *that the human soul of Christ* (as he termed it) existed before it was united with a body" (page 34, emphasis added). And, yet, as indicated above, the pre-existence of the human soul of Christ is not actually addressed in the second edition of *An Address to the Christian Churches*. Is this particular way of looking at the pre-existence of the Son of God not part of Stone's theology, when it was clearly so much part of the Trinitarian position of Isaac Watts?

What is notable is that in the first, 1814 edition of *An Address to the Christian Churches*, on pages 17–19, including the asterisked footnote on the bottom of 19, Stone did make mention of the pre-existence of the human soul of Christ, directly linking it to Colossians 1:15 and the idea that if Christ is the firstborn of all creatures, and if his becoming firstborn occurred in his pre-existence, it must have occurred with the origin of his *human soul,* as it clearly did not happen with his body. Nonetheless, it is still a bit baffling as to why Stone would in the second edition cite witnesses concerning the longevity of his teaching and preaching of the pre-existence of the Son's human soul when he does not mention the issue in the second edition. Perhaps he felt that his discussion of the pre-existence of the Son of God would be taken by his knowledgeable readers as amounting to a discussion of the pre-existence of the human soul of Christ. Or, perhaps, he really thinks that he is concurrently addressing the subject of the pre-existence of the human soul of Christ in the discussion. However, this would certainly not be clear to those who may read only the second edition.

Additional Monographs or Separate Publications

As stated above, Barton Stone's *An Address to the Christian Churches* is taken as the key document from which to ascertain Stone's position on the Trinity. Not only is it the most intentionally directed Trinitarian statement Stone composed, but it is also the latest (save his *Letters to James Blythe,* which are essentially a response by Stone to a reply to his *An Address to the Christian Churches* written by Thomas Cleland[70]). Therefore, it can be taken to supersede those things he previously wrote.

Stone's other lengthier works that contain anything substantial on Trinitarian doctrine include *A Short History of the Life of Barton W. Stone, Written by Himself* from 1847;[71] *Atonement, The Substance of Two Letters*

Written to a Friend;[72] *A Reply to John P. Campbell's Strictures on Atonement;*[73] *A Letter to Mr. John R. Moreland, In Reply to His Pamphlet;*[74] and *Letters to James Blythe, D.D., Designed as a Reply to the Arguments of Thomas Cleland, D. D. Against My Address, 2d. Edition, On the Doctrine of Trinity, the Son of God, Atonement, &c.*[75] The latter two warrant treatment here.

A Letter to Mr. John R. Moreland

A Letter to Mr. John R. Moreland, In Reply to His Pamphlet includes Stone's responses to the charges made against *An Address to the Christian Churches* by a Presbyterian minister who had read Stone's second edition. The last four pages of the fourteen-page document merely deal with the history and chronology of Stone's interactions with the synod of Kentucky, whereas Stone answers Moreland's accusations on pages four through ten.

Stone first says of Moreland, "You charge me with denying the divinity of Christ," after which Stone assesses his own perspective on Christ as placing the Son at a higher status than what Moreland himself does.[76] From here, Stone logically argues as he did in *An Address to the Christian Churches* that there are several contradictions that must be simultaneously held if the Son is both the one only true God and at the same time a separate intelligent being. Since this is the case, Stone says, anyone holding the traditional position must think of the Father, Son, and Spirit in modalities and not as separate beings, meaning Trinitarians must adopt a position that is essentially Sabellian.[77]

Further, Stone addresses the charge Moreland has made concerning what he sees as Stone's denial of the humanity of Christ. Moreland argues that instead of asserting Christ possessed a fully human soul, Stone claims Christ's soul is identical with the Son of God with whom the flesh was united, meaning that—in Moreland's view—Stone must assess Christ as not being fully human for he had no human soul.[78] Stone responds by saying that, indeed, Moreland has read him correctly, but that there is no scriptural warrant for thinking Jesus possessed a fully, purely human soul. Moreland does not mention here the position of Isaac Watts, nor does Stone, but clearly standing behind the discussion is Stone's link to Watts.

Another issue raised by Moreland is one to which Stone had previously addressed himself, that of the divine names, titles, and attributes given to

Jesus in Scripture, along with the actions he performs that are credited to him as God. Stone answers by saying the Son was united with a body and was indwelled by God so that the whole fullness of God, as a Spirit without measure, entered into the human body conjoined with the Son. "Jehovah," then, is a permissible name for Christ because he possessed the presence of Jehovah and was able to perform the mighty works that only Jehovah could do. That Christ would credit the Father as having worked when such great deeds were accomplished by him only makes the point; clearly the Son is not equal to the Father, nor is he to be identified with him, lest he simply be crediting himself.[79] Ultimately, Stone argues, Moreland joins together an inferior presence with humankind when he joins the second person of the Trinity to a human body, for in Stone's view of things, when the Son of God is joined to a body and then the full divinity of God comes into a human being, even more than the second person of the Trinity has conjoined with a human—God the Father has entered into and indwells humanity.[80]

Stone closes out his responses to Moreland by addressing two of Moreland's claims: (1) that Stone mistakenly accuses Trinitarians of saying that the very God suffered; (2) that Stone claims that the Son of God was a created, mutable being in a way identical to the Arians. In the first charge, Stone quotes *The Doctrines and Discipline of the Methodist Episcopal Church in America*, indicating it does say that the Christ, who is very God, suffered, and wonders how Moreland could deny that Trinitarians hold this view. On the second point, Stone denies that he is at all an Arian, for an Arian would claim that Christ was created, but Stone's view is that the Son *derived* His existence from the Father in the process of being begotten.[81]

It is on this final point concerning the *derivation* of the Son, rather than the *creation* of the Son, that I prefer to speak of Barton Stone's position as *Quasi-Arian*. If scholarship has correctly identified the position of Arius as asserting that the Son was created, there is a distinction between this view and that of Barton Stone, who clearly takes *begotten* in a sense other than "created." For Stone, there was a pre-existing, created human soul that was joined together with the begotten Son of God prior to the creation of anything else, but the Son of God is not, himself, created—hence Stone's use of the word *derived*. Perhaps the point at which Arius and Stone are most closely linked is in their common conception that the Son cannot be the one only true God.[82]

Letters to James Blythe

Barton Stone's *Letters to James Blythe* from 1824, although ostensibly written to a longtime Presbyterian acquaintance of Stone's who had been a careful observer and critic of Stone's defection from Presbyterianism, is actually a book-length response to Thomas Cleland's *Letters to Barton W. Stone, Containing A Vindication Principally of The Doctrines of the Trinity*. . . . Cleland's work was a book-length response from an orthodox Trinitarian to the second edition of Stone's *An Address to the Christian Churches*. The portion on the Trinity in *Letters to James Blythe* covers 116 pages, with the balance of the work addressing the doctrine of the atonement. *Letters to James Blythe* is typically considered significant for its reiteration and clarification of what Stone had written in *An Address to the Christian Churches*, not because new or alternate thoughts are presented within. It also possesses some elements that warrant discussion because they do offer new insights into Stone's analysis of Trinitarian doctrine.

Letters to James Blythe is divided up into a series of stylized "Letters," the first eight of which directly concern Trinitarian doctrine. Stone's approach is to deal point-by-point either with what he wrote in *An Address to the Churches*—and with what Cleland had to say in *Letters to Barton W. Stone*—or Stone addresses Cleland's own position. The document amounts, then, to a long polemic. In 116 pages of response to Cleland, Stone deals with nearly all of Cleland's arguments one-by-one, frequently repeating his positions and arguments, as these are applicable.

Letter I. Stone begins this letter, which is nothing more than a brief introduction, by reiterating his basic position: there is but one God the Father and one Lord Jesus Christ, who is the Son of the Father, and he rejects the ideas that there are three equal Gods and that Jesus Christ is, himself, the Supreme God.[83] As will be seen in Chapter Four, this is still the crux of his position and this is significant for establishing the most important influences on Stone's basic Trinitarian position.

Letter II.—*Of Trinity*. Here Stone consistently applies the same sort of syllogistic reasoning and close attention to biblical propositions that are seen in his other theological writings. First he expresses his frustration with Cleland's discussion of "person," reiterating the position he had taken in *An Address to the Christian Churches*.[84]

Second, Cleland's critique of *An Address to the Christian Churches* allows Stone here to say a bit more about 1 John 5:7 than he did in his previous work. In addition to citing further evidence that this verse as it stands in the King James Version should not be included as a text original to 1 John, he includes Calvin among those witnesses who think that the agreement of the Three expressed in this verse, if the disputed additional words are original, references an agreement of mind or will and not a oneness in ontology. Stone also offers a lengthy critique of the interpretive extrapolation that occurs when the word "God" is added at the end of the disputed words in 1 John 5:7, saying that not only does θέος not fit with the ἑν that stands at the end of the disputed words, but that neither this verse, nor John 10:30, nor John 17:22 fit with Cleland's suggestion that θεῖον fits the context as an extrapolation. In John 17:22, Jesus prays for the oneness of believers to be the same as the oneness of Father and Son, but, of course, this oneness for which Jesus prays cannot be unity in *human* θεῖον.[85]

Over the next few pages, Stone adds to his argument on 1 John 5:7, John 10:30 and John 17:22 by considering evidence from the early church Fathers (Tertullian, Cyprian, Novatian, Origen), indicating that they interpreted as the oneness between Father and Son nothing more than agreement in mind and will.[86] Following a reiteration and further defense of what he had written in *An Address to the Christian Churches* concerning *Elohim* and other pluralized Hebrew names, descriptions, and pronouns that refer to the majesty of a singular God,[87] Stone critiques Cleland's use of several biblical texts to defend an orthodox Trinitarian perspective; e.g., Isaiah 48:6 and 61:1; Matthew 3:16, 17; 28:19–20; John 6:38; Acts 2:32–33; 1 Corinthians 12:4–6; and 2 Corinthians 3:14.[88] These quotations support the suggestion made in Chapter Four regarding Barton Stone's dependency on Samuel Clarke for his own Trinitarian perspective. On pages 18–20 Stone quotes Samuel Clarke five times, using Clarke's *The Scripture Doctrine of the Trinity* as a sourcebook for Stone's references to early church Fathers. In the remaining portions of *Letters to James Blythe* in which Stone addresses the Trinity, he references Samuel Clarke an additional 71 times, for a total of 76 references in 116 pages. Although Stone references other writers—most often Moses Stuart—Samuel Clarke is clearly his favorite source for evidence from a non-Trinitarian perspective. It will be argued in Chapter Four that Stone's dependence upon Samuel Clarke is a key element shaping his doctrine of the Trinity.

"Letter III—The Trinity—continued." This section begins as Stone suggests it will, with thoughts on the opinions of the ancient Fathers about the singularity of substance and the tri-personality of God. Quoting Daniel Whitby, who had also been influenced by Samuel Clarke, Stone makes the point that according to the ancient church Fathers there is only a *specific* [or specified] *unity* of the three persons and not a unity among them in *individual nature, essence or substance.* In other words, the unity is a unity in *like* nature but not a unity in the single substance that is actually the Father's exact ontological Being.[89] Stone also quotes Bishop Bull, Moses Stuart, and Johann L. Mosheim for the same purpose, which is interesting in that Bull was an ardent supporter of the orthodox position. He further makes the point that although the Creed of Constantinople of AD 381 did specifically discuss the identity of the nature of the three with the nature of the one, Nicea did not do the same, so that in AD 325 all that was said was that there was unity of substance, not that there were three in one.[90] Because it was only in response to Cleland—after Cleland critiqued Stone's view of the singularity of God—that Stone constructs his own argument about the *specific* [or specified] *unity* of the three persons vis à vis God's unity in *individual nature, essence or substance,* this is the first time we have seen this argument in Stone.

Moses Stuart is used by Stone to make the point that for the early Fathers, the Son of God was actually begotten at a period not long before the creation of the world rather than from eternity. Shepherd of Hermas, Justin Martyr, Athenagoras, Tatian, Theophilus, Clement of Alexandria, Tertullian, and Dionysius are, according to Stuart—and Stone—unanimous in denying the eternal nature of the Son and in their collective opinion that the Son was begotten only briefly before the creation of the universe. The Trinitarians, then, according to Stone, disagree with the Fathers who say that God alone existed from eternity, that the λόγος was not a distinct person equal to the Father in power and glory, that the Son is not self-existent and independent, that the Son is not eternally begotten, and that the divinity of the Son is derived or communicated.[91]

Furthering his point that the Son is not the *same individual substance* as the Father, but only the *same specific substance* with God, Stone says he will "select a few more quotations, taken from the ancient Fathers by Doct. Samuel Clarke, Scrip. Doct. of Trinity; in order to settle this matter beyond fair debate."[92] He actually proceeds to quote Clarke fifty-five times in the next eight pages, making reference to Athanasius, Origen, Irenaeus, Justin Martyr, Clement of Alexandria, Tertullian, Novatian, Eusebius, Basil, Hilary, Gregory of Nazianzus, Victorinus, Alexander of Alexandria, and Constantine. As part of this litany, Stone includes Clarke's mention of Bishop Bull and Bishop Pearson, both of whom, Clarke claims, made the point that the Son cannot be the one only true God.[93]

"**Letter IV—Of the Son of God.**" Stone begins this section by naming his intentions:

> In order to avoid confusion on this important subject, I shall endeavor to state my own view of the Son of God, as exhibited in my Address 2d edition, with Mr. C[leland]'s objections; and then to consider his arguments in proof of the supreme divinity of the son; or more properly, that he is the Supreme God.[94]

The summary that Stone offers here from *An Address to the Christian Churches* is helpful in identifying what he considers to be the most salient points in his Trinitarian position.[95] However, the greatest value of "Letter IV" is the clarity with which Stone separates himself from the classically accepted Trinitarian position, especially regarding the pre-existence of the Son. Cleland had accused Stone of denying the Lord's divinity—a charge that Stone denies. Following two quotes from Alexander of Alexandria and Athanasius that Stone and Samuel Clarke (from whom Stone takes the quotations) believe support the idea of the Son's derived divinity, Stone discusses Cleland's charge that his conception of the Son's divinity is a *communicated* divinity. Stone actually accepts the charge, even though *communicated* divinity is not language Stone uses, preferring to speak of the Father's divinity *indwelling* the Son.[96] Cleland also claims Stone makes no distinction between *begotten* and *created*, implying that Stone really is an Arian. Stone specifically denies the accusation, but he admits that in his first edition of *An Address to the Christian Churches* he did make the mistake of identifying *begotten* with *created*.[97]

Cleland had charged that because Stone accepted the idea (from Isaac Watts) that the Son possessed a pre-existent soul prior to creation, that Stone necessarily denied the real humanity of Jesus because he would not accept the principle that the Son took for himself a reasonable human soul. Stone replies that he does not believe the Son took for himself a reasonable human soul because he already had received a pre-existent human soul prior to his birth, at which point he also took on a human body, dwelling within it.[98] For Stone, if there were two complete, combined realities within the man Jesus, so that the Son received a fully human soul upon his earthly birth instead of possessing only a pre-existent soul, there would be two full natures within the Son. However, Stone contends that Scripture says nothing of the Son existing as two, complete natures nor anything about the Son receiving a human soul at the time of the incarnation.[99]

Further, for Cleland, the Son's pre-existence includes his eternality as the λόγος, a notion that is unacceptable to Stone on the grounds that eternality is an attribute only of the Father and not of the Son. In fact, for Stone, it is proper to call God eternal but not to use the expression "eternal Father" because there is no eternality in the Son, and, therefore, no sense of God being Father until the Son is begotten sometime before the creation of the world.[100] Where Cleland argues that the pre-existence of the Son entails his eternality and unity with God, Stone sees the pre-existence of the Son as inclusive of his *origin* as the One begotten by the Father *prior to creation*, who then comes to be born of Mary and is joined with flesh.[101] Additionally, Stone here made use of the work of Samuel Clarke to establish that (1) what some Trinitarians believe actually comes close to the view of the Unitarians, because only a proper man was born of a virgin; and (2) they tend to think of the Son and Spirit as being part of the same self-existent Being with the Father, dissolving the reality of Son and Spirit. When Trinitarians say that it was a man who died on the cross and that the impassable and incorruptible God in him did not die, they essentially say the same as the Socinians—that the Son of God was a mere man who did not exist prior to the birth of Jesus from Mary.[102]

"Letter V—Same Subject Continued." Stone claims in this section that Cleland's criticisms of his position on the pre-existent Christ are off base because Cleland mistakenly supposes that Stone's position cannot be proven from Scripture.¹⁰³ Stone, then, offers proof for his position that the Son pre-existed as *an intelligence inferior* to the Supreme God. Arguing from Colossians 1:15, Hebrews 1:6, Ephesians 1:3, and 1 Peter 1:3, Stone asserts that *firstborn* and *first begotten* cannot apply to the one only true God, because he was never born. Nor can they apply to Jesus as a mere man, because he was not the firstborn human being. But they appropriately apply to the Son who was born and united with a pre-existent soul prior to creation, and because he was the begotten Son, he was therefore inferior to the one and only true God before creation, in direct contradiction to Cleland's denials of this fact.

Continuing his pattern of syllogistically applying reason to Scripture, Stone argues that: because God created by the Son, the Son must have been pre-existent; but he could not be the one true God while also being the One the true God used to create all that has been created.¹⁰⁴ He could not pray to receive glory he had before the world was if he was not pre-existent; but neither could he be praying to God if he was God, nor could he be merely a man offering such a prayer. He could not be *set up* as God or man before the world began as in Psalm 8, and as Trinitarians often argue. Thus, 2 Corinthians 8:9 could not apply to Christ, for God is unchangeable. John 1:15 could not apply to Jesus the man, for only the Son was "before" John the Baptist chronologically. Christ neither as God nor man could ascend to where he was before, but John 6:62 appropriately speaks this way of the Son. The One who is humbled according to Philippians 2:6 cannot be God for he is unchangeable and could not be humbled. The Father cannot covenant with himself in the Son, per Isaiah 42:6. He came to do God's will, not his own, according to Hebrews 10:5, 7, but certainly this teaches that there were two separate wills operating in the Father and Son.¹⁰⁵

Finishing his discussion of the Son's pre-existence, Stone moves on toward the conclusion of the fifth letter by analyzing Cleland's critiques of Stone's position regarding the Son's instrumental role in creation. He begins by applying several quotes from Samuel Clarke in which the opinions of the early Fathers are used to build a case for the Son's instrumentality in creation.¹⁰⁶ Further, where Cleland applies various biblical texts to indicate the Son's direct role in creation, Stone believes these Scriptures simply indicate that God was the one creating, using the Son as the means by which he carried out creative acts. Letter V ends with a brief summary by Stone of both his and Cleland's positions that can serve as a helpful abstract of their positions.[107]

"Letter VI—Of the Supreme Divinity of the Son." Stone gives recognition here to Cleland's positive attempts to prove from Scripture the full unity of the Son with the Father, claiming that Scripture indicates that the Son is the one only true God. Stone says he, "shall take his [Cleland's] arguments in his own order,"[108] but as part of his response, Stone actually offers some of the clearest, most concise exposition of his own Trinitarian position. This comes in the form of comments on biblical texts that have been explained by Cleland as part of his defense of Trinitarian orthodoxy.[109]

"Letter VII—Of the Equality of the Son with the Father." Stone here applies to various biblical texts the syllogistic logic he has applied throughout his writings on the Trinity. He begins by reiterating his basic premise concerning the equality of Father and Son: God is one infinite Spirit without parts, which means that another cannot be equal, for equality implies a comparison of two, and there cannot be two infinite Spirits without parts. They cannot both equally possess the divine perfections, or there would be two Gods. Although at places in the redemptive plan Christ is said to possess an authority equal to the Father's, in each case that authority has been granted by the Father as the supreme source of such prerogatives.

Stone indicates that, contrary to Cleland's claims, only John 5:18 and Philippians 2:6 need to be addressed as texts that teach the equality of the Son with the Father. Cleland had accused Stone of omitting several passages that look like they assert equality, but Stone asserts that in each case the text is simply indicating the presence of God within the life and ministry of the Son, not indicating something of his ontology. So, the Son does what the Father does: the Son quickens the dead; the Son has been given judgment. But these are instances of the Son only being equal *as a representative* doing work on behalf of another. The Son receives honor, but only as the Father who is within him and who is working through him is honored. With respect to John 5:18, where the Jews accuse Jesus of claiming to be God, Stone again asserts that the claim of the Son's equality with the

Father is only an accusation made by the Jews, not a claim actually made by Jesus. In fact, here Jesus labored to show that he is not God.

As he had done in *An Address to the Christian Churches,* Stone addresses Philippians 2:6 as a text that many claim indicates the equality between God and the One who chose not to cling to God's divinity. Here he argues as he has elsewhere, citing Drs. Whitby, Doddridge, and Mcknight, all of whom translate ἴσα as "as" instead of "equal" in Philippians 2:6. Again he asks, how could the one true God form himself, be equal to himself, or die and be exalted? Even if μορφήν means nature, was the one true God humbled, did he die, and was he risen and exalted? Clearly, to be in the form of God is not the same as possessing the exact nature or being of God.[110]

"Letter VIII. The Same Subject Continued." The final section on the Trinity in *Letters to James Blythe* includes Stone's continued attempts to deal with Cleland's proofs of the Son's equality with the Father. For example, Cleland has interpreted Ephesians 3:19 as indicating that all of God's fullness is in the Son, entailing their exact equality, where Stone interprets this text as saying only that the Son is *filled unto or into* the fullness of God. Further, Stone says, Cleland's idea is that the unoriginated divinity of the divine λόγος or second person of the Trinity dwelt in the man born of Mary, whereas Stone's idea is that the unoriginated divinity of the Father, or all the unoriginated fullness of the Godhead, dwelt in the Son born of Mary. On this score, Stone thinks, his argument must carry the day because Jesus only mentions the Father as one who indwells him, but he says nothing of the λόγος doing so.[111]

Further, Cleland tries to prove that the Son is eternal by saying that the eternal life mentioned in 1 John 1:2 is actually the Son, himself, meaning that the Son is eternal; but for Stone a comparison of 1 John 1:2 with 1 John 5:11 reveals that the eternal life mentioned in 1 John 1:2 is simply the eternal life received by believers and is not the Son, himself. This kind of refutation by Stone of the biblical evidence Cleland presents on behalf of the eternality of the Son carries him almost to the end of his section on the Trinity, as summarized in the list below.

- Clelend uses John 17:5, 24 as evidence of the Son's unity with God, but according to Stone the one who prays such things cannot be God. If he is the one only true God, what glory could he now receive back that he previously had? Did God lose his glory? Further, if he is just a man, what glory could he now receive back that he had before?

- As Stone had mentioned previously, Cleland uses Proverbs 8:23, 30 to argue that the Son was *set up* or *anointed* from everlasting. But was the Supreme God *set up* from the beginning?
- Where Cleland argues that Proverbs 8:23, 30 show that the Son was *set up* from *everlasting*, Stone has previously shown that the Hebrew word *olem* often refers to an *indefinite* period of time, and not an *infinite* period of time. If Proverbs 8, then, is referring to the Son, it is simply saying that he was *set up* from some *indefinite* point in the past, but not from an infinite past.
- Cleland applies Proverbs 30:4 to prove the Son's omnipotence and eternal nature. Stone says, "If this text *surely* teaches these things [as Cleland says] . . . I must really confess that language would be of no use."[112]
- Cleland's position regarding the worship of the Son is that the Son only is the object of Christian worship, just as is the Father; therefore the Son must be God *alone*. Stone counters: There are, indeed, two beings who are to receive worship, but the one is worshipped on behalf of the other, not for himself. One of them is slain, but this atoning work is performed on God's behalf, not as the actual death of God. To worship the Son, then, is to glorify the Father without giving worship to the Son as if he *really is* the Father. Stone then shows by quoting Samuel Clarke that the Fathers, too, both believed that the Son is worshipped on God's behalf and that the Father and Son were worshipped in the early church as two distinct beings. The redeemed in heaven are shown in the Revelation to be doing the same.
- Stone critiques Cleland's use of the image of a tree to illustrate how the Son and Father are of the same nature.[113] Branches, trunk, and root are all one nature, but they are not identical. For Stone, the weak point of Cleland's argument is that the three trees or branches are three distinct particular instances of the

same specific nature, but they are not of the same exact, identical nature. As he indicated before, to possess the same individual nature or substance is different from sharing the same specific, specified nature. In the first case, there is identity. In the second case, there is simply similarity or likeness. Further, no one branch can be equal to the whole of the other parts; so if the Son is merely a part of the tree, he is not fully equal to the nature of the One God who is represented by the whole tree.

- Cleland tries to prove that the two natures, divine and human, were united in the one person, Christ, so that Christ not only possesses divinity but has the nature of the Father within himself. He uses Zechariah 13:7 as evidence, but for Stone this text is actually evidence that the Father and Son are two individual personalities, and he quotes Isaac Watts as proof.[114] Stone indicates that having examined several passages that Thomas Cleland uses to defend the doctrine of two natures, he finds that the doctrine is simply an expedient conveniently applied in theological "emergencies" to defend a doctrine that only came about in the church after centuries of frustrating discussion. In Scripture there is no proof for it. There is, instead, a view of Christ presented in Scripture whereby two different wills are possessed by the Father and Son ("not my will, but yours be done"), and the fact that there are two wills indicates two separate distinct beings with two distinct intelligences. The idea, then, that the Son possesses the complete being of the Father with himself, so that the Son can be said to be the one only true God, is not proved by the doctrine of two natures.[115]
- Cleland catalogues a list of biblical texts that Stone and others use to argue against the orthodox view of the Trinity, asserting that such texts are misinterpreted or misapplied. Stone remains incredulous, convinced that 1 Corinthians 8:6, Ephesians 4:5–6, and John 17:3 really do serve as proof that the Father and Son are not the same intelligent Being. The sender and the sent cannot be the same Being; the One who is sent cannot wish to do His own will and the will of the One who sent Him if they possess only one will and are only one person. John 5:19 specifically states that

the Son can do nothing of himself; John 14:28 specifically says that the Father is greater than the Son. Mark 13:32 specifically says that the Son does not know what the Father knows. If Jesus is the mediator between God and man, how could he be God himself, mediating on his own behalf? Matthew 19:17 is proof that God is *one unique person* because there is no *person* who is good, but *one person,* that is God, and Jesus decisively separates himself from that one Person who is the Father. Cleland's assessment of 1 Corinthians 15: 24–28, in which the Son is described by him as the Supreme God, is infinitely mysterious and contrary to reason and plain language; 2 Corinthains 8:9 says of the Son that he was rich and became poor, but then he could not be the one only true God who is unchangeable. Cleland has implied that the loss of richness spoken of here is really the veiling or covering of his richness and not a real loss or change. To this, Stone responds by saying it must have been a real loss or Christ would not have prayed for his former glory to be restored. Where Cleland sees Colossians 1:15 as proof of the common identity of Father and Son, for Stone the image of a thing, no matter how closely it duplicates its source, is still not the thing itself. He further wonders how that which is *firstborn* can be eternal. Revelation 3:14 simply teaches that Christ is the instrumental cause of all that is created and not that he was created. Cleland makes a similar point against the Arians, and in agreeing with Cleland on this final point, Stone attempts to show that he is, indeed, not an Arian, or he would take this text to indicate that the Son was created.

Each of these texts are, according to Stone, unsatisfactorily explained away by Cleland and other Trinitarians as they willfully deny the obvious implications of such texts.[116]

Articles in Which Stone Addresses the Trinity

We find Barton Stone discussing the Trinity in several places in Christian journals. In some, he makes only passing reference to Trinitarian doctrine, and the bearing of these articles on his place in Stone-Campbell

Trinitarianism seems minimal.[117] In others, Stone takes considerable space to express his Trinitarian opinions or significantly interacts with others, such as Alexander Campbell. The most pertinent journal articles for investigating his thoughts on the Trinity are delineated below.

"Objections to Christian Union Calmly Considered" (December 25, 1826)

Stone here addresses the Trinity as part of a discussion of the factors that divide Christians. On most peripheral matters, dissonant opinions are overlooked, but barriers to fellowship are still being erected with respect to the Trinity, Christology, and the atonement. Stone first delineates the traditional view, citing Nicea as the point at which the belief *"that there are three persons in the same one Being, substance, or nature, which Being is God"* was first inculcated. He begins by simply making the point that such teaching is not found in the Bible and so was never a term of fellowship prior to A.D. 325.[118] While the Fathers consistently referred to the issue of the Trinity as an "incomprehensible mystery," various firm opinions were nonetheless expressed at Nicea, and binding conclusions were reached. Although none of these conclusions are reasonable, according to Stone, they are claimed by Nicea's adherents to represent orthodoxy. The result of the conference, he says, is that all agreed in some form that God is one intelligent Spirit, one infinite intelligent mind.[119]

Rather than expressing his own view or critiquing the various Trinitarian positions, in the remainder of the article Stone examines how the decisions at Nicea enabled judgments to be made of those who held differing opinions. His concern is that opinions that can best be classified as mysteries have become criteria for determining what and who is *orthodox*. Those considered unorthodox are condemned, but their condemnation is "unreasonable, and entirely arbitrary" because the judges are unable even to define their own terms.[120] Alluding to the controversy over whether or not the Son is eternally begotten, he reiterates the arbitrary nature of ecclesiastical judgments, drawing attention to the inconsistency present when authorities declare some Christians unorthodox who are from differing fellowships, when every Christian fellowship consists of those who hold disparate conceptions of Trinitarian relationships.[121] He clearly rejects the premise that "the *orthodox* notions of the Son of God should be considered so essential as to justify the exclusion of all who do not receive them,"[122] particularly when "the majority of professors of religion reject, or do not believe" the traditional speculations about the Son.

He provides as a specific example the belief that Jesus Christ is the eternal son of God, indicating that Adam Clarke and Moses Stewart have led many away from that which is now considered "absurd and foolish" regarding the position that the Son is eternal and eternally begotten.[123] He ends the article by drawing attention to the foolishness of disputing about such matters when human beings are both dying without Christ and are being saved without any knowledge of such disputed doctrines. Those things that can be believed by all about the Son of God deserve the attention of all, while disputed matters should be avoided.

"To The Christian Baptist" (July 25, 1827)

With this article we view from Barton Stone's side the discussion identified in Chapter Two that took place between Stone and Alexander Campbell in several issues of *The Christian Messenger* and *The Christian Baptist*. The series began with a letter to Campbell from "Timothy," to which Campbell responded in the May 1827 issue of *The Christian Baptist*. Stone then responds to Campbell in *The Christian Messenger*, remarking on his disappointment that Campbell has "speculated and theorised on the most important point in theology, and in a manner more mysterious and metaphysical than your predecessors."[124]

Stone responds to Campbell's delineations about the divine λόγος in the May 1827 article by making the same kind of arguments previously seen throughout Stone's Trinitarian reflections. For Campbell to refer to the λόγος as eternal in an attempt to avoid saying the Son of God is eternal is to make the same error—Campbell is still identifying the Word as eternal, and in the process he is identifying the Word with the "one, self-existent, and eternal God himself."[125] Since whatever is eternal is self-existent and independent, it must stand as God Supreme, of which there can without contradiction be only one. Further, Campbell speaks of a relation between the λόγος and God, and the very notion of relationship implies at least duality, not unity. Therefore, Campbell must believe that there are two eternal Gods. This, Stone says, puts Campbell in the same Trinitarian place as the Calvinists, whose view Campbell himself rejected.

Stone also challenges Campbell with the idea that if the λόγος is thought by Campbell to be a separate, intelligent being, then he must be either another eternal God or less than a separate intelligent being, since there is only one true God. In this case, Campbell's λόγος must be an unintelligent relation or sign or image of an idea, but cannot be the only one true God.[126]

Stone finishes his query of Campbell with a series of questions that Stone intends to be more than just rhetorical. Does the language of the Son of God ascending and descending not indicate that the *Son* existed prior to the incarnation? How could the only true God say that he came down to do the will of the One who sent him? How could the one true God pray to himself to receive the glory that he had with him before the world began; and if it was a human who prayed this, how could he have glory with God before the world began? How could it be the one true God who, though he was rich, became poor, since God is unchangeable; this could not be Jesus, for he was never rich? Who is mentioned in Philippians 2:6-10; the whole context indicates that it was not the one true God? Who said, "A body you have prepared for me, O God"? In line with the writing of Samuel Clarke, was the Lord not just the instrumental cause of creation, and not the only true God? Did the Son of God actually not exist until he was called Jesus?

What is striking with this series of questions, and with the material that precedes them in the article, is the way in which Stone in such short order brings to bear the majority of the issues he outlined in *An Address to the Christian Churches*. Stone has brought the full force of his position against Campbell in just six brief pages of *The Christian Messenger*.

Alexander Campbell's "From the Christian Baptist, To the Christian Messenger" (November 1827) and Stone's "Reply," (November 1827)

These two articles were published sequentially, with the second of the articles serving as Stone's response to what Alexander Campbell had written. Campbell had answered the criticisms and queries that Stone had presented to him in the July 25, 1827 issue of *The Christian Messenger*. On page 8 of his article, Campbell specifically defends his view (and in the process the view of classical Trinitarianism) by saying, "no man as *philosopher*, or as a *reasoner*, can object to the Trinitarian hypothesis, even should it say that the Father, the word, and the Spirit, are three distinct *beings*, and yet but one God.—There is nothing unreasonable about it."[127]

After all, Campbell asserts, there is nothing reasonable about the existence of God, but this does not make his existence unreasonable. The best course of action is to not get involved in speculation where reason cannot go, nor to align with or defend a particular theological party, nor to use language that goes beyond what the Bible says. Despite what I see (and discussed in Chapter Two) as the inconsistencies with which Campbell was able to abide by his own instructions, this was vintage Alexander Campbell, and Stone responds in his own article.

The crux of Stone's article concerns Campbell's statements that "I [Campbell] once told you [Stone] that I could conscientiously and devoutly pray to the Lord Jesus Christ as though there was no other God in the universe than he," and "They who tell me that they supremely venerate and unequivocally worship the King, my Lord and Master, and are willing to obey him in all things, I call brethren." These principles, then, allowed Campbell to call Stone "brother." Stone is clear, however, that Campbell must have misunderstood, for certainly Stone was not able to pray to Christ as if he is the only true God, nor could he *supremely* venerate him.[128] Beyond this, Stone agrees with Campbell on the value of reason and revelation, saying that revelation is supreme but that reason should never tolerate "human contradictions and inventions."

By taking to the absurd extreme the apparent reasonableness, according to Campbell, of the multiplication of persons within God, Stone mockingly claims that there could then be 300 or 30,000 distinct beings that are all the one only true God, claiming that reasoning such as Campbell's is "too metaphysical," and he suggests that they should abide by Bible terms alone. Stone further replies to Campbell's fear that Stone's Christians will soon be classified as a sect along with the Arians and Unitarians—with the name "Christian" having a meaning that comports with a particular speculative view of the Trinity—as a possible outcome that he (Stone) simply cannot control.[129]

Spencer Clack's, "From the Baptist Recorder" (December 1827) and Stone's "Reply" (December 1827)

In 1827 Elder Spencer Clack wrote several letters to *The Christian Baptist*, and Stone replies to the one from October 13. Clack had criticized Campbell for not defending in *The Christian Baptist* a biblical position on the Trinity—contra Stone—and in the process Clack makes several accusations against Stone, including calling Stone and the Christians "the Arians of the West."[130] This appellation Stone vehemently rejects, saying, "Does it not argue something worse than ignorance, to apply this name to us, to whom, of all others, it least applies?"[131] Stone proudly accepts some of Clack's accusations, including that Stone and his followers "preached and prayed against creeds and confessions." Other accusations Stone rejects, or, at least gives explanations for, such as the charge that Stone rejects the notion of there being three persons in one God. Stone again argues that to accept the individual intelligence and personhood of the Son leads to tritheism and to deny the Son's full individuality means he and the Spirit would be mere unintelligent beings or properties. Further, Stone suggests to Clack that he should use only biblical language, in which no other "oneness" of the Father and Son is maintained aside from the oneness that is like that of human beings, for which Jesus prayed in John 17:21.[132]

Clack, like others, accused Stone and his followers of denying the divinity of Christ, and Stone says that despite the claim being made from "Dan to Beersheba" it has been denied and refuted, although it is certainly true, he admits, that he does deny that "the *Son of the living God*, was the living God himself, or the only true God which is the Father." He then positively states for Clack his own position: "Remember that we understand the divinity of Jesus to be this, that he was God's OWN son, his ONLY begotten, and that in him, (the son) dwelt all the fulness of Godhead bodily."[133] Stone ends this article by suggesting he will write to Clack again, this time proving from the Scriptures that worshipping the Son of God as a being distinct from the Father is not only not idolatrous but is a duty enjoined on believers by the Father to his [the Father's] glory.[134]

"Letter II To Elder S. Clack," (January 1828)

Barton Stone's second installment to Spencer Clack takes up where his previous article finished, answering additional accusations that Clack had made in *The Christian Baptist* against Stone's Trinitarian position. Clack had accused Stone of not believing that Jesus Christ is God, giving Stone opportunity to present his position in a way that may be unique. As has been seen, Stone frequently makes the claim in his writings that Jesus Christ is divine, being indwelled with the presence of God. This indwelling is not eternal, but it is substantial and complete so that the fullness of God bodily indwells the Son.

However, in his second response to Clack, Stone actually says, "All acquainted with us and our writings, know that we have not denied that Jesus is *God*, but that we maintain this truth, as stated and explained in the scriptures, but not as explained in the *orthodox* creeds of the day."[135] This is a bit confusing in that Stone does not at this point explain exactly how he defines "God," and he makes this statement even while making it clear he is not saying the Son is in fact the one, only, true God. One could legitimately ask Stone at this point, "So there is another God, and Jesus is this God, but not the one only true God?" Based on everything else Stone wrote, the conclusion must be made that in this case he is stretching the definition of "God" to refer to the Son *who is fully indwelled with the Father's presence,* permitting him to receive the divine title.[136]

Stone further answers a query from Clack about whether Stone and his followers actually worship Jesus Christ, with Clack implying that if Stone does worship the Son as God that he must inappropriately worship him, for Stone does not view the Son as one with the Father. Stone's answer to this question requires most of the remainder of his article as he enumerates several points explaining how he does worship the Son of the only true and living God in whom the Father dwells, where Clack and the orthodox inappropriately worship him as the only true God.

In framing his answer, Stone makes direct applications from biblical propositions. First he cites several passages indicating that in the New Testament Jesus is worshipped by the apostles and others but never as the supreme, self-existent, only true God. Clearly, for Stone, if this had been idolatrous, the "faithful and true witness" would not have permitted it.[137]

As further evidence of the appropriateness of worshipping the Son, Stone shows that the Father sanctioned such worship to be directed to Jesus, that the angels worship him, that from Philippians 2:8–11 all creation in heaven and on earth is to exalt him, that the church consistently gave to him honor and glory and claimed for him dominion, and that in the Revelation the heavenly host ascribes to him honor and worship.[138] However, Stone rounds out his survey of Scripture by saying, "In the whole Bible there is not an instance of Christ being worshipped on the ground of his being the self existent, or only true God; but on the ground of his being God's *own* Son, and the *constituted* Lord and Savior of the world."[139]

Clack had indicated that if Stone worships Christ only as the Son that he commits idolatry because worship should not be ascribed to any besides the one, only, true God. Stone takes a long paragraph to reply that worship of the Son is worship of the Father through the Son, and so is not idolatry but is fulfilling a command received from the Father.[140] He closes his second response to Clack by insinuating that in worshipping the Son as the only true God, Clack and the orthodox are worshipping God as one who was emptied, humbled, dead and alive again, giving worship to a *mutable* God (who would not, then, be God at all). Further, if Christ is the only true God, worship directed to the Son would take place as worship of the one only true God with the purpose of giving glory to God the Father—an absurdity![141]

"Remarks on the Preceding Communication" (April 1828)

Barton Stone here responds to "Timothy" whose article on "The Spirit of Orthodoxy" was printed in the same issue of *The Christian Messenger*. In Timothy's article, he wrote disparagingly of a preacher he had heard who espoused the traditional Trinitarian position about the Holy Spirit (that he is a separate, fully divine Person within the Trinity) vis à vis those who think him not to be a person at all.[142] In the process, Timothy mentioned several Christian writers who would agree with his basic premise, including John Locke and Isaac Watts. From there, Stone proceeds to offer his own thoughts on Timothy's article and on those who take the orthodox position, especially with reference to the Holy Spirit.

The article is divided into two halves, with the first half taking up Timothy's statement that Isaac Watts did not take the orthodox Trinitarian position on the personhood of the Holy Spirit, and, therefore, did not hold the orthodox position on the Trinity. Stone takes as his chief source for his comments Isaac Watts's publication, *A Faithful Enquiry After the Ancient and Original Doctrine of the Trinity, Taught by Christ and His Apostles.*[143] From this work, Stone quotes several passages that indicate Watts did not accept the personhood of the Holy Spirit.[144] Stone obviously agrees with Watts's sentiments. Stone then prints a lengthy quotation from a reviewer of Watts's book who denigrates the traditional Trinitarian position as nothing but "a matter of words and phraseology alone."[145] For the reviewer, the Trinitarian position is nothing but semantics, on which even committed Trinitarians cannot agree. In fact, Watts, himself, according to the reviewer, was considered orthodox and accepted by Trinitarians because he used acceptable language, even though Watts had departed in his later publications from his earlier position on the Holy Spirit's personality. This constitutes the sum of Stone's response to Timothy.

This article is quite interesting in that Stone clearly believes both Timothy and the reviewer he quotes on pages 129–130 have given accurate assessments of Watts. And, in fact, Stone's comments on page 128 make it clear that he takes Watts to have departed from a Trinitarian position late in life, as proved by a reading of *A Faithful Enquiry After the Ancient and Original Doctrine of the Trinity, Taught by Christ and His Apostles*. However, while I think it is clear from *A Faithful Enquiry* that Stone is correct about Watts's taking a perspective on the Holy Spirit that denies the Spirit's personhood, I think it doubtful that Watts's opinion about the relationships within the Trinity, particularly the relationship between the Father and Son, run in the same "non-Trinitarian" direction as Watts's opinion about the personhood of the Spirit. In fact, I will argue in Chapter Four that Barton Stone's opinions about the subordination of the Son—a position he also ascribes to Watts—is at least partially grounded in a misreading of Isaac Watts in *A Faithful Enquiry* and that Watts to the end of his days held the Son of God to be the one only true God. My claim is that the central place for Stone in his denial that the Son is the one, only true God is at least partially grounded in Stone's reading of others, such as Samuel Clarke, and that this causes him to see the same in Isaac Watts, when I am not convinced that Watts ever actually held this same position.

Summary

This chapter and the previous one have presented writings from three of the four thinkers typically classified as the most significant voices in the early days of the SCM, with the goal of displaying their positions regarding the Trinity in a readily accessible way. This, of course, does not tell the whole story of SC Trinitarian thought, but focusing on these three progenitors helps those interested in a historical theology of SC Trinitarianism understand the Movement's Trinitarian ethos. This chapter has shown that despite their hesitancies to speak in language that is not specifically biblical, Thomas and Alexander Campbell were essentially classically orthodox in their Trinitarian positions but that Barton Stone would not readily embrace or inculcate an orthodox Trinitarian position. This knowledge about the SCM's theological heritage allows those in the Movement to react from an informed perspective and offers a partial explanation for SC hesitancies regarding an openly orthodox position on the Trinity.

It is in light of the Trinitarian statements of these writers—Thomas Campbell, Alexander Campbell, and Barton Stone—that the roots of the Trinitarian perspectives held within the early SCM may be outlined. Chapter Four will continue down this path by indicating the Trinitarian antecedents to these SC fathers, and Chapter Five will establish where SCM Trinitarianism went after the Movement's earliest decades, offering a perspective on where SC Trinitarianism stands at the beginning of the twenty-first century.

Notes

[1] D. Newell Williams, *Barton Stone: A Spiritual Biography*. During Stone's life, his unorthodox Trinitarian position generated much discussion among Presbyterians and others following his defection from Presbyterian ministry, and the subject was discussed extensively as his relationship with Alexander Campbell and the Disciples developed. As an anecdotal note, whenever I held conversations with others from the SCM about my work on this project, the two best-known features of SCM Trinitarianism were that (1) little had been written on the subject, SC and (2) there was some kind of issue related to Stone's Trinitarian orthodoxy. The general direction of Stone's Trinitarian position became even better known following the Williams biography of Stone.

[2] Barton W. Stone, *Biography*.

[3] See Williams, *Barton Stone*, 9–28.

[4] Ibid., 29.

[5] Ibid., 30–32.

[6] Ibid., 44–45.

[7] Ibid.

[8] Ibid., see 65–120 for the exacerbating doctrinal conflicts between Stone and the Presbyterians.

[9] Barton W. Stone, *Atonement*.

[10] Williams, *Barton Stone*, 115.

[11] Ibid., 116.

[12] John P. Campbell, *Vindex*, 45–46; quoted in Williams, *Barton Stone*, 118.

[13] Barton W. Stone, *A Reply to John Campbell's Strictures on Atonement* (Lexington, Kentucky: Joseph Charles, 1805), 19.

[14] Williams, *Barton Stone*, 44.

[15] Barton W. Stone, *An Address to the Christian Churches*. The second edition of 1821 is corrected and enlarged. Differences between the two editions are catalogued in Williams, *Barton Stone*, 150–53. References to *An Address to the Christian Churches* will hereafter be to the second, 1821 edition, unless otherwise indicated.

[16] Barton Stone, *An Address to the Christian Churches*, iii.

[17] Ibid., 1.

[18] Ibid., 3.

[19] Ibid.

[20] Ibid., 6. It will be argued in Chapter 4 that the most likely source for Stone's rigid commitment to this principle—which he regards as entirely reasonable—is either Samuel Clarke or someone who argues as Clarke does.

[21] Ibid.

[22] Ibid., 6–7. See Chapter Four for an analysis of Stone's use of the word "Trinity."

[23] For more on these differences, see Chapter Four.

[24] Ibid., 7; cf., 11–12.

[25] Ibid., 7.

[26] Ibid., 8.

[27] Ibid., 7.

[28] Ibid., 9.

[29] Ibid., 8.

[30] Ibid., 9.

[31] Ibid., 9–10.

[32] Ibid., 11. By his second to the last sentence in this quotation, Stone is apparently referring to his comments about the oneness of mind and agreement of purpose that is intended with 1 John 5:7, John 10:30 and 17:21, to which he had referred on pages 8–9.

[33] Ibid., 12.

[34] Ibid., 13.

[35] Cf., ibid., 11.

[36] Ibid., 13. He also quotes *The Doctrines and Discipline of the Methodist Episcopal Church in America* from 1798, as written by Thomas Coke and Francis Asbury.

[37] Ibid., 14.

[38] Campbell consistently maintained that Stone and those like him who asserted that there was a logical error in the idea that one divine Person—the Father—could at the same time be three persons, failed to allow for a difference to exist between divine Persons and human persons. Stone and others, out of a failed imagination, were unable to allow Trinitarians to maintain what they thought was a logical misunderstanding of the capabilities of personhood, where Campbell thought Stone inappropriately applied natural limitations to God, missing the ways in which what was unreasonable regarding human personhood was quite reasonable with respect to divine personhood. It is interesting that the claim by Campbell about Stone parallels what Rowan Williams says of both Newman's and Harnack's assessments of Arianism. Both assert that Arianism suffered from something like a penchant toward rationalistic, irreverent speculation and pure philosophical monotheism. Rowan Williams, *Arius: Heresy and Traditon*, 5–10.

[39] Stone, *An Address to the Christian Churches*, 14.

[40] Ibid.

[41] Ibid., 15.

[42] Ibid. This is essentially the same argument that Stone makes on pages 6–7 concerning the unreasonableness of the Trinitarian position that must either assert that in God one being is comprised of other beings, or that if there is more than one divine person or being there must be more than one God.

[43] Ibid.

[44] Ibid.

[45] Ibid.

[46] Ibid., 16.

[47] Ibid.

[48] Stone, *An Address to the Christian Churches*, 16.

[49] Ibid., 17.

[50] Ibid., 17–18.

[51] Ibid., 18–19.

[52] Ibid., 19.

[53] Ibid., 19–20.

[54] Ibid., 20–21.

[55] Ibid., 21.

[56] Ibid., 21–22.

[57] Ibid., 22.

[58] Ibid., 23.

[59] Ibid., 24.

[60] Ibid.

[61] Ibid.

62 Ibid.
63 Ibid., 26.
64 Ibid., 27.
65 Ibid., 28.
66 Ibid., 29.
67 Ibid., 30.
68 Ibid., 30–31.
69 Ibid., 30–31.
70 Thomas Cleland, *Letters to Barton W. Stone*.
71 The most easily accessible version of Stone's autobiography may be found at the Restoration Movement website founded by Hans Rollmann, which is now under the oversight of Abilene Christian University's Center for Restoration Studies. See https://webfiles.acu.edu/departments/Library/HR/restmov_nov11/www.mun.ca/rels/restmov/texts/bstone/barton.html, (February 12, 2014). The version of Stone's autobiography used for the electronic edition found here is from Rhodes Thompson, ed., *Voices from Cane Ridge*, 31–134. Those interested will find references to Stone's position on the Trinity on pages 43–45, 60, and 90 of the *Voices from Cane Ridge* edition.
72 Stone, *Atonement*. There is actually little here with ramifications for Stone's position on the Trinity, but one should consult page 16, numbered point 8. Stone's point here is that in order to purchase pardon for sinners through substitutionary atonement, Christ would have had to be a distinct, independent God, but since there is only one true God, he could not be a distinct, independent God, and, therefore, did not purchase for sinners their salvation through a substitutionary atonement—what Stone calls the "surety-righteousness of Christ."
73 Stone, *A Reply to John Campbell's Strictures on Atonement*. See pages 19–20 concerning the equality of God and the Son.
74 Stone, *A Letter to Mr. John R. Moreland*.
75 Stone, *Letters to James Blythe*.
76 Stone, *A Letter to Mr. John R. Moreland*, 4.
77 Ibid., 6.
78 Ibid., 7.
79 Ibid., 8.
80 Ibid. 9.
81 Ibid., 10.
82 Cf. Rowan Williams, *Arius: Heresy and Tradition*, 95–116. Quasi-Arian is used in this paper to describe Stone's position, rather than semi-Arian, because of the historically specific description of semi-Arianism as the position of those who in the fourth century argued for the use of ὁμοιούσιος instead of ὁμοούσιος. See Jaroslav Pelikan, *The Emergence of the Catholic Traidition (100–600)*, vol. 1 of *The Christian Tradition: A History of the Development of Doctrine* (Chicago: The University of Chicago Press, 1971), 209–210.
83 Stone, *Letters to James Blythe*, 3.
84 Ibid., 6–12.
85 Ibid., 15–17.
86 Ibid., 17–20.
87 Ibid., 20–29.
88 Interrupting his assessment of these verses, Stone on pages 23–25 evaluates several texts concerning the personhood of the Holy Spirit, indicating that none of these texts,

as suggested by Cleland, refute his contention from *An Address to the Christian Churches* that the Holy Spirit should not be considered a proper person.

[89] Stone, *Letters to James Blythe*, 30–31. Although he does not say it, my take on this is that Stone is making the point that the majority of early church Fathers would have chosen to support ὁμοιούσιος instead of ὁμοούσιος. Stone wants to attribute to the Son the Father's divinity, but not his exact same oneness in nature.

[90] Ibid., 31–32.
[91] Ibid., 32–38.
[92] Ibid., 39.

[93] Ibid., 39–46. For the purposes of Chapter 4 and determining the roots of Stone's doctrine of the Trinity, this cascade of quotations of Samuel Clarke is significant, not only as evidence of dependence but also to establish Stone's specific dependence on Clarke regarding the unity of God and the separate personality of the Son. The ending quotes from Bull and Pearson, on page 46, which come from Clarke, illustrate well Clarke's emphasis and Stone's agreement with it, in that these quotations focus on the *one God* and *one true God, alone*, with Stone italicizing just these words for emphasis.

[94] Ibid., 47.
[95] Ibid., 47–50.
[96] Ibid., 51–52.
[97] Ibid., 54.
[98] Ibid., 55–56.
[99] Ibid., 57–58.
[100] Ibid., 59–61.
[101] Ibid., 62–64.
[102] Ibid., 64–65.
[103] Ibid., 70–71.
[104] Ibid., 71.
[105] Ibid., 71–73.
[106] Ibid., 74.
[107] Ibid., 75–76.
[108] Ibid., 77.

[109] Stone's analysis of these portions of Scripture is found in pages 77–93. Biblical verses here addressed by Stone include (in the order in which Stone addresses them): John 1:1–3, 10; John 1:18; John 17:5; Colossians 1:15; Romans 9:5 (Stone's dependence here upon Samuel Clarke is notable); 1 Corinthians 15:24ff.; Hebrews 1:8–9; 1 John 5:20; Acts 7:59; Acts 9:3–6; John 20:28; Isaiah 44:6 and Revelation 22:19; Isaiah 8:13, 14 and Isaiah 23:16; Isaiah 6:5 as quoted in John 12:41; Psalms 78:56; Colossians 2:8:9.

[110] Ibid., 99–103.
[111] Ibid., 104–5.
[112] Ibid., 108.
[113] Ibid., 110.
[114] Ibid., 111.
[115] Ibid., 112.
[116] Ibid., 113–14.

[117] Cf., Barton Stone, Untitled Editorial Comments, 18, 21; "The Creed of the Waldenses," 56; Untitled Comment, 82, 83–86; "History of the Christian Church in the West—VI," 194; "History of the Christian Church in the West—No. VIII," 265, 268–69;

Untitled Review of a May 1830 Article on the Trinity, 169–73; "Reply," *The Christian Messenger*, 6, 118–21; "To Elder Thomas Campbell," 205; and Unnamed Author, "'The Trinity' from Spark's Inquiry," 75–79.

[118] Barton Stone, "Objections to Christian Union Calmly Considered," 29.

[119] Ibid., 30.

[120] Ibid., 31.

[121] Ibid., 31–32.

[122] Ibid., 32.

[123] Ibid., 33.

[124] Barton Stone, "To The Christian Baptist," 204. That Stone refers to discussion of the Trinity as the most important point in theology is interesting given the general lack of attention given to this subject for most of SC history. The Movement would have been served by followers of Stone and Campbell taking these words seriously and acting upon them.

[125] Ibid., 205.

[126] Ibid., 206.

[127] Alexander Campbell, "From the Christian Baptist, To the Christian Messenger," 8.

[128] Barton Stone, "Reply," *The Christian Messenger* 2 no. 1, 10–11.

[129] Ibid., 11–13.

[130] Spencer Clack, "From the Baptist Recorder," 28.

[131] Barton Stone, "Reply: To Elder Spencer Clack," 30.

[132] Ibid., 32–33.

[133] Ibid., 33–34.

[134] Ibid., 35–36.

[135] Barton Stone, "Letter II.—To Elder S. Clack," 53.

[136] Ibid. Of course, as seen previously in this chapter, Stone has frequently made the claim that the indwelling of the Father's fullness in Jesus Christ is responsible for Scripture applying to Christ all sorts of divine names and titles.

[137] Ibid.

[138] Ibid., 53–55.

[139] Ibid., 55.

[140] Ibid., 56.

[141] Ibid., 57.

[142] "Timothy," "The Spirit of Orthodoxy," 124–28.

[143] Isaac Watts, *A Faithful Enquiry*.

[144] Barton Stone, "Remarks on the Preceding Communication," 128–29.

[145] Ibid., 129.

4

The Historical/Theological Roots of
Early Restorationist Trinitarianism

Few studies have examined the links between nascent SCM theology and pre-nineteenth-century Protestantism, and little has been done from the perspective of historical theology to determine the specific influences that most directly contributed to the Trinitarian positions of Thomas Campbell, Alexander Campbell, and Barton Stone. Newell Williams's reflections on what I have in other parts of this book labeled Barton Stone's "quasi-Arianism" partially meet the need. However, even when rigorous and historically critical examinations of early SC theology have been conducted, such as the work done by the Disciples of Christ's W. E. Garrison, who in 1900 published his University of Chicago Ph.D. dissertation under the title *Alexander Campbell's Theology: Its Sources and Historical Setting*—the foundations of SC Trinitarianism for the most part have been left out of the discussion.[1]

Likely the chief reason for this is a concern over the relatively sparse evidence available in the writings of the Campbells and Stone to trace theological connections related to their Trinitarian views. As mentioned in Chapter One, they simply offer relatively few sustained Trinitarian discussions, providing largely inadequate foundations for a continuing Trinitarian dialogue. So, it is not surprising that there are relatively few places in their writings where either of the Campbells or Stone overtly state the *historical/theological influences* that shaped their Trinitarian thinking.[2]

At the very least, the progenitors of the SCM were uninterested in such discussion; but more to the point, they intentionally avoided exploration of the topic because it ran opposite their orientation toward denigrating speculative theology. For present-day historical theologians, then, to examine the connection between early Restorationists and their Trinitarian theological predecessors runs against what the Campbells and, to an extent, Stone wanted to do—and apparently what they would have desired be done with their work. Such research would look to assert a dependency on the speculative theologizing of others that they, for the most part, specifically, intentionally, and overtly attempted to avoid in favor of looking to the Bible as their only source for doctrine.

Reluctance to Admit Trinitarian Influences

It would have been surprising if they had not held such an attitude toward the Trinitarian influence of their predecessors, given several factors. First, there is the simple fact that few of us are ever aware of all the influences shaping our positions; such factors often can only be delineated in retrospect. Second, in the case of the Restorationists, this factor is compounded with the fact that the Campbells and Stone were largely convinced that their reading of biblical texts was what *exclusively* influenced them. They claim to rely upon no creed but the Bible. And, since Scripture offers no systematic, clearly delineated perspective on the Trinity, most early Restorationists were typically not just reticent to construct their own systematic Trinitarian perspectives, but they rebelled against doing so. This is especially true of Alexander Campbell.[3]

Third, if Scripture does not provide abundant and clear exposition regarding the Trinity, Restorationists would certainly hesitate to construct a position grounded in what they perceived as the *humanly* originated theologies of their predecessors. Of course, their readings of the biblical text were, in turn, shaped by the numerous factors, including the reader's horizon that postmodern hermeneutics now generally take into account in evaluating any text. Nonetheless, they perceived they were being true to their objective of reading the Bible with no humanly originated presuppositions. From their common perspective, they had before them only the "facts" of the biblical text, and they now believed only what they found specifically stated there.[4] This Restorationist, primitivistic hermeneutic by nature precludes readers of the Bible from seeing and acknowledging human influence on the conclusions they reach concerning the text. Hence, early Restorationists said little about the influences on them which we can now historically trace, preventing today's historical theologians from reaching unequivocal conclusions on the backgrounds of early SCM Trinitarian thought.

Fourth, given Thomas Campbell's experiences both in Ireland and in the United States, he would have been somewhat hesitant to acknowledge who had influenced his thinking on a number of matters. The previous response of the Anti-Burgher Seceder Presbyterians who knew of his associations with thinkers, speakers, and writers outside their own sect would have made a man bent on achieving Christian unity and promoting nonsectarian doctrinal formulation reluctant to name those who influenced him, particularly about something as volatile as a Trinitarian position.[5] Perhaps Campbell's relatively weak subordinationism (discussed in Chapter Two) was not enough to have given him much anxiety concerning the potential reaction to this particular issue within his personal theology. However, the Seceder General Assembly in Scotland previously had specifically stated their concerns that in his dealings with others he had left himself open to Latitudinarianism, which in his day many coupled with Socinianism and Unitarianism.[6] Having previously experienced such acrimony, he may have thought it best not too readily to disclose those whose thinking influenced his own, even if their influence was slight or very general, and even if his own position on the Trinity met with the approval of his critics, as his *Circular Letter* of 1816 apparently did.

Fifth, Alexander Campbell would have been influenced by his father's experiences and discussions regarding the matter of disclosing where one stood on the Trinity, including whether to disclose the steps that led him to his conclusions.[7] Such likely discussions, perhaps combined with what

Alexander may have witnessed or read concerning the troubles of self-acknowledged non-Trinitarians—such as Locke's famous difficulties with Stillingfleet and Edwards—would likely have caused him to hesitate to say much concerning his own views or the factors that influenced his thinking, whether he was basically Trinitarian or not.

And as a sixth factor, there was always standing above all other reasons the Restorationists' concern for Christian unity. It is clear that they believed disunity and sectarianism would result from aligning with a specific, speculative Trinitarian position—especially if such an alignment formed any part of a creedal summation required as a test of fellowship or church membership. This factor alone would have been enough to cause Restorationists to remain circumspect about any backgrounds to their Trinitarian or non-Trinitarian positions. To align themselves with any previous position would have only invited rejection and separation.

Finally, Barton Stone, even while he was taking steps to move out of Presbyterianism, was challenged as to his views on the Trinity, as seen in Chapter Three. In light of the kind of direct challenges that came his way, it is not surprising that he would eventually resolve to have little to do with such controversies, including remaining relatively silent about the roots of his Trinitarian views. Stone did, of course, acknowledge the link between his own thinking and that of Isaac Watts, but he no doubt recognized that such an acknowledgement had repercussions among his critics, in that they could and did simply categorize him as being a theological descendent of Watts, of whom they were already suspicious. Thus, he would have understood that a clear acknowledgement of his dependency on one like Samuel Clarke would have fostered only an escalation of criticism. Fortunately for the purposes of this study, as seen in Chapters Two and Three, Stone was quite public about his Trinitarian perspectives from about 1805 until after he began serious discussions with Alexander Campbell regarding unifying the Disciples and Stone's Christians. Even at these places, Stone for the most part discusses his Trinitarian views by arguing from the Bible, referencing an established Trinitarian like Calvin or Bishop Bull, or referencing theologians who explicate and apply the Trinitarian positions of the early church Fathers (which is how Stone applies his reading of Samuel Clarke).[8] Perhaps in referencing these sources without acknowledging direct dependency on any non-Trinitarians for his conclusions, Stone hoped to escape the charge that heretics had shaped his thoughts on the Trinity.

Parallels to Previous Trinitarian Thoughts

Even considering all the above factors, the striking parallels that occur between the Restorationists' positions and previous Trinitarian thought should have obviated their hesitancy to connect their positions with that of previous theologians, whether this antecedent Trinitarianism comes in the forms of creedal dogmatisms, systematic theologies, Trinitarian monographs, polemical pamphlets, or published sermons. At some points, such as in Thomas Campbell's 1816 *Circular Letter* to the Redstone Baptist Association, such connections take the form of a positive view of traditional Trinitarianism. In other cases, such as Stone's *An Address to the Christian Churches,* a non-Trinitarian perspective is argued, one that finds parallels in Isaac Watts and others, such as Samuel Clarke. Although early Restorationists largely avoided admitting parallels between their own positions and those of their predecessors, these parallels can be demonstrated. Neither the Restorationists' desire to ground their theological positions entirely on the Bible nor historical naiveté on the parts of historical theologians today should hinder close examination of SC Trinitarian roots.

Of course, there are *some* references made by early Restorationists to antecedent Trinitarian theology, at least in the case of Barton Stone. But early Restorationists, understandably, typically did not assert a significant *dependence* upon previous writers (except for Stone's acknowledgement of Watts's influence). Instead, they note the works of others in constructing their own positions, most frequently citing the thoughts of others as *supporting evidence* for the Trinitarian positions they themselves hold.

The question is, "At what point does *evidential support* become *dependence?*" Are the apparent connections strong enough for historical theologians to speak of *direct dependency* by Restorationists? Even if this is not the case, can Restorationist Trinitarian thought be closely associated with a general style of Trinitarian thinking arising from seventeenth and eighteenth century theology in the United Kingdom? Is there a historical milieu that is to a great extent responsible for the thoughts of the Campbells and Stone concerning the Trinity?

The irony is that the claims made by the Campbells and Stone to rely on Scripture alone find precedent in the voices of the many biblical primitivists who went before them and who claimed for themselves the same importance. In the case of Trinitarian theology, neither the Restorationists' methodological choice to ground their thoughts in Scripture alone, nor their specific Trinitarian conclusions, nor their aversion to experiencing or propagating the disunity often created among Christians by the formulation of Trinitarian doctrine is without precedent. And Restorationists' references to the thoughts of others—even if such references constitute only supporting evidence and not an admission of dependence—help establish the sources for their perspectives.

Because the Campbells and Stone intentionally deemphasize the doctrine of the Trinity, and say relatively little about the influences on their Trinitarian doctrine, there must be at least some element of speculation in piecing together the intellectual background of their thoughts on the Trinity. While this factor lends a sense of tentativeness to any conclusions about such sources, there is at least some evidence on which to base an opinion. Much of this evidence concerns what was happening among Anglicans, Presbyterians, and Independents of England, Scotland, and Ireland prior to the beginning of the SCM.

The remainder of this chapter will examine how Thomas Campbell, Alexander Campbell, and Barton Stone were influenced by their theological predecessors, including the cumulative impact from what may be simply characterized as the intellectual climate of the day. Some of these influences have in recent years become so much a part of SC reflection on its own history as to be thought of as virtual truisms.

Following a delineation of these general aspects, more specific historical and theological influences that likely played a role in early SC Trinitarian theology will be considered, and a proposal will be made regarding the specific Anglican, Presbyterian, and Independent forces at work.

Post-Reformation Influences

Whatever one may finally say of the Trinitarian positions of the Campbells and Stone, they certainly de-emphasize Trinitarian thought in comparison to the remainder of Christendom considered at virtually any point in post-Nicean Christian history up until the rise of Socinianism. Even if a solidly orthodox Trinitarian position may be established for some early Restorationists, their writings and sermons scarcely touch on Trinitarian doctrine. What general factors within the broad scope of their intellectual history affected this reluctance? How might such factors have even moved the Campbells or Stone in a direction away from traditional Trinitarianism?

One direct factor is the Reformational ancestry from which Restorationists descended. Although Trinitarian reflection is included in, for example, the commentaries on the Gospel of John penned by Luther and Calvin,[9] or in Calvin's *Institutes*,[10] early reformers are relatively terse regarding Trinitarian theology. This brevity does not constitute a rejection of Trinitarianism, but rather an acceptance of the traditional creedal position, so that Luther and Calvin and other reformers *assume* a Trinitarian theology and pay it relatively little attention. Thus, those who descended from the great reformers were made partially vulnerable to a de-emphasizing of the Trinity, and to non-Trinitarian positions. Despite the presence of carefully and thoughtfully worded Trinitarian theology among those who followed the reformers—*The Augsburg Confession, The Second Helvitic Confession, The Thirty-Nine Articles, and The Westminster Confession of Faith* all contain carefully worded statements about the Trinity—the major issues during the nascent days of the Reformation typically centered on matters other than Trinitarian orthodoxy. When, in the seventeenth and eighteenth centuries, Arianism and Socinianism began to significantly impact the Presbyterian ancestors of Restorationists, especially the Presbyterians in England, there was at least some room for such influences to work given the lack of emphasis on Trinitarian doctrine in the thought of the magisterial reformers.

Sola Scriptura

Of course, another way the reformers (including their precursors Wycliffe and Huss) affected later Trinitarian thinking stems from their emphasis on *sola scriptura* and the obligation of all Christians to sort out for themselves their own theological positions. Free thinking on religious matters in the post-Reformation era derives from those who became willing to question Catholic orthodoxy on the basis of Scripture. Further, as early as the fourth century, claims were made concerning what some believed to be the paucity of evidence within the Scriptures for the position accepted at Nicea. It is not surprising, then, that when Scripture was placed at the forefront for establishing orthodoxy, any weaknesses in the scripturally based case for orthodoxy would be discovered, exposed, and exploited by non-Trinitarian thinkers taking advantage of the freedom they had to think theologically for themselves.[11]

The influence of *sola scriptura* and the freedom to think theologically eventually led to the sometimes anticreedal, antisubscriptionist, Restorationist spirit present in some parts of the United Kingdom during the seventeenth and eighteenth centuries. In many places, what were considered human accretions to the pure church and pure gospel were being rejected in favor of the free practice associated with Puritanism. This attitude included not just a rejection of the strictures placed on Christians by Catholicism, but, for some, the rejection of any and all creedal statements, save Scripture, and the Protestant confessions mentioned above were seen by some as impositions and illegitimate fetters binding their abilities to live in light of what they perceived to be biblical truth. It is important for the purposes of this study to see that these nonconformists and nonsubscriptionists felt the freedom to reject even the *Protestant* statements of faith that possessed a clear affirmation of Trinitarianism if they did not feel the statements were supported by Scripture. The rejected systems constituted by creeds and confessions were replaced by many Puritans (and their heirs) with what we know as biblical primitivism.[12] This attempt to ascertain from the New Testament the earliest beliefs and practices of the Christian church, and to follow them, meant that primitivists felt the freedom, and even the call, to reject traditional Trinitarianism in favor of whatever theological positions they discerned within the primitive, biblical church.

For Restorationists, their post-Reformational freedom to reflect for themselves on biblical theology in order to restore the primitive church amounts to a trademark of their entire ethos as a movement.[13] And, as indicated, there was abundant room and opportunity for traditional Trinitarian theology to be affected by the general attitudes associated with the post-Reformation period. Certainly this context forms the general theological background for American Restorationists, and no doubt this influence is present in the writings and preaching of the Campbells and Barton Stone.

Lockean Empiricism and Emphasis on Reason

One other general element should be noted for contributing to the intellectual climate of the post-Reformation period and helping to form the milieu for Trinitarian thinking in the United Kingdom during the seventeenth and eighteenth centuries. Although there is a direct connection between this factor and early Restorationists, the pervasiveness of this influence in the United Kingdom and the United States prior to the nineteenth century means it should be treated within the category of general influences. This influence is the rationalistically/empirically oriented thought of the day,[14] especially the writings of John Locke, and the perspectives of Locke and others on the centrality of rational thought and on tolerance.

To state that Lockean empiricism and Locke's perspective on reason was widely influential on those speaking English in the seventeenth and eighteenth centuries is to drastically understate the case. Lockean-like perspectives on the place of reason quite simply dominated the thinking of the period we are considering.[15] The place given to reason by Locke drew into question propositions, including theological ones, that were difficult to square with a rational outlook. To the extent that Trinitarian doctrine seemed to rely on metaphysical speculation, having little support from reason, it became questionable. In fact, it would appear that the vast majority of Arian and Socinian thinking taking place at the end of the seventeenth century and within the eighteenth century is somehow theoretically linked to Locke's empiricism—or at least to someone echoing comparable thoughts.[16]

Not to be missed is how Lockean thoughts of toleration influenced the potential for variances in Trinitarian thinking during the eighteenth century. Locke calls for a unity that transcends ideological differences and leads to a rejection of sectarian attitudes that had been maintained on the basis of inherently speculative doctrinal principles. On these grounds, many naturally de-emphasized the Trinitarian doctrines that had led through the centuries to so much disunity among Christians. With thinkers as ecumenically minded as the Campbells and Stone, any idea that a strictly orthodox Trinitarian teaching could contribute to Christian sectarianism, especially if it were couched within a humanly originated creed, would lead them to reduce their commitment to such teaching.[17]

This kind of rationalism directly influenced Barton Stone to move in the direction of Arianism. And there is a sense in which Locke's rationalism also stands behind any relaxation on the part of the Campbells of Trinitarian orthodoxy. Not only is Locke's thought a major factor in the general thinking of the day, but both Campbells were well-versed in Locke, with Thomas insisting while Alexander was still a teenager that he read Locke's *Essay Concerning Human Understanding* and *Essay on Toleration*. To both the Campbells and Stone, Locke's *Reasonableness of Christianity* was available, and here Locke argues that only an acceptance of Jesus as Messiah should be considered a belief to be necessarily held. Although Trinitarian formulas are not named, it is clear Locke included them as speculation and rejected them as a necessity on this basis.

It seems, then, that Barton Stone and the Campbells would have been both indirectly and directly influenced by the pervasiveness of the Lockean rationalism and toleration of the day and its impact on Trinitarian thinking. First, they would have been indirectly affected by their general culture. Second, they would have been directly influenced by their actual reading of Locke: Thomas read Locke at the University of Glasgow in the late 1700s and during his later theological study; Alexander read him at home and in his own studies at the University of Glasgow in 1807–08 and later consistently committed himself to read Locke; and Stone was influenced by Lockean ideas during his association with Caldwell's Academy in the 1790s.

While reading Locke may have contributed directly to the perspectives of Stone and the Campbells, were there other influences that may have caused them to read Locke with an openness toward a non-Trinitarian perspective? Were they heirs to a history of Lockean interpretation, that, when combined with the general influences delineated above, helped shape SC Trinitarian thought, however little or great?

What seems to be the case is that a coalescing of the general principles of Reformation thought, the specific influences of a Lockean type rationalism, and the influence from the ecclesiastical/theological events of the eighteenth century all impacted the early Restorationists. Locke's rationalism/empiricism had been influencing Christian theology for over a hundred years when Stone and the Campbells began writing about being Christians only and restoring the ancient order. A century's worth of rationalism's impact on Anglicans, Presbyterians, and Independents preceded and influenced whatever the Campbells and Stone thought in nineteenth-century America concerning Trinitarian doctrine, even apart from any direct contact they had with John Locke.

Seventeenth- and Eighteenth-Century Theological Influences

In the United Kingdom, in the last decades of the seventeenth century, particularly in 1690 and the years immediately following, controversy developed among Anglicans, Presbyterians, and Independents, over subscription, nonconformity, and the doctrine of the Trinity. Those who eventually became non-Trinitarians consistently and increasingly linked together these ideas as the decades passed. In addition, there was a steady rise in the application of rationalism and empiricism to church doctrine, as seen, for example, in the works of John Tillotson and the other Latitudinarians, with Isaac Newton, and, of course, with Locke.[18] It is important to set forth some of the major events and patterns of this developing non-Trinitarianism to place in their historical, theological contexts the parallels and direct connections between this period and early SC Trinitarian thought.

First, it should be noted that neither antisubscriptionists[19] nor nonconformists[20] were necessarily non-Trinitarian, and the Trinity appears not to have been a source of widespread conflict before about 1690. The earliest of those who came to be called Latitudinarians were committed to orthodoxy regarding the Trinity, and so they allowed speculative language about the nature of God, even if they were generally opposed to human speculation and creedal language. For instance, Herbert Croft's *The Naked Truth of the True State of the Primitive Church* (1675) called for a return to a simple, biblically primitivistic faith free from the creeds, and he further suggests that only biblical expressions be used to assert doctrinal formulations.[21] But Croft also specifically speaks negatively about the Arians and supposes that their position would have simply died out had there been no Council of Nicea.[22]

Croft was not alone in being both Latitudinarian and Trinitarian, and little non-Trinitarianism is evident among the writings of most of these *early* Latitudinarians (whose works by and large were published prior to

1700—Tillotson, Stillingfleet, Fowler, Kidder, Tenison, et al.). What they *did* possess was openness toward the application of rationalism to Christianity, even if their adherence to Trinitarianism necessarily included a level of toleration concerning speculative doctrine.[23] Hunt says, "Before the dialogue closes, it is shown that they (the Latitudinarians) adhere firmly to all the essentials of Christianity, but that on minor questions of speculative doctrine, church government, and modes of worship, they 'persuade men to peace and moderation.'"[24]

These early thinkers, who predate the Restorationist work of the Campbells and Stone by about 125 years, are seen to parallel in a nascent way the concern for toleration and unity present among the Restorationists. That the early Latitudinarians were essentially Trinitarians who adopted a rational approach to faith that fits with that of Locke especially parallels the thinking of Thomas Campbell, who not only is quite obviously Trinitarian, but who also shared with the Latitudinarians a background which included Anglicanism (Church of Ireland), university education, and a love of the rational mind.[25]

The Naked Gospel

A next step in the seventeenth- and eighteenth-century progression we are following pertains to the well-known Trinitarian controversy among early Latitudinarians that began with the 1690 publication in England of Arthur Bury's *The Naked Gospel*. This volume, along with the publication in the same year of the first of three series of anti-Trinitarian tracts published by Thomas Firmin, created a significant furor and brought about several published responses, along with the burning at the University of Oxford of certain anti-Trinitarian publications. In Bury and in Firmin's tracts, there was a summation of natural, rational religion that included a protest against speculation about the person of Christ.[26] Here Calvinism was denigrated, the efficacy of the sacraments was denied, biblical primitivism was promoted, creeds were either rejected or relegated to insignificance, faith was viewed as an act of intellectual reasoning along Lockean lines, speculation was said to be injurious to the faith, the notion of the three Persons being in One was described as irrational, the Son was said to be inferior to the Father, the Nicean and Athanasian creeds were rejected, and a simple form of the gospel was proclaimed.[27] In addition, in response to attacks on Bury, Le Clerc wrote—also in 1690—*An Historical Vindication of the 'The Naked Gospel,'* which argued that the concept of the Trinity had been borrowed from Plato, that the notion of hypostasis came from Plotinus, and that Christians would be far better off keeping to the language of the New Testament.[28]

An investigation of this time period indicates that a spirit of ecclesiastical and theological revolution was everywhere present in England, despite attempts by the English monarchy and the Anglican church to suppress the numerous free thinkers who continued to challenge the status quo. Clearly, this theological revolution included the fact that Latitudinarianism had taken a Socinian turn.

With the dawning of the eighteenth century, Latitudinarian-like change and an increased number of departures from orthodoxy were abundantly evident, indicated, for example, in publications by William Whiston (*Historical Preface to Primitive Christianity,* 1710) and the non-Trinitarian Samuel Clarke (*The Scripture Doctrine of the Trinity,* 1712); by the semi-Arian controversy of 1710; by the Salter's Hall Synod in February 1719; by the Exeter subscription controversy of May 1719 that specifically pertained to a rejection of subscription on the basis of the first of *The Thirty-nine Articles;* by the Arminian and High Arian revision by James Strong of *The Westminster Shorter Catechism* in 1735 and its 1738 publication by Samuel Bourn;[29] and by numerous other events and publications. It is also significant that there are signs of the existence of such controversy throughout the United Kingdom, with Drysdale noting its presence in both Scotland and Ireland.[30]

The second half of the eighteenth century is significant for this study, not because of numerous key events that occurred during the period, but more because of the sense of ferment that developed concerning non-subscription, nonconformity, and non-Trinitarianism. There were some important publications, like Francis Blackburne's *The Confessionals,* which came from the press in 1766; and there was the meeting at Feather's Tavern in 1771 and its subsequent petition, presented to Parliament as a plea asking that clergy be allowed to interpret the Bible in the light of reason and conscience instead of according to creedal formulas. But most significant is the continued spread of nonconforming ideas, including a gradual drifting of many nonconformists toward a Unitarian position.[31]

Non-Trinitarianism in Presbyterians

This nonconformist, nonsubscriptionist trend led to the domination of non-Trinitarian doctrine among English Presbyterians in the latter half of the eighteenth century. G.R. Cragg says:

> Presbyterians were usually against subscription, and in due course their name became a synonym for freedom of thought, even for laxity of opinion. Arianism steadily gained ground among them. By 1770 barely half the Presbyterian congregations were Trinitarian in belief; thereafter they rapidly veered toward Socinianism, and in due course became explicitly Unitarian. Thus the Presbyterians passed from Calvinism to Arminianism, then to Arianism, and so to Socinianism. Many of the ablest dissenters became Arians.[32]

It is a startling fact that in just over half a century, between 1720 and 1770, about one half of the English Presbyterians became essentially Unitarian in orientation. As early as 1719, at Salter's Hall Synod, the majority of Presbyterians voted against subscription, which indicated a decidedly non-Trinitarian perspective among them. Liturgical forms among English Presbyterians during this period ran along the same lines.[33]

The academies, too, played a role in promoting a mindset among English Presbyterians (and some Independents) that was fertile ground for Arianism and Socinianism. Best-known among these as a home for non-Trinitarianism were Daventry and the Warrington Academy, the first of which trained Joseph Priestley, and the second of which employed Priestley as a tutor.[34] In fact, it is notable that Philip Doddridge was an instructor at Daventry, that he was known for doing nothing to discourage the moves made by many toward Unitarianism, and that numerous Daventry and Doddridge students, including Priestley, later became prominent Unitarians.[35]

This trend among eighteenth-century Presbyterians has been noted by numerous others, and there seems to be little question about its existence.[36] What must now be shown is any connection between this history and the early Restorationists, which includes an element of speculation but also represents an informed extrapolation stemming from what is known of the setting from which early SCM Trinitarianism arose.

Specific Influences on Thomas Campbell's Trinitarianism

As was seen in Chapter Two, Thomas Campbell's view of the Trinity is essentially in line with traditional orthodoxy, which is no surprise based on his background, which was also detailed in Chapter Two. Obviously, despite being influenced in whatever other ways he was by his fellow Seceder Presbyterians and Independents with whom he was in touch at Rich Hill, Campbell essentially maintained the Trinitarian perspective of *The Westminster Confession*. At least on this point he remained committed to the position held by the Anti-Burgher Seceder Presbyterians of Ireland and Scotland.

The question arises, whence the dichotomy that was apparently present in the thought of Thomas Campbell? How is it that he is both Latitudinarian and staunchly Trinitarian, even classically so? Were there others who shared a similar position who could have had direct impact upon him?

It appears some of the Latitudinarian Independents—particularly those at Rich Hill—to whom Thomas Campbell was exposed, held both Latitudinarian and orthodox Trinitarian positions. It is well-known from the events of Salter's Hall in 1719 that many Latitudinarian Independents remained subscriptionists, meaning they supported the Trinitarianism of *The Thirty-nine Articles* and *The Westminster Confession*.[37] Although Campbell was called before the Associate General Synod of the Anti-Burgher Presbyterian church in July 1799 in Belfast, where he was accused of associating with the Latitudinarians of the Evangelical Society of Ulster—which included Latitudinarian Anglicans, Independents, and all sorts of Presbyterians—there is was no indication he had given himself over to non-Trinitarian Latitudinarianism, as the council no doubt figured he either had or would. True, he adopted much of the Latitudinarianism around him, but like the Independents of Salter's Hall and some later Latitudinarian Presbyterians, *he remained Trinitarian*.

Much of Thomas Campbell's theology meshes with that of the Latitudinarian, nonsubscriptionist English Presbyterians of his day, but he is not a good fit with the non-Trinitarian stance that dominated the English Presbyterians of his era. Neither does he appear to have been directly dependent upon later, non-Trinitarian Latitudinarians, such as Samuel Clarke or Francis Blackburne, and he makes no references to them. Further, although there are clear parallels between Thomas Campbell and the early Trinitarian[38] Latitudinarians, his departure from Anglicanism and acceptance of nonconformity runs contrary to their defense of and adherence to the Anglican communion.

It seems safe to say, then, that the general outlook of Thomas Campbell may best be described as later Trinitarian Latitudinarianism. In Campbell's case, this inherently flexible category includes biblical primitivism, his anticreedal position, his Lockean, Arminian-like soteriology, his concern for unity, his rational orientation, and a view of the Trinity that is essentially traditional and orthodox. In positing the roots of Thomas Campbell's Trinitarian theology, then, one cannot simply fall back on his background among the Irish/Scot Anti-Burgher Seceder Presbyterians, who were inherently Calvinistic and subscriptionist. His acquaintance with (and adoption of) a Latitudinarianism that included an essentially orthodox Trinitarian stance was decisive for Thomas Campbell's perspective on the Trinity.

Specific Influences on Alexander Campbell's Trinitarianism

At one level, it is very difficult to separate whatever specific influences may have contributed to Thomas Campbell's Trinitarianism from the factors that led Alexander Campbell to take his own position. They were recipients of a common religious heritage and were both influenced by the general features of that heritage, as chronicled in Chapter Two. They worked together and initiated the Restoration Movement as a common cause between them. On the day that Thomas Campbell presented his Trinitarian position before the Redstone Baptist Association, son Alexander was there, giving him encouragement. Thomas Campbell was a frequent contributor to both Alexander's *The Christian Baptist* and *The Millennial Harbinger* and the source of reference and inspiration for Alexander's theological ruminations. Three things set them apart.

First, Thomas Campbell was directly confronted by the Anti-Burgher Seceder Presbyterians for his association with Latitudinarianism, but Alexander never had to face that kind of tribunal. Hence, there was not the kind of pressure from his own heritage that challenged Alexander to remain *overtly* orthodox. He was, from the time he arrived in the United States, part of no denominational structure with a governing body that required him to adhere to a theological formula, and his theology was largely worked out in a context of religious freedom. He was, as was seen above, essentially orthodox, but there was no compelling reason for him to focus on his Trinitarian position or to explicate his views; conversely, refusing to focus upon Trinitarian doctrine was actually part and parcel of his ecumenical mission.

Second, because Alexander had no need to devote allegiance to a party line, he was far more vocal than Thomas about his Lockean-like hesitancy regarding speculation and the Trinity.[39] Alexander was more thoroughly Lockean in his approach to hermeneutics and toleration, and his consistent commitment to Locke's empiricism is not so easily pushed aside in light of his religious traditions as Thomas's Latitudinarianism was in light of the criticisms that came his way. Locke's influence was far more direct on Alexander, which resulted in his deep rigidity with respect to either writing about or arguing about Trinitarian theology. In fact, it is Alexander Campbell's hesitancy regarding speculative language and his emphasis on toleration that makes it difficult to delineate his Trinitarianism or the influences on his position. Alexander was actually committed to *not* writing something akin to Thomas Campbell's *Circular Letter*. It is no wonder that Alexander Campbell's adamant opinions about the detrimental effects of Trinitarian speculation eventually caused Barton Stone to cease from arguing about Trinitarian doctrine.

Third, Alexander Campbell was directly taught by his father. To the extent, then, that Thomas passed on to Alexander any hint of a less rigid Trinitarianism, a weak subordinationism, or a lessened emphasis on Trinitarian creedal formulas, it is not surprising that the son would simply take this position one step further, as sons are prone to do. Thomas had hinted at his rejection of the creeds as standards for Christian unity; Alexander directly augmented that with a firmer commitment to Lockean empiricism, which, in turn, led him to a heightened denigration of theological speculation.[40]

Alexander Campbell and the Issue of Eternal Sonship

More can be said regarding the roots of Alexander's perspective on the Trinity, especially with reference to the Eternal Sonship of Christ. In Campbell's 1827 letter "To Timothy," in *The Christian Baptist*, he makes clear he believes the language "Eternal Son," as taken from *The Westminster Confession of Faith* (Chapter 2, Section 3), is insufficient in that it uses nonbiblical language instead of biblical language about "the Word" from John 1:1. I suggest we see the influence of others upon Alexander Campbell revealed in this letter, although there is no overt mention here of such dependence. In fact, in his statements directed against the doctrine of the Eternal Son, Campbell adamantly denies dependence on any other writer or conversation partner, saying he had held such views for sixteen years prior to the letter.

However, two writers on whom Campbell relied for understanding the Scriptures were major figures in the Eternal Sonship controversy occurring after about 1816. Adam Clarke, the Methodist theologian and commentator on whom Campbell and others from his era often relied for biblical commentary, finished his multivolume commentary between 1810 and 1826, with a key volume on Matthew–John coming forth in 1817.[41] Clarke's perspectives on Eternal Sonship can be seen at the end of his comments on Proverbs 8, Acts 13:33, and his "Observations on the Divinity of Christ" at the end of Hebrews 1, but they are most clearly presented at the commentary on Luke 1:35. His comments here created a significant stir and reaction, particularly among Methodists. Richard Watson published in 1818 a response to Clarke,[42] followed by Robert Martin, who in 1821 also published a much-read volume directed against Clarke's perspective on the Eternal Sonship of Christ.[43]

Campbell also read much from Moses Stuart, whose rejection of the Eternal Sonship of Christ was a well-known feature of his theology. By 1819 Stuart was writing and being criticized for his perspective on Eternal Sonship,[44] and he argues his case in both his commentary on Hebrews, published in 1827–28, and his commentary on Romans, published in 1832.[45]

It is certainly possible that by 1817 Campbell had already independently possessed thoughts leading to a firm perspective concerning the Eternal Sonship of Christ and the wording he found in *The Westminster Confession,* but, was he totally unaware and uninfluenced by the controversy? I believe it likely that Campbell was aware of the Eternal Sonship controversy and Clarke's and Stuart's views on the matter, and that, at the least, his own perspective was confirmed by his use of Adam Clarke's commentary and his reading of Stuart. I base that opinion on several factors: (1) the ten years between the publishing of Clarke's commentary on the gospels and Campbell's dialogue with "Timothy"; (2) the significant controversy and publications that came about in response to Clarke; (3) the fact that Campbell was quite aware of Clarke's work and used it; and (4) the fact that Stuart's view of Eternal Sonship and responses to him were published as early as 1819. In addition, it is known that by December 25, 1826, Barton Stone took note in *The Christian Messenger* of both Adam Clarke's and Moses Stuart's positions on Eternal Sonship.[46] Is it not likely, then, that when Campbell asserts five months later in *The Christian Baptist* that he is void of anyone's input concerning the Eternal Sonship of Christ, he is reacting to the fact that some of his readers are quite familiar, like he is, with the Eternal Sonship controversy involving Clarke and Stuart?

Antecedents to Barton Stone's Quasi-Arianism

The Trinitarianism of Thomas and Alexander Campbell stands in significant contrast to what may be called the quasi-Arian position maintained by Barton Stone, which was detailed in Chapter Three. From whence does Stone's position derive?

Without question, one must first look to the general character of post-Reformation Protestantism—including the gradual movement toward an emphasis on Scripture alone as the basis of Christian doctrine, a denigration of creedal formulas, and the rational/empirical approach to Scripture and doctrine advocated by John Locke. Stone's conclusions are so much in line with the course of this whole theological flow that he can easily be placed within this stream. In a general way, then, the theological moves of English Presbyterians and Independents toward Socinianism detailed at the beginning of this chapter serve as the backdrop to the Trinitarian perspectives of Barton Stone. However, more can be said about the specific influences impacting Barton Stone's Trinitarian thought.

Isaac Watts's Influence on Barton Stone

As Newell Williams has made clear, there is abundant evidence linking Barton Stone to Isaac Watts, who was very much part of the events chronicled above pertaining to English Presbyterians and Independents early in the eighteenth century.[47] A "treatise" by Watts came out of this milieu, and Stone mentions reading it prior to his examination for ordination.[48] In addition, Stone specifically quotes Watts on the Trinity, and in his autobiography he mentions Watts's influence on his own Trinitarian perspectives.[49] There is no doubt, then, that certain aspects of Barton Stone's view of the Trinity, including his view of the pre-existent human soul of Christ, owes a major debt to Isaac Watts's view of the human soul of Christ being created and existing before the foundation of the world and being indwelled by the mind of God prior to the creation of the universe. We are indebted to Williams for delineating a relationship between Stone's Trinitarian views and those of Isaac Watts.

However, some important clarifications must be made concerning Stone's dependency on Isaac Watts, especially with reference to Newell Williams's conclusion that Watts's "treatise" *The Christian Doctrine of the Trinity* was at the time of their ordination "'read with pleasure and understanding'" by Stone and Samuel Holmes and that they then "accepted Watts' views."[50]

Although Stone does not identify in his autobiography which treatise by Watts that he and Holmes read, I agree with Williams that this was likely *The Christian Doctrine of the Trinity*, in that this was Watts's best-known work and the one that would serve best as preparation for an ordination examination. It was the most likely work of Watts to which Henry Patillo would have pointed Stone and Holmes, given their dissatisfaction with Witsius. But Stone's perspective on the Trinity—as seen in the second edition of his *An Address to the Christian Churches*, several articles published in *The Christian Messenger*, and defenses of his position directed to J. R. Moreland and James Blythe—significantly diverges from and goes further in an Arian direction than does Watts's *The Christian Doctrine of the Trinity*.[51]

Differences between Watts and Stone

On at least four different points of Trinitarian doctrine in his second addition of *An Address to the Christian Churches,* Stone ultimately differs with Watts's *The Christian Doctrine of the Trinity.* First, although it is a relatively minor point, it should at least be mentioned that Watts freely uses the word "Trinity" to reference the Godhead, and capitalizes the word Trinity in every instance. For Watts, "Trinity" functions as a divine title referencing God, and it is, therefore, given divine capitalization. Stone, although he does title his first section "OF TRINITY," and uses the term "trinity" in several places, asserts that the term is extrabiblical.[52] Of course, Watts, also, was aware the word "Trinity" is absent from Scripture, and on this basis the point may be made that by using the term Watts is *intentionally* taking a position on the justifiability of traditional, orthodox terminology in referring to God. But more to the point is the way in which Stone uses the word "trinity," particularly with reference to its capitalization. If quoting a source that capitalizes the word, or in referring to the "doctrine of the Trinity" as the title of a specified body of teaching, Stone uses the word in its capitalized form. However, in his own discussion of trinity, Stone uses the lowercase form of the word. Stone appears to be intentionally avoiding the capitalized form of the word as a title or name of deity, and, in fact, he avoids putting the definite article before "trinity," ensuring that no one would miss his point.[53] Stone does in places describe the Son as the second one of a "trinity" of individualities, but in these cases he is intentionally using "trinity" as a mere descriptor of number indicating "threeness."[54]

The "One True God"

A second departure of Stone from Watts concerns the idea that the three persons of the Trinity together comprise "the one true God." Watts takes great pains in *The Christian Doctrine of the Trinity* to make the identity of the three persons and the one true God a key principle in his Trinitarian perspective, stating it explicitly in six of twenty-two propositions and explaining or justifying the idea in several others. It is his core idea.[55] But this idea is in direct contrast to Barton Stone's reflections in the second edition of *An Address to the Christian Churches,* particularly in his second section, "Of the Son Of God."[56] Stone's first section, "Of Trinity," actually begins with the proposition that "there is *none other God but one,*" and here he quotes 1 Corinthians 8:6, making the point that Jesus Christ is the one Lord, but that he is not the one true God. Stone goes on to assert that, "If all agree that this *one only* God is *an infinite spirit without parts;* all must agree that this infinite spirit is not a compound of two or three spirits, beings, or Gods."[57] Then, in Section 2, Stone plainly states that Jesus as the begotten Son of God cannot be at the same time the one, eternal, true God who begat the Son, or he would have begotten himself.[58] So a logical conflict exists between the ideas that the Son of God is begotten and that he is also the eternal God who shares common eternal substance with the eternal Father. The Father is clearly *not* begotten, since the substance of the Father is eternal.[59] The Son, who *is* begotten, cannot be begotten *and* share the eternal substance of the begetter, both because a substance cannot beget itself and would, if eternal, have no need to do so, and because if the Son shares the eternal substance with the Father, by definition of the word "eternal" the Son's substance cannot be begotten.

Further, either the Son is a real, eternal being, in which case there must be two real, eternal beings—and, therefore, two Gods, since only a true God is a real eternal being—or the real, eternal being of the Son must be denied, since the real, eternal being of the one true God cannot be denied, otherwise there would be no eternal Father from whom the eternal Son could be begotten.[60] Further still, is it the case that the same God was sending and sent at the same instant in eternity? If so, he was active in sending and passive in being sent; which is impossible. Or was the one and only true eternal God born of Mary, so that Mary is the mother of the eternal God?[61] Or did the one and only true God suffer on the cross, submitting himself to true death?[62] Stone says:

> Here is certainly the notion of two distinct Gods held forth—the one an unchangeable God; the other a changeable one—The one a living God; the other a dead, buried one—the one reconciling; the other reconciled! But as all acknowledge, that there is but one only *living* God; therefore we must conclude that the one that was dead was not that one only living and true God. And as all acknowledge the one and only living and true God is *without*

passions; therefore he that suffered such exquisite *passion* on the cross, was not the only living and true God.[63]

Clearly, there is a stark contrast here between Watts and Stone with respect to the identification of the Son (and the Spirit) with the one and only eternal, true God. This difference is crucial, and it raises questions as to why, where, and how Stone derives his understanding that the Son and Spirit cannot be the one and only true, eternal God. If Stone did not reach this understanding completely on his own, and if he did not get it from Watts's *The Christian Doctrine of the Trinity*, then did he derive it from something else Watts later wrote or did he derive it from someone else?

The "Person" of the Trinity

Third, there is a difference between the willingness of Watts in *The Christian Doctrine of the Trinity* to use the word "person" to describe each of the three individualities as distinct intelligences, beings, minds, or wills within the one personhood of God and Stone's overt rejection of such language. Watts says regarding the three persons:

> The word person signifies in the common language of mankind, one single intelligent voluntary agent, or a principle of action that has understanding and will. So three men, or three angels are properly called three distinct persons; and the Father, the Son and Spirit, who are all one God, yet having three such distinct sort of actions and characters attributed to them, as may properly be ascribed to three distinct intelligent agents, we make no scruple to call them three persons. For it is sufficiently evident, that three mere names, three attributes, three modes or manners of being, three relations, or three sorts of conception of one and the same single or individual being, are not sufficient to sustain the three different offices, or to perform the three different sorts of actions which are attributed to Father, Son, and Spirit: Nor can we account for them, without supposing three distinct intelligent agents.[64]

This language is echoed throughout Watts's propositions, and his upholding of the idea that there are three persons that comprise the Godhead is a central feature of *The Christian Doctrine of the Trinity*. Stone, however, by the time of the second edition of *An Address to the Christian Churches*, had significant doubts about the reasonableness of there being three distinct persons within one God, who, too, is a person.[65] For Stone, the issue is of major importance, and his rejection of the language of "person" to describe each of the three individualities in the Godhead forms a major portion of those sections devoted to the Trinity in his *Address*. On page 7 Stone says:

> It is commonly stated, that there are three persons in one God, of one substance, power and eternity. To me it is evident that they who maintain this proposition, do not—can not believe, that these three persons are three distinct spirits, beings or Gods, each possessed of the personal properties of intelligence, will and power; for this would not only contradict the Scriptures, but also those sections of their creeds just quoted, which declare that there is but one only living and true God, without parts. They must understand the term *persons* in God, not in the proper and common sense of the word *person;* but in such a qualified sense as to exclude the notion of three distinct spirits or beings. What this qualified sense should be, has long puzzled divines; and in no proposition are they more divided. The cause of this perplexity is obvious, because no idea of it is to be found in revelation nor reason. Revelation no where declares that there are three persons of the same substance in the *one only* God; and it is universally acknowledged to be above reason.[66]

For Stone, God the infinite spirit without parts cannot be "a compound of two or three spirits, beings, or Gods" without denying God's singularity, and he disallows the term "person" if it means this kind of independency of the three.[67] For him, God the one and only possesses singular personhood, and on the basis of reason, three persons cannot comprise another singular person.

Nor, he says, does Scripture describe any of the divine three using terms that indicate the kind of individuality denoted by "person." This does not mean that Stone never uses the word "person" to describe the three divine personalities, but he does so on his own terms rather than the terms of traditional Trinitarian doctrine, refuting the common arguments that attempt to establish the biblical legitimacy of using "person" as a descriptor for the Three.[68]

The Mystery of the Trinity

Fourth, in *The Christian Doctrine of the Trinity*, Watts at several points is content to assert the mystery that is the Trinity and default to the mysterious nature of Trinitarian relationships when trying to describe matters that clearly transcend human comprehension.[69] Watts ends *The Christian Doctrine of the Trinity* by saying:

> Let us be constant and zealous in paying these divine honours to the sacred three, which the word of God hath appointed, and upon which scripture hath taught us to expect eternal life: And then if God be faithful, and his gospel true, eternal life shall be our portion in the other world, though we know not how to explain all divine mysteries in this.[70]

But for Barton Stone, this is exactly what a Christian must not do. He says:

> I am confident that mystery will be urged as the argument to refute and cover these difficulties. But shall we cover ourselves in the mantle of mystery, woven by our own hands? Shall we cling to a mystery which strikes at the very existence of the Son of God?—a mystery which destroys the efficacy of his blood—the commendation of God's love to sinners and involves so many absurdities and contradictions? Mystery is one of the names of the whore of Babylon, written in large letters on her forehead. Her daughters have the same mark. Rev. 17.[71]

The above paragraphs indicate that there are significant divergences between Barton Stone's most complete and intentional work on the Trinity—*An Address to the Christian Churches*—and Isaac Watts's *The Christian Doctrine of the Trinity*, even if at other points there is dependency. Therefore, even if, as Stone himself indicates, he accepted Watts's view as found in *The*

Christian Doctrine of the Trinity, on the day of his ordination in 1793, he did not continue to hold that perspective throughout his career. At the very least, if Stone continued to think of himself as dependent upon Isaac Watts for his Trinitarian views, he would have to have read Watts's later works and to have changed his views as he was convinced Watts had changed his own views. This is apparently what Stone did.[72]

However, the view presented here is that: (1) Stone's interpretation of Isaac Watts's later Trinitarian perspective, as seen in Stone's reading of *A Faithful Enquiry After the Ancient and Original Doctrine of the Trinity*, was mistaken at certain points; and (2) ultimately there are differences between Watts and Stone that demonstrate Stone was influenced by others. The delineation of these two points constitutes the remainder of this chapter.

Stone's Mistaken View of Watts's Later Works

A sustained look into Barton Stone's Trinitarian reflections reveals his continued dependency on Isaac Watts, but only as Stone—mistakenly, I believe—thought that Watts had altered his perspectives after *The Christian Doctrine of the Trinity.* For our purposes, the most significant of Watts's later works is *A Faithful Enquiry After the Ancient and Original Doctrine of the Trinity.*[73] Stone points to this work as an example of Watts's departure from the positions he took in *The Christian Doctrine of the Trinity*, and Stone specifically refers to this work in delineating his own perspective.[74]

Most importantly, it is Barton Stone's view that Isaac Watts in *A Faithful Enquiry* departed from his insistence in *The Christian Doctrine of the Trinity* on the identity between the one and only true God and the Son and Spirit.[75] Watts's material on this subject in *A Faithful Enquiry* consists of only a couple of paragraphs, but these are, admittedly, very closely in line with Stone's opening paragraphs of Section 1 on the Trinity in *An Address to the Christian Churches,* so that there is no mistaking the connection. Watts in his work says:

> IN [sic] all our conceptions of God, or of the divine nature, this must be laid down as a solid and unmoveable foundation, that *there is and there can be but one true God,* One supreme, almighty, and eternal Being or Spirit who is often times called

> *God the Father* in Scripture, as the first of Beings and prime Agent in all things.... 'Tis our truest notion or conception of God, that he is a *Spirit,* that is, an invisible and thinking Being most perfect in all his properties ... This is the notion or idea which the light of nature or right reason would give to all mankind concerning the one true God, and this is the notion which Scripture gives us both in the Old Testament and in the New.... This idea or conception of *God the Father,* is in all ages the same, and in all true religions.[76]

As biblical evidence, Watts mentions Deuteronomy 6:4 and Mark 12:29, and, in light of his comments it is perhaps understandable how Stone could conclude that Watts was no longer so closely identifying the Father with the Son and Spirit. Stone's perspective on Watts's view becomes even more understandable in light of page 8, where Watts says, among other things, that "there are sufficient guards in the New Testament, that this ancient doctrine of the eternal *Unity of God* must have no inroad made upon it by *Christianity.*"

Stone in *An Address to the Christian Churches* makes essentially the same point:

> That there is but one living and true God, is a plain doctrine of Scripture.... This doctrine is also contained in the creeds of every sect of christians [*sic*] with whom I am acquainted.... If all agree, that there is but one only living and true God; all must agree there are not two or three such Gods. If all agree that this *one only* God is an *infinite spirit without parts;* all must agree that this infinite spirit is not a compound of two or three spirits, beings, or Gods. These things are abundantly evident, concerning which there can be no dispute.[77]

However, as discussed above, there is a stark contrast between Stone and *The Christian Doctrine of the Trinity* on exactly this point, where Stone apparently believes there is congruence. My position is that Stone has actually misinterpreted Isaac Watts in *A Faithful Enquiry* (which was written in 1745 although not published until 1802), and that in this work Watts still asserts that the Son and Spirit are the one true God, just as he did throughout all his previous and later Trinitarian works.[78]

Misreading of *A Faithful Enquiry*

Rather than *A Faithful Enquiry* being a departure from Watts's typical perspective, it is mostly a very brief summation of what is presented at length in his other works, without adequate context and explanation for readers to easily see the congruence between it and his entire body of work on the Trinity. I believe Stone, perhaps influenced by others, has read into *A Faithful Enquiry* what he wished to see there, misconstruing his predecessor and asserting a major shift in Watts's thinking that never really occurred.

At least three features of *A Faithful Enquiry* bear this out. First, on pages 8, 10–11, and 14 of *A Faithful Enquiry*, Watts unequivocally asserts that the Son possesses the same Godhead as the Father and that the Son and Spirit are the one true God. For Stone to suppose, then, that Watts is demarcating a separation between the one true God and His Son and Spirit in his comments on pages 6–8 is to misconstrue Watts's points about the plurality of persons within the one true God.[79] Watts does wish in *A Faithful Enquiry* to protect the unity of God, but, significantly, he is not denying the identity of the Son and Spirit with the one true God.

The Three Divine "Persons." Something similar is the case regarding Stone's view of the three divine "persons" in *An Address to the Christian Churches* and Watts's early and later works. As shown above, Stone challenges the legitimacy of describing the Three as persons within the one God and contradicts *The Christian Doctrine of the Trinity* on exactly this point. However, Stone's position actually echoes quite closely the position the later Watts takes on "persons" in *A Faithful Enquiry*. So is Stone clearly following the Isaac Watts of 1745, at least on this point? It would appear not. Although Watts does take a different position on the use of the word "person" when applied to the Three in *A Faithful Enquiry*, his later view is still not congruent with that of Barton Stone. Watts says,

> Those writers who call the Sacred Three by the name of *three persons* do not assert or maintain that this very word or

expression of *three persons* is found in Scripture, nor is the word *person* expressly applied to them all three.

And though in our translation the word *person* be ascribed both to the *Father* and the *Son,* who (as we find in Scripture) are proper persons, yet none pretend that this word is so expressly applied to the *Holy Spirit,* though he be represented often in a personal manner.

Now this word *person* having been a great bone of contention in the churches, both in ancient and later times, and not agreed upon by all Christians to this day, I shall by no means think it necessary to use that word which may be so offensive to some very good Christians.

And this is certain further, that our most orthodox divines, though they sometimes call them *proper and real persons,* yet they do not pretend to use the word person, in this scriptural doctrine of the Trinity, in the very same intire [sic] and complete sense as when we say, *Peter, Paul* and *John,* are three persons. A distinct person, in the full and proper sense of the word among, men, must be a distinct spirit; for a distinct spirit person requires at least another distinct consciousness, with another distinct will, which seems to infer another different spirit. And surely the Deity is not made up of three such distinct and different spirits.[80]

There are affinities here between Stone and Watts, especially with reference to the different way in which the word *person* is used when referring to the divine Three and the way it is used when referring to *person* "among men." Stone and Watts also both specifically say that the notion of "three persons" in the Godhead is not found in Scripture. However, where Stone uses this fact to deny the reality of three *persons in one God,* Watts uses the same language to deny the reality of there being *three* persons in God, calling into question the scriptural personhood of only the Holy Spirit. Perhaps Stone is trying to follow what he believes is the position of the later Watts with respect to the application of the word "person" to the three individualities of Father, Son, and Spirit, denying the notion that there are three distinct "persons" within one transcendent person, but this simply does not appear to be Watts's position. Watts does say that it is not *necessary* to use the word "person" in describing the individualities within the Trinity, but on page 10 of *A Faithful Enquiry*, he clearly states that he has no problem with using the word "person" for each of the divine Three.[81]

The Divinity of the Son. In a third instance, Stone thinks he has followed the later Watts, but without taking into account the full breadth of Watts's position. In *A Faithful Enquiry*, Watts emphasizes the indwelling of divinity in the Son,[82] whereas in *The Christian Doctrine of the Trinity*, the divinity of the Son and Spirit is a necessary feature of these two sharing in the singular divinity of the Father. In both the Watts of *A Faithful Enquiry* and in Stone's *An Address to the Christian Churches* the divinity of the Son and Spirit is a function of the Godhead of the Father *indwelling* the Son and Spirit through the willful volition of the Father.[83]

However, there is a difference between Stone and Watts on this point. For Stone, the indwelling of divinity in the Son and Spirit constitutes a separation between the Three, so that divinity *only* indwells the Son and Spirit in a way that relegates their divinity to something derived and less than that of the Father.[84] For Watts, indwelling is simply the means by which the Son and Spirit possess divinity, with this indwelling in no way preventing Son and Spirit from being considered the one true God. Stone does not tell us where he derives this idea, but if he *does* think that he is following Watts from *A Faithful Enquiry*, I would judge his perspective as actually quite different from that of both the early and later Watts.

Stone's Divergence from Watts

Given the above, the question must be asked: Does the perspective of Isaac Watts as found in either *A Faithful Enquiry* or any of his other Trinitarian works adequately account for the depiction of the Trinity that Barton Stone offers in his *An Address to the Christian Churches*? I believe it does not. At the very least, although Isaac Watts was interested in *A Faithful Enquiry* in protecting the unity of God, he did not do so at the expense of the full deity of the Son and Spirit. In every one of his published works, Watts uses, contends for, and defends language that equates the Son and Spirit with the one true God. He never reveals a hint of hesitancy on this point, even if he sometimes is guilty of muddled communication as to how the unity of God and the full natures of the Son and Spirit as one true God can be maintained.

Instead, I would argue that if Stone was still attributing his position on the Trinity to the influence of Watts when writing his autobiography in 1843, that at least on some points Stone misread Isaac Watts's intentions, perhaps due to presuppositions Stone held. I believe Stone's reading of Watts's *The Christian Doctrine of the Trinity* in 1793, as recorded in his autobiography, initiated his lifelong study of the Trinity, including the writings of Watts. And, certainly, Stone derived elements of his Trinitarian theology from Watts, especially his position on the pre-existent human soul of the Son. However, there is ultimately separation between Stone and Watts on the identity of the natures of the Son and Spirit with the one true God. Stone's movement away from Watts—particularly when he seems to have thought he was following Watts—begs for an explanation. Why was Isaac Watts's depiction of the unity of the one true God in *A Faithful Enquiry* read by Barton Stone as including the idea that the Son and Spirit were to be thought of as in some way distinct from the one true God?

If the above construal of Watts and Stone and the agreements and divergences of their Trinitarian works are accepted, then it is likely that additional influences beyond Stone's own reading of the Bible and the later Watts caused him to move further in an Arian direction. If nothing else, Stone's use of Watts shows he could be further influenced by that cadre of late seventeenth- and eighteenth-century British Independent and Presbyterian theologians who held views that departed from traditional Trinitarian doctrine. It could be expected, then, that historical theologians would find the roots of Stone's accelerated Arianism wherever Stone indicates his contact with such sources. Stone has been characterized as holding a non-Trinitarian theology, which fits perfectly with the English Presbyterian, English Independent, English Dissenter, and English Latitudinarian character of much Trinitarian theology written during the late seventeenth and eighteenth centuries. I conclude that this background, even beyond his reading of Watts, directly influenced Stone's Trinitarian views.

Influences Beyond Watts

That contact with this theological milieu beyond Watts would be a source of influence precisely fits with Stone's familial upbringing and environment, which, according to Newell Williams, were essentially New World Anglican/English, with an Anglican connection on both sides of Stone's parentage.[85] Further, the rationally oriented training he received at David Caldwell's academy and the ethos of Henry Patillo, his examiner for ordination and the one who introduced him to Watts, has the ring of a fairly open English Presbyterian attitude. Patillo, in fact, is the impetus for Stone making use of the Adopting Act for the purposes of passing his ordination.[86] Since the Adopting Act was instituted in the colonies in 1729 in direct response to the later Latitudinarian moves being made there,[87] it seems quite safe to say that Henry Patillo's orientation, as a mentor for Stone, paralleled a fairly radical version of English Presbyterianism, especially when it came to the questions of subscription and the Trinity. Were it not for the organizing that Presbyterians did in the years prior to Stone's ordination, such as the union of 1758 (which accentuated subscription) and the holding of their first General Assembly in 1789, it is perhaps questionable whether Stone would have had to submit to an ordination examination or worry about his position on the Trinity.

As it was, with the Latitudinarian Patillo serving as his mentor and examiner, Stone's position on the Trinity ultimately mattered very little in the course of his ordination. Nevertheless, his perspective during this entire time—clearly discernible from his later departure from the Presbyterians and his conflicts with the hierarchy—indicate there was most likely a strong English Presbyterian New Light influence on Stone from the outset of his life as a Presbyterian minister. Stone himself references writers in addition to Watts and their works, to which some attention should be paid.

Despite the demonstrated differences on the Trinity between Isaac Watts and Barton Stone, it appears that—in addition to the direct influence of personal acquaintances—Watts represents the major direct influence on Stone's Trinitarian views, certainly early in Stone's ministerial career. As pointed out above, Stone's autobiography bears this out.

Paul Cardale, Adam Clarke, Moses Stuart

But Stone also makes reference to Paul Cardale, Adam Clarke, Samuel Clarke, Philip Doddridge, Daniel Waterland, Daniel Whitby, Bishop John Pearson, Dr. Daniel Scott, Moses Stuart, and others, making it safe to conclude that Stone was quite familiar with contemporary Trinitarian literature and was not afraid to apply what he read to his own theological understanding. He may wish only to acknowledge such sources as *supporting evidence* for his own views, but based on correlations between Stone and Watts and Stone and Samuel Clarke, it seems reasonable to speak of Stone's *dependency* upon earlier theologians. Some explication of this influence is warranted, although there is neither space to deal with each of Stone's references nor sufficient transparency in those references to clearly identify every way in which those writers shaped Stone's Trinitarian perspective.

For instance, twice in the second edition of Stone's *An Address to the Christian Churches*, he refers to Paul Cardale's *The True Doctrine of the New Testament Concerning Jesus Christ*. Cardale (1705–1775) was an English Presbyterian minister, trained at the Dissenting Academy of Ebenezer Latham in Derbyshire, who in the midst of his career abandoned Calvinistic doctrine for a position that associated him with Nathaniel Lardner and Joseph Priestley. Cardale seems to be a classic example of the previously described move made during this period by Presbyterians to a non-Trinitarian position. Stone refers to Cardale's work when demonstrating Calvin's distaste for the word "Trinity"[88] and when mentioning Tertullian's perspective on the absurdity of the idea that the presence of the sovereign God could have resided in the womb of Mary.[89]

Stone also makes reference to those who are significant for his Trinitarian perspective on the eternality of the Son. This issue of the eternality of the Son was, as mentioned above in the discussion of the roots of Alexander Campbell's Trinitarianism, an often debated topic of the day. Consequently, it is not surprising that Stone would reference Adam Clarke and Moses Stuart, two of the most prominent voices rejecting the eternality of the Son. Although Stone says little of Adam Clarke beyond simply referencing him in connection to the issue, Stone several times mentions Moses Stuart in this context, referencing him as a source for what early Christian Fathers believed on the matter.[90] That Stone references these two, along with the others mentioned above, indicates his awareness of contemporary writers on the Trinity and his willingness to cohere with their sometimes controversial views.[91]

Samuel Clarke

An English predecessor whom Stone cites seventy-six times in his *Letters to James Blythe* and once in a letter to Alexander Campbell,[92]—is Samuel Clarke, the author of *The Scripture Doctrine of the Trinity*, which served as *the* major English non-Trinitarian work from its first edition in 1712 through the first half of the nineteenth century. Although Clarke throughout his life remained an Anglican and so does not support a connection between Stone and English Presbyterianism, he was *the* classic English Arian/Semi-Arian of the day. Stone's reliance upon Clarke, the most prominent Trinitarianly unorthodox church leader in England from 1690 to 1800, is significant. *The Scripture Doctrine of the Trinity* was revised three times after it was initially published in 1712—1719, 1732, and 1738—and Clarke's work can be counted most responsible for setting off the Trinitarian controversy that dominated both Anglican theology and much of dissenting, later Latitudinarian thought in those years. For most of those who tended in an unorthodox direction, Clarke established a benchmark in terms of the comprehensive manner in which he dealt with New Testament passages impacting Trinitarian doctrine, the strength and clarity of his argument, and his ability to hold a prominent position of authority and responsibility in the Anglican communion despite his well-known nontraditional Trinitarian views.

Stone's references to Clarke demonstrate that he was interested in and influenced by more than Isaac Watts's perspective on the Trinity. Watts's work is important in the history of non-traditional Trinitarian thought— Clarke's is monumental. One may disagree with Stone's Trinitarian conclusions; one cannot doubt his acquaintance with the pertinent literature on the subject nor his willingness to acknowledge his sources.

Stone's references to Clarke's *The Scripture Doctrine of the Trinity* are especially instructive, if for no other reason than their number. Stone's section on the Trinity in *Letters to James Blythe* is 116 pages long; that he quotes Samuel Clarke seventy-six times in these 116 pages is remarkable.

Granted, the majority of these references consist simply of Stone using Clarke to show where the early church Fathers stood on various Trinitarian issues. Nonetheless, it is evident that Barton Stone was clearly a careful reader of *The Scripture Doctrine of the Trinity*.[93] In addition, Stone uses Clarke at places where Clarke had been arguing the same non-Trinitarian points Stone wishes to defend. In other words, Samuel Clarke is not just a source book for reading the Fathers, he is a source book for reading the Fathers *in a non-Trinitarian direction*. In fact, Samuel Clarke is used by Stone at several places in *Letters to James Blythe* to show that the Son could not be the one only true God—the dominating point in Samuel Clarke's *The Scripture Doctrine of the Trinity* and a point that dominates Stone's thinking in *An Address to the Christian Churches.*

Besides the plethora of references to Samuel Clarke in *Letters to James Blythe*, there is one later reference that I regard as quite an intriguing one, for three reasons. First is the nature of the reference itself, written in *The Christian Messenger* to Alexander Campbell:

> The Greek fathers of the second and third centuries, commenting on those texts above quoted, say that *hupo* means the original, or first cause, and that *dia* signifies the second, or instrumental cause. Thus Philo, Origen, Eusebius, and Cyril, who certainly better understood their language better than we do. (Clarke on Trin. p. 91.92). Doctor Clarke also remarks that this was the constant and unanimous sense of the primitive church. If these observations be true, will it not follow undeniably, that the *Word (di'hou) by whom* all things were made, was not the only true God, but a person that existed with the only true God before creation began; not from eternity, else he must be the only true God; but long before Augustus Caesar?[94]

The question is, who is the "Clarke" to which Stone is referring, Adam Clarke, the well-known Methodist commentator, or Samuel Clarke, the Anglican philosopher? Elsewhere I have shown there is little doubt that the reference is to Samuel Clarke.[95]

Second, here Stone somewhat casually and comfortably references Clarke, pointing in the direction of a telling familiarity, both on his part and on what he apparently expects will be Alexander Campbell's part. He is clearly unafraid of making clear to Campbell his familiarity with and apparent agreement with Clarke and his views on the Trinity. That Stone doesn't hesitate to make the reference shows his willingness to allow Campbell to see the kinds of influences impacting Stone's Trinitarian perspectives.

The third intriguing element in Stone's reference in *The Christian Messenger* is simply that this reference stands alongside Stone's use of Clarke in *Letters to James Blythe* as a witness to the parallels between the specific features of Stone's Trinitarian position and Samuel Clarke's argumentation in *The Scripture Doctrine of the Trinity*, especially and specifically vis à vis Stone's divergences from Isaac Watts's *The Christian Doctrine of the Trinity*.

Barton Stone's use of Samuel Clarke's work in *Letters to James Blythe* and in *The Christian Messenger* provide evidence that he is following Samuel Clarke in making essentially the same argument about the Trinity that Clarke makes. In fact, in my opinion, there are enough references to Samuel Clarke in Stone's writings and sufficient parallels between Stone's and Clarke's Trinitarian views that it appears likely Stone is intentionally following a scheme and using language patterned after, if not directly dependent upon, Samuel Clarke's *The Scripture Doctrine of the Trinity*. The most obvious similarity between Stone and Samuel Clarke is simply the general denial that the Son and Spirit are identical with the one only true God. As has been shown above, this was Stone's leading proposition in *An Address to the Christian Churches* and in *Letters to James Blythe*, and it is clearly the one great point to which Samuel Clarke consistently returns in *The Scripture Doctrine of the Trinity*. It is my position that Barton Stone at least partially derived support for his view about the Son not being identical to the one only true God from his reading of Samuel Clarke. Parallels between their works are such that if Stone did not reach his conclusions from reading Clarke, he at least followed a similar intellectual and spiritual path and then found common ground in Samuel Clarke.[96]

I think it quite reasonable, based on the above, to assert that Stone's view of the Son as being distinct from the one true God who is the Father derives from Stone's familiarity with other English non-Trinitarians in addition to Isaac Watts, with Samuel Clarke being exhibit A. Stone obviously read Clarke and referenced Clarke, and in answering his critics it appears possible that Clarke's form of argument and position on the singularity of the Father becomes as much a part of Stone's thinking about the separation between the one true God and the Son as did Watts's view on the pre-existence of the Son and the human soul of Jesus Christ.

One other parallel between Barton Stone and Samuel Clarke should be mentioned here. Whereas Isaac Watts asserted the divinity of the Son *because of* the oneness the Son shared with the one and only true God, Barton Stone believed in the complete divinity of the Son *despite* the singularity of the one only true God who is the Father.[97] As it turns out, Stone shared this view with Samuel Clarke. Clarke says:

> For He is the One God, [or, God is One,] and the Only one, and the First. And yet these things do not destroy the Divinity of the Son: for He also is in that One and First and Only One, as being the Only Word and Wisdom and Brightness of the Glory of Him who is the One, and the Only one, and the First.[98]

The juxtaposition of these ideas—of both the singularity of the one only true God, distinct from the Son, and the full divinity of the Son—is explicitly framed in Clarke and Stone in a way not found in any of Watts's works on the Trinity. More than likely, then, if these thoughts on the part of Stone are not original, he is relying here on Samuel Clarke (or someone that shares Clarke's position) rather than on Isaac Watts.

Space does not permit further delineation of the connection between Barton Stone's Trinitarian perspective and that of Samuel Clarke. My impression is that further study of the two side by side would reveal additional parallels. Although more could be said, the above sufficiently makes the point concerning the roots of Barton Stone's opinion that the Son was not to be identified with the one only true eternal God. Despite having previously gone unnoticed in the literature on Stone's Trinitarian thought, the likelihood of Stone's connection to Samuel Clarke's *The Scripture Doctrine of the Trinity* seems to me assured.

Conclusion

Despite their claims only to be interested in biblical statements regarding the relationship between the Father, Son, and Spirit, the above has indicated places where the Trinitarian perspectives of both the Campbells and Barton Stone are connected to their predecessors. Thomas Campbell's orthodox Trinitarian stance largely derives from his Anglican/Presbyterian background. Alexander Campbell, while retained a lifelong commitment to his father's orthodox Trinitarianism, was at least ostensibly committed to a hesitancy regarding expressing his position. He did, however, frequently lapse into traditional Trinitarian language, meaning he was, at least to some extent, dependent on the Trinitarians who preceded him, and his position regarding the eternal Son paralleled the works of Adam Clarke and Moses Stuart, which were familiar to him. Both Campbells were most influenced to be circumspect and hesitant regarding their Trinitarian views by the general climate of the time that required theological conclusions to be solely based on what were considered to be biblical *facts*. While they clearly thought that the orthodox Trinitarian position was in line with the teaching of the Bible, the contemporary disunity within the Christian communion over Trinitarian doctrine pushed them to refrain from speculative language and the creation of an overtly stated Trinitarian position.

Barton Stone, who came from an intellectual background similar to the Campbells, and who also ultimately decided not to speculate upon the Trinity, was greatly influenced by the impulses of English non-Trinitarianism that came his way first through his academic training and mentors and in the form of Isaac Watts's *The Christian Doctrine of the Trinity*. However, eventually Stone clearly departed from Watts at several points, even when he appears to have thought that he did not, and was in the end significantly influenced by others, most particularly Samuel Clarke, who was perhaps the most significant English quasi-Arian writer from 1690–1800.

Notes

[1] This happens in Garrison's work, *Alexander Campbell's Theology: Its Sources and Historical Setting*, even though he specifically discussed in his final chapter the early Restorationists' perspectives on God. As was noted in Chapter One, it was not until the second half of the twentieth century that ICC/CC and CCa began to fully appreciate their own characters as historical movements, thus the critical, historical study of the SCM was chiefly relegated to the work done by those in the Christian Church (Disciples of Christ). Currently, there is abundant scholarly work being conducted on the history of the SCM, with theologians and historians from all three branches of the Movement significantly contributing. For those in ICC/CC and CCa, particularly, it is as if they have in the last fifty years been awakened to find they have a history to be investigated. Most intriguing is the way in which this kind of critical, historical investigation is altering the manner in which conservative Restorationists have viewed the discipline of theology—including the entire area of Trinitarian studies.

[2] There is far less material for the Campbells than for Stone. See Chapter Three for information about Stone's description of Isaac Watts's influence on his thinking. Stone acknowledged his indebtedness to Isaac Watts but would never say that Watts was the source of his position on the Trinity. From Stone's perspective, Watts simply helped Stone see what was in the Scriptures—the only real source for his doctrinal positions.

[3] Campbell insists in "To Timothy," that his view of the Trinity he got from no one and no book; he wants to adhere only to the words of Scripture, and so he frames his position with reference to the Apostle John's depiction of the *Logos*. In the same article, he cites his refusal to create a system of Trinitarian thought (page 334).

[4] Thomas Olbricht has drawn attention to how this approach to the Bible affected the overall ability of Restorationists to think theologically. Their neglect of the Trinity is a prime example of how a nontheological reading of Scripture prevented Restorationists from being influenced by the grand themes of Scripture typically delineated in systematic or Biblical theology. See Olbricht, "The Bible as Revelation," 228–30.

[5] See Hiram J. Lester, "The Form and Function," 181ff.

[6] Ibid., 184–85. For the Socinian and Unitarian tendencies of *later* Latitudinarianism, see Gerald R. Cragg, *The Church and the Age of Reason*, 169.

[7] Given Thomas's appearance before the Redstone Baptist Association in 1816, at which Alexander was present, it is impossible to suppose that the two did not discuss such issues.

[8] Cf. James M. Mathes, *Works of B. W. Stone*, 51–56. Stone at various places does mention the influence of Isaac Watts, as will be discussed below, but he offers no lengthy depiction or exposition of Watts's views, nor does he constantly quote Watts or even name one of Watts's works aside from *A Faithful Enquiry after the Ancient and Original Doctrine of the Trinity*, a work considered of less significance for his view on the Trinity than nearly anything else Watts wrote on the subject. Instead, in Stone's works, the references most often made are to Moses Stuart and Samuel Clarke, typically because they quote the early church Fathers with reference to particular Trinitarian issues. Even in these instances, Stone never acknowledges that he has derived his own views directly from a predecessor.

[9] See Martin Luther, *Sermons on the Gospel of John*, 15; John Calvin, *Commentary on the Gospel According to John*, 29.

[10] See Book 1, Chapter 13 of Calvin's *Institutes of the Christian Religion*, 120ff. Although Calvin discusses in several places the Father (e.g., Book 1, Chapter 14), the Son (e.g., Book 2, Chapter 6), and the Spirit (e.g., Book 3, Chapter 1), his actual discussion of the Trinity is relatively brief in comparison to Aquinas and Augustine, especially the latter.

[11] For the general impact of the Reformation, the magisterial reformers, and their immediate ancestors on Restoration thought see Thomas H. Olbricht, "Continental Reformation Backgrounds," 157–71.

[12] See Theodore Dwight Bozeman, *To Live Ancient Lives*. Cf. Richard T. Hughes and C. Leonard Allen, *Illusions of Innocence*.

[13] See Hughes and Allen, Chapter 7: "Freedom from Dogma: James S. Lamar and the Disciples of Christ," 153–69.

[14] The earlier work of Francis Bacon and the work of Locke's contemporary, Isaac Newton, should also be mentioned as an influence. Newton, particularly, has been directly linked to non-Trinitarian views. See John Hunt, *Religious Thought in England*, 191–93.

[15] Ibid., 192.

[16] Horton Davies says, "A consequence of this interest was a tendency to omit all those mystical and aesthetic elements of experience which are incapable of being displayed in the lucid, consecutive, and convincing form which is proper to mathematical demonstration. Such an age will inevitably relegate to the background whatever is paradoxical and remote from the ordinary ways of thinking. In religion this will mean a reduction of revelation to the limits of the rational and a distaste for such a speculative doctrine as the Holy Trinity, and such a mystical doctrine as salvation through the atoning sacrifice. Horton Davies, *Worship and Theology in England*, 52.

[17] It is just this factor, I believe, which comes to separate the *early, Trinitarian* Latitudinarians and the *later, non-Trinitarian* Latitudinarians. Although I do not see in the literature this distinct nomenclature used to describe the Latitudinarians, there seems to me to be this kind of distinction. The seventeenth-century Latitudinarians, although they generally come right at the end of the century, hold a noticeably different perspective than their eighteenth-century counterparts, even though the significant work done by many of these later Latitudinarians, such as Samuel Clark, comes as early as 1712. Concern for unity and tolerance among the early Latitudinarians, despite their loyalty to Anglicanism, seems to have progressed in the later Latitudinarians to less concern about subscription and adherence to the church's position on the Trinity. This change came for some in only a couple of decades.

[18] Hunt, on page 183 of *Religious Thought in England*, draws attention to Locke's pre-eminence among these religious rationalists, saying, "The best representative of the theological spirit of this age was John Locke." Although he also makes it clear that Locke is not the first to explicitly apply reason to religion. he says Locke is "the most thorough." Cf. Hunt's comments concerning Newton, Hunt, 191–93.

[19] Defined here as those who rejected the need for clergy—and in some cases, church members—to accept the doctrines of *The Thirty-nine Articles* or *The Westminster Confession of Faith*.

[20] Defined here as those who after 1662 did not claim allegiance to the Anglican communion.

[21] Hunt, *Religious Thought in England*, 11–13.

[22] Ibid., 12.

²³ For a thorough treatment of the early Latitudinarians see Martin J. Griffin, Jr., *Latitudinarianism in the Seventeenth Century Church of England*.

²⁴ Hunt, *Religious Thought in England*, 130.

²⁵ For recent discussion regarding the impact of Thomas Campbell's time with the Church of Ireland, see Richard Phillips, "Thomas Campbell: A Reappraisal Based on Backgrounds," 78–87. Phillips focuses on the background leading up to Thomas Campbell's plea for unity in the *Declaration and Address*, but his reference to Campbell's background in the Church of Ireland, his conversion to Presbyterianism, and the development of Latitudinarianism within these communions speaks to the milieu from which Thomas Campbell developed his own Trinitarian version of Latitudinarianism.

²⁶ Hunt, *Religious Thought in England*, 197f.

²⁷ Ibid., 194ff.

²⁸ Ibid., 199.

²⁹ Bourn also published in 1736 *An Address to Protestant Dissenters*.

³⁰ A.H. Drysdale, *History of the Presbyterians in England*, 499.

³¹ See Cragg, *The Church and the Age of Reason*, 169.

³² Gerald R. Cragg, *Reason and Authority in the Eighteenth Century*, 37.

³³ Davies, *Worship and Theology in England*, 89.

³⁴ Cragg, *Reason and Authority*, 38.

³⁵ See Drysdale, *History of the Presbyterians in England*, 515, 524. It is noteworthy that Drysdale is insistent that Priestley, who is given credit for later starting the first Unitarian congregation in the United States, was actually an Independent. The Presbyterians and Independents often joined together in their common nonconformity and nonsubscription (hence many at the Salter's Hall Synod in 1719 were Independents), and in 1690–1694 they officially joined with each other in a "Happy Union." See Drysdale, 459–68. The phenomenon we are tracking, then, was also present among the Independents, although perhaps not at the same rate as among the English Presbyterians. We have noted Drysdale's opinion that the Independents were more affected by Arianism in the case of the academies. However, Cragg makes it clear that the Independents were less attracted to Arianism than the Presbyterians; see Cragg, *Reason and Authority*, 37–38. Because Drysdale may be more easily suspected of bias, one tends to think that perhaps Cragg gives the truer version of the tendencies of the two groups.

³⁶ See Davies, *Worship and Theology in England*, 83ff. Cf. Drysdale, *History of the Presbyterians in England*, 489–542.

³⁷ See Cragg, *Reason and Authority*, 36–37; Cragg, *The Age of Reason*, 137; and Robert Davidson, *History of the Presbyterian Church in the State of Kentucky*, 503. By voting for subscription, these Independents were revealing their essentially Trinitarian position.

³⁸ For a description of these see Hunt, *Religious Thought in England*, 11–13.

³⁹ Cf. Alexander Campbell, "Trinitarianism, Arianism, & Socinianism," 153–60.

⁴⁰ Ibid.

⁴¹ Adam Clarke, *Containing the Gospels Matthew, Mark, Luke, and John*.

⁴² Richard Watson, *Remarks on the Eternal Sonship of Christ*.

⁴³ Robert Martin, *The Doctrine of the Eternal Sonship of Christ Considered*.

⁴⁴ See Moses Stuart, *Letter to the Rev. Wm. E. Channing*; and Samuel Miller, *Letters on the Eternal Sonship of Christ*.

⁴⁵ See Excursus 1 on Romans 1:4 in Moses Stuart, *A Commentary on the Epistle to the Romans*; also see Excursus 2, 3, 4, and 5 dealing with Hebrews 1:2; 1:3; 1:4; and 1:5, respectively, in Stuart's *A Commentary on the Epistle to the Hebrews*.

⁴⁶ Barton Stone, "Objections to Christian Union Calmly Considered," 33.

⁴⁷ See Davidson, *History of the Presbyterian Church in the State of Kentucky*, 503.

⁴⁸ See Newell Williams, *Barton Stone: A Spiritual Biography*, 30–32. Cf. Barton W. Stone, *The Biography of Eld. Barton Warren Stone*, 13.

⁴⁹ See Stone, "Remarks on the Preceding Communication," 128; and *Biography*, 13–14.

⁵⁰ Newell Williams, *Barton Stone: A Spiritual Biography*, 32. Cf. Williams, 31, note 9, where he draws attention to the change in Watts's perspective in his later publications and mentions Stone's awareness of these developments. It is significant that Williams mentions that for the later Watts, only the Father and Son are considered the two Persons in whom the Godhead subsists. Williams apparently does not think, contra Stone, that there is a significant move by Watts in *A Faithful Enquiry* toward the idea that the Son and Spirit are not the one only true God. If this is the case, I am in agreement with Williams with respect to developments in Watts's thinking in *A Faithful Enquiry* and the apparent misinterpretation of Watts by Barton Stone, as will be seen later in this chapter.

⁵¹ Throughout this book, mentions of Watts's *The Christian Doctrine of the Trinity* will refer to the edition listed in the Bibliography.

⁵² Stone, *An Address to the Christian Churches*, 6.

⁵³ See Stone, *An Address to the Christian Churches*, 6, 7, 13 (Trinity); 11, 12, 15, 17 (trinity).

⁵⁴ Cf. Stone, *A Letter to Mr. John R. Moreland*, 9.

⁵⁵ Cf. Isaac Watts, *The Arian Invited to the Orthodox Faith*, 216, and especially the footnote on 219.

⁵⁶ Stone's position regarding the singularity of the one true God and what he asserts about the misidentification on the part of Trinitarians of this one true God with the Son is also briefly summarized in *A Letter to John R. Moreland*, 5–6. Here Stone is even more clear and pointed about the distinction between Father and Son, describing the Son as a distinct, intelligent being separate from the Father, who is the only very, true, living God. Cf. Barton Stone, "To the Christian Baptist," 205–9.

⁵⁷ Stone, *An Address to the Christian Churches*, 6.

⁵⁸ Ibid., 14.

⁵⁹ Ibid.

⁶⁰ Ibid., 15. Cf. *A Letter to Mr. John R. Moreland*, 6; "To the Christian Baptist," 205–6.

⁶¹ Ibid.

⁶² Ibid., 16.

⁶³ Ibid; cf., 19–22, 25. On page 25 Stone says, "It is generally believed that the Father made a covenant with the Son, concerning the redemption of sinners, before the Son came into the world; in which covenant the Father promised to hold his hand, help him in the great work, and preserve him till the salvation was accomplished, &c. Isaiah, 42, 6; 49,8. We cannot see how the one only living and true God could covenant with himself; nor how the Father could make such promises to the Son as very God. But if we conceive the person to whom the promises were made, to be the Son of God, the application is easy, and natural."

⁶⁴ Watts, *The Christian Doctrine of the Trinity*, 163.

⁶⁵See Newell Williams, 241. Cf. Stone, *An Address to the Christian Churches*, 26–28.
⁶⁶Stone, *An Address to the Christian Churches*, 7.
⁶⁷Ibid., 6.
⁶⁸Ibid., 8–11. E.g., despite provisionally accepting the textual authenticity of 1 John 5:7, Stone argues that it does not actually teach that the three are one God, but that the three are one in spirit, purpose, and mind, as in agreement with one another. In addition, he rejects the proposal by many that the inherent plurality of *Elohim* and *Adonim*, along with the plural pronouns occasionally used for God—e.g., Genesis 1:26—indicate a plurality of persons within the one and only true God.
⁶⁹E.g., Watts, *The Christian Doctrine of the Trinity*, 178–79.
⁷⁰Ibid., 206.
⁷¹Stone, *An Address to the Christian Churches*, 17–18.
⁷²There is an indication of this in Barton Stone, "Remarks on the Preceding Communication," 128, where Stone mentions that he was familiar with *A Faithful Enquiry After the Ancient and Original Doctrine of the Trinity*, in which he believes Watts reveals he had moved away from an orthodox Trinitarian position.
⁷³Isaac Watts, *A Faithful Enquiry After the Ancient and Original Doctrine of the Trinity*.
⁷⁴See Stone, "Remarks on the Preceding Communication": 128. While there are some genuine agreements between the later Watts and the later Stone, the second edition of Stone's *An Address to the Christian Churches* is demonstrably at odds with views published by Watts subsequent to *The Christian Doctrine of the Trinity*. This is particularly the case with reference to the Son and Spirit being identified with the one and only true God. Watts simply never relinquishes his position that there is identification between the one and only true God and the Son and Spirit, a position Stone refuses to accept even though he apparently thinks he is in congruence with the later Watts. However, all of Watts's works at all points in his writing career, assert an identification between the one and only true God and the Son and Spirit. This occurs so often in Volume 6 of *The Works of the Rev. Isaac Watts, D. D. in Nine Volumes*—in which are found his Trinitarian publications—that likely over one hundred such references could be cited. As representative examples, see these pieces from that volume: *The Arian Invited to the Orthodox Faith*, 219–20; *Dissertation III*, 244, 246, 268; *Dissertation IV*, 306, 308, 310; *Dissertation V*, 338, 349; *Dissertation VII*, 386–87; *Useful and Important Questions Concerning Jesus the Son of God*, 409–10, 417, 420, 425; *An Essay on the True Importance of Any Human Schemes*, 476, 478–79; *The Glory of Christ as God-Man Displayed*, 522, 532, 544, 583, 616. It is especially noteworthy that *The Glory of Christ as God-Man Displayed* was published in 1746, one year after Watts wrote *A Faithful Enquiry*.
⁷⁵See Stone, "Remarks on the Preceding Communication," 128.
⁷⁶Watts, *A Faithful Enquiry*, 6–7.
⁷⁷Stone, *An Address to the Christian Churches*, 6.
⁷⁸Is it not telling that in all of his published works on the Trinity, both those written before and after *A Faithful Enquiry*, that Watts consistently and clearly emphasizes the identity between the one true God and Jesus Christ? This is, in fact, *the* decisive difference between the Trinitarian perspectives of Isaac Watts and Barton Stone, and it is the chief reason that it is inaccurate to conclude that the Trinitarian perspective of Stone and Watts are the same.
⁷⁹Even on page 13 of *A Faithful Enquiry*, where Watts says, "He was born as a man here on earth, he lived and died as a man; having a human body with a rational soul,

and in this view he was a being far inferior to the true and eternal God," his reduction of Jesus to inferior status is a reference "in this view" to the humanity of Christ, not with a view to his entire personhood.

[80] Watts, *A Faithful Enquiry*, 8-10.

[81] Ibid., 10; cf., 9; Watts, *The Arian Invited to the Orthodox Fatih*, 363-70. On pages 20-22 of *An Address to the Christian Churches*, Stone does apply the word *person* to the Son, and on page 20 refers to the Son as a distinct being, but he uses such language only if *person* is applied with the understanding that the Son is not the true God, but is a *person* distinct from the one true God. Perhaps Stone would think this echoes Watts on page 13 of *A Faithful Enquiry*, where Watts twice refers to the Son as "another distinct person" while also asserting that "He was born as a man here on earth, he lived and died as a man; having a human body with a rational soul, and in this view he was a being far inferior to the true and eternal God." But Watts's emphasis at this point is clearly on the Son as incarnate, not on the Son as the One who is also the one true God. Where Watts clearly affirmed the Son as both incarnate and the one true God, Stone would accept only the first of these affirmations, saying that the Son possesses divinity, but only in a derived way that did not include His status as the one true God. Watts asserted the derivation of the Son, but not in a way that precluded him from also being the one true God.

[82] Watts, *A Faithful Enquiry*, 15.

[83] Ibid. Also see Stone, *An Address to the Christian Churches*, 26-27.

[84] Ibid.

[85] For details of Stone's English heritage, see Williams, *Barton Stone: A Spiritual Biography*, 9-16.

[86] Ibid., 30, 44-45.

[87] See Andrew C. Zenos, *Presbyterians in America*, 56.

[88] See Stone, *An Address to the Christian Churches*, 6.

[89] Ibid., 15.

[90] Cf. Stone, *Letters to James Blythe*, 32-39.

[91] Barton Stone, "Objections to Christian Union Calmly Considered," 33.

[92] Stone, "To the Christian Baptist," 208.

[93] An edition of Clarke's work obviously read by Barton Stone is Samuel Clarke, *The Scripture Doctrine of the Trinity*, 2nd ed., (London: James Knapton, 1719). For a detailed argument see Kelly D. Carter, "The Trinity in the Stone Campbell Movement: Historical/Theological Analysis and Constructive Proposal," PhD. dissertation, Southern Methodist University, 2012: 243-248.

[94] Stone, "To the Christian Baptist," 208.

[95] See Kelly D. Carter, "The Trinity in the Stone Campbell Movement," PhD Dissertation, 243-248.

[96] Having carefully examined both Deacon Morrell's edition of Samuel Clarke's *The Scripture Doctrine of the Trinity—Clarke on the Trinity*—and Stone's *An Address to the Christian Churches*, it is my judgment that Stone *may* be reflecting throughout his *Address* upon his reading of Samuel Clarke. Admittedly, this claim includes a significant level of speculation, both because Stone never references Clarke in his *Address* and because parallel thoughts in the works of two writers may exist because they are dealing with a common subject, using common vocabulary, arising from a common milieu, and ultimately holding similar perspectives. Therefore, parallels and dependency of one upon the other may be coincidental. Nonetheless, we know that Stone read and referenced

Clarke on the Trinity. I would even say it is likely that parallels between Stone's *Address* and Clarke's *Scripture Doctrine* reflect Stone's familiarity with and use of Clarke's most significant work. Clarke's work was perhaps more significantly influential on English-based non-Trinitarianism, following Salter's Hall, than any other work, so it makes sense he could have significantly influenced one like Stone, who reflects a Trinitarian perspective that so clearly derives from this post-Lockean, English Presbyterian, non-Trinitarianly oriented milieu.

[97] See Stone, *An Address to the Christian Churches*, 13.

[98] Clarke, *The Scripture Doctrine of the Trinity*, Deacon Morrell's edition, entitled *Clarke on the Trinity*, 2.

5

The Impact of Prior Trinitarian Perspectives on Trinitarian Theology in the Later Stone-Campbell Movement

Until this point, this book has been almost exclusively historically descriptive. The goal has been to accurately describe the earliest history of Trinitarian thought within the SCM, as I believe an understanding of these beginnings is vital to understand the Movement's contemporary Trinitarian tendencies. In addition, this book intends to provide not just description of the crucial early period, but also an assessment of what this history has meant for subsequent generations and its significance for SC churches in the present and future. An early history of Trinitarian doctrine has helped SC churches define who they presently are, how they think, and what they do. With this history in view, an altered present and future are possible, partially dependent upon how SC churches respond to the challenge to take seriously their perspectives on Trinitarian doctrine.

This chapter will (1) offer further description of SC Trinitarian thought in the period from about 1850 to the present; (2) identify the status of Trinitarian theology among ICC/CC and CCa situated in the second decade of the 21st century; and (3) further delineate the idea that certain theological and ecclesiastical deficiencies exist within SC churches because of their approach to Trinitarian theology.

For three reasons this chapter will narrow its focus to Trinitarian doctrine present within ICC/CC and CCa, essentially ignoring the subject for the Disciples of Christ. First is simply the fact that I am vastly more familiar with and interested in ICC/CC and CCa, living among them on a daily basis. My own experience is in CCa, and I am an instructor in an institution founded by Independent Churches of Christ/Churches of Christ. Christian fellowship for me, including the collegial, theological conversations and ecclesiastical events in which I regularly participate and am most interested, includes abundant interaction with those from both ICC/CC and CCa. I have less interaction with Disciples of Christ.

The second reason for this exclusive focus is what seems to be the theological correspondence between the ICC/CC and CCa, including the parallel courses they have followed in responding to the liberal/fundamentalist controversies that arose early in the twentieth century and continue today, their approaches to the interpretation of Scripture, their styles of "doing" theology, and the dialogue between the two fellowships that has been taking place since the 1980s. Their attempts to reconstruct a positive relationship, grounded in their common heritage and theological/ecclesiastical parallels, indicate the appropriateness of addressing a discussion of Trinitarian theology in the context of both fellowships.

Third, this chapter will specifically treat ICC/CC and CCa because, to a large extent the shared core theological and practical issues that face these two fellowships stand enough apart from those of the Disciples of Christ to warrant separate treatment. Common details in the existence of ICC/CC and CCa—separate from the Disciples of Christ—mean that the needs of both these fellowships can be conjointly delineated without significant risk of missing the mark when assessing their current ethos or proposing ways to address inadequacies of either fellowship through renewed Trinitarian reflection.

By 1846, when Alexander Campbell wrote the last of what I take to be his most important pieces that included a Trinitarian emphasis, the blueprint for subsequent Restorationist Trinitarian doctrine was largely established.¹ Despite being quite traditional in his own Trinitarian perspective, Alexander Campbell was able to convince not only Barton Stone but also the majority of their theological descendants of the merits of concentrating on issues other than the Trinity. Thus, within the SCM as a whole relatively little was written about the Trinity after the 1832 merger of Campbell's Disciples with Stone's Christians.

That does not mean later Restorationists wrote absolutely nothing about the Trinity, but that slight attention is given to Trinitarian thought within the SCM in comparison with other Christian traditions. One searches in vain among Restorationists for a multiplicity of weighty, theologically informed monographs exclusively delineating Trinitarian nuances. Given its primitivistic, noncreedal ethos, neither early ecumenical statements of faith nor later Protestant confessions centered on the Trinity significantly influenced SCM churches. Virtually anything ICC/CC and CCa authors wrote about the Trinity was almost exclusively biblically focused, including little speculative, philosophical language, and there was no significant interaction with the works of recognized Trinitarian theologians.² Trinitarian thought had minimal influence upon the ministries of SC churches when compared to the ways Trinitarian doctrine shaped the ministries of many denominations. In fact, because early Restorationists had so directly and intentionally repudiated their Protestant roots, statements reflecting Trinitarian doctrine, like those found in the Westminster Confession of Faith, were more likely to foster rebuttal than subscription.

Therefore, the most significant impact of overt Trinitarian theology upon Restorationists and the SCM was that the speculative, technical, philosophical, nonscripturally-based language that often ended in paradox, mystery, and ecclesiastical schism pushed a biblicist, propositionally oriented, rationalistically-delineated theology further from overtly stated Trinitarian doctrine. Negative assessments and derogatory remarks about Trinitarians and Trinitarian theology are not uncommon in early SC history, not because Restorationists held a non-Trinitarian perspective, but because they took no consistently stated Trinitarian position, choosing to separate themselves from anything resembling a theological standard. For many in the SCM, overt Trinitarian theology and the corresponding disputes that accompanied Trinitarian speculation served as the epitome of what they hoped to avoid by using only biblical words to define only biblical positions that were hermeneutically established through rationalistic principles applied to the results of biblical induction.

In light of the nondenominational, autonomous ecclesiastical ethos and anticreedal orientation of the SCM, identifying a representative, standard view of some theological positions within the Movement is difficult. Extensive diversity exists, and because formulating authoritative theological statements runs against the grain of the entire Movement, there is no statement of faith to assess. Additionally, because attention given to the doctrine of the Trinity within the SCM is largely absent after 1846, minimal documentation exists regarding Trinitarian thought among Restorationists for much of the Movement's history. Nonetheless, while a representative Trinitarian stance among the ICC/CC and CCa may be somewhat difficult to document, it is not impossible to identify.

Some documentation of a pattern of Trinitarian thinking following 1846 can be found, first in some articles and monographs written by Restorationists. Douglas Foster and John Mark Hicks presented two unpublished studies to the Restoration Theological Research Fellowship in 1999 that indicated the most valuable written sources for establishing the SC Trinitarian general tendencies after the era of the Campbells and Stone.[3] I have also been assisted in identifying other sources by Jack Cottrell, who has greatly contributed to knowledge of Trinitarian theology from within the ICC/CC.

These sources and others are examined below in order to establish that there is a pattern of Trinitarian thought within ICC/CC and CCa. Additionally, it will be demonstrated that SC Trinitarian doctrine in these two fellowships suffers from deficiencies, with the most significant deficiency being the absence of overt, clear, readily identifiable, consistent, nuanced, applicable Trinitarian theology. Constructive Trinitarian theology is called for in order for SC churches to most profitably benefit from the resurgence in Trinitarian theology currently taking place. A Movement that has been hesitantly, almost reluctantly, Trinitarian stands to be revitalized if those now thinking theologically among ICC/CC and CCa will tackle the task of constructive Trinitarian theology.

Due to the relative scarcity of published Trinitarian works, the process of identifying *a* Trinitarian position for the SCM may be supplemented with anecdotal reflections and extrapolations from SCM theologians and historical theologians and by assessing what individual congregations believe about the Trinity. The caveat assumed here is that each individual Christian, Christian theologian, and church ultimately will hold a distinct position concerning the Trinity; thus, what Restorationists believe concerning the Trinity can only be a summation of these combined perspectives. Answering the question about Trinitarian thought among SC churches requires an insider's perspective and experience, so that a perception of SC Trinitarian thought can be grounded in *contextual description* coalesced from years of conversations and relationships; from time spent in congregational life, Bible study, and worship services; from participation at fellowship-wide conventions and lectureships; and through years of hearing sermons and reflecting on their import.[4] Further, where contextual description falls short, such as when there is no direct experience with particular congregations, direct affirmations of belief from individual, autonomous congregations can provide evidence for their views on the Trinity. Some such affirmations will be listed below.

In order to be complete and accurate in evaluating Trinitarian trends among Restorationists, more must be considered than just the relatively sparse number of published theological works that include ruminations on the Trinity. These works are important, but they are not decisive, particularly because no matter how erudite, informed, thorough, historically and theologically astute, biblically grounded, well-reasoned, well-stated, or well-accepted one particular Trinitarian statement or perspective may be, it will only constitute the opinion of one writer, editor, theological think-tank, or working group of theologians at a certain conference or convention at a certain time in history, with no binding ecclesiastical authority.

Therefore, the assessment offered in this chapter finds its basis in (1) anecdotal reflections made by the author, after about thirty years of serious reflection on SC theology; (2) anecdotal reflections made by interested, qualified, informed people personally consulted by the author; (3) statements of belief found in the documentation of representative churches; and (4) written works on the Trinity by Restorationists. The combination of these kinds of information can provide a comprehensive, current contextual description of Trinitarian thought among ICC/CC and CCa, even in the absence of authoritative creedal statements and widely accepted monographs of theology. The following examination will move from the most subjective means of assessment to the least subjective, beginning with anecdotal reflection and progressing to an analysis of contemporary SCM Trinitarian works.

The Author's Contextual Description

While the experience of an individual member of the SCM is not sufficient to determine the general Trinitarian ethos of the Movement, such experience can be consequential, depending on the scope of the individual's experience, his or her role within the Movement and relationships with others in the Movement, and the observer's ability to assess and compare various Trinitarian views and perspectives.

My own observations consist of hundreds of conversations over thirty years with many individuals in ICC/CC and CCa, including recognized church leaders; theologians and biblical scholars; seminary, university, and graduate school professors; journal editors; authors of theological literature; elders of numerous congregations; ministers; Bible teachers; and many Christians interested in Trinitarian doctrine from a wide array of age groups, geographical locations, and congregational types. While the accuracy of my observations and assessments must be evaluated by others, I offer the following as a summary statement of my perceptions regarding SC Trinitarian thought.

The history of SC theology has often relegated serious reflection on the Trinity to a place of insignificance, if not excoriation, yet I would assess the general position of SC Trinitarian doctrine as being essentially Trinitarian, but in an almost covert sense, much like the position of Alexander Campbell that was examined in Chapter Two.[5] SC adherents are generally Trinitarian, believing in the full deity of all three members of the Trinity, being quite willing to refer to Jesus Christ as One who is the same as God, or simply as God, but without holding a carefully delineated Trinitarian perspective and being unwilling or unable to evaluate their own perspectives against classically held Trinitarian positions. Very few theologians and scholars within the RM would take for themselves Trinitarian positions that would be significantly at odds with Nicea or Constantinople or Chalcedon or the Westminster Confession or the Heidelberg Confession. They would, then, generally be Trinitarian, even if they are somewhat ignorant of this fact, and would not particularly care that they could not articulate a classically held Trinitarian position or give an account of the differences between their own positions and other Trinitarian views. Few would know whether their positions resemble more closely that of the Campbells or Barton Stone. Many SC churches have statements of faith, but few members of these churches, including the church leaders who developed the faith statements, would have spent considerable time reflecting on the nuances and ramifications of the generally Trinitarian views included in those statements.

Perhaps one significant difference, then, between contemporary SCM members and Alexander Campbell would simply be that Campbell had carefully considered his Trinitarian perspective and knew well the issues involved, but, primarily for the sake of Christian unity, he decided to say little about Trinitarian matters. In contrast, most contemporary Restorationists, choose to say little about the Trinity because they are somewhat ignorant of what they believe rather than because they fear attention to the Trinity will propagate division. They would be able to refer to Scriptures that speak of Jesus and the Father being one, or mention being baptized in the name of the Father, the Son, and Holy Spirit, or ask questions about why Jesus exclaimed, "Why have you forsaken me?" But even most church leaders and ministers in SC churches would not be able to formulate careful argumentation concerning a particular Trinitarian view.

Thus, the question arises: *how is it that a generally Trinitarian position has come to dominate in SC churches?* First, I would suggest that, true to their heritage and ethos, SC churches have generally adopted traditional orthodox Trinitarianism because they take this to be *the biblical position*. This position has been little nuanced because they wish to avoid convoluted theological language and extrapolations and they perceive Scriptural witness to the Trinity to be vague and confusing. Alexander Campbell may have specifically avoided speculative, nonbiblical language primarily for the sake of Christian unity, but I believe the majority of those in the SCM today would be *most* interested in using only biblical language and asserting only biblical teaching when discussing the Trinity. They view this approach as theologically and hermeneutically proper, and generally view the Bible as giving witness to a traditionally orthodox, divine oneness of the three individualities Father, Son, and Spirit rather than to a separateness or to variegated levels of divinity among the Three.

Second, the question of Christian unity would actually play a role in *enabling* Restorationists to take some kind of generally Trinitarian stance in that SC churches (most particularly ICC/CC and CCa) are today greatly influenced by North American Christianity. Most specifically, they now typically view themselves as part of North American evangelicalism, which is typically Trinitarian in nature. Although there are contemporary denominations that loosely fall within the category of a Christian worldview that are also non-Trinitarian (e.g., United Pentecostals, Jehovah's Witnesses, The Church of Christ of Latter-Day Saints, Christadelphians), the vast majority of North American Christianity is generally Trinitarian. Even in cases where CCa desire to remain distinct from evangelicalism or conservative fundamentalism, I surmise that the SC Trinitarian position has been greatly influenced by North American Christianity, particularly in its evangelical form. Most in SC churches simply and unreflectively accept the Trinitarian position they typically see inculcated around them, even if they are somewhat unclear as to the nuances of this position.

My own anecdotal experience and an attempt at contextual description leads me to observe that one will not find in ICC/CC and CCa significant space or attention given to Trinitarian thought, particularly to the nuancing of Trinitarian theology. Extended dialoguing over others' Trinitarian theologies is scarce, and sometimes specifically avoided, and the overt impact of the doctrine of the Trinity on SC churches has been minimal. Nonetheless, those in ICC/CC and CCa are generally Trinitarian in line with the evangelicalism around them, even if it is difficult to adequately document this fact through monographs or denominationally authoritative statements of faith.

Additional Anecdotal Input

Although relatively little has been published that specifically and at length addresses Trinitarian doctrine in the SCM, there are those within the

Movement today who are qualified to provide input on the subject. In addition, technology permits anecdotal reflections and other types of input to be communicated in a way that is most valuable. In previous generations, this kind of anecdotal research would have been quite difficult, and researchers would have to wait for an extended period for theological and historical reflections to be published. In contrast, the current electronic age allows questions easily to be posed to a number of potential respondents and answers to queries to be received quickly and in a form that can easily be recorded and applied. Immensely valuable information can be quickly and easily assembled, including reflections that were made only weeks, days, or even minutes before being included as part of the research for this chapter.

Therefore, research for this work included gathering and assessing anecdotal reflections from qualified individuals who offered their perspectives on the status of Trinitarian doctrine within the contemporary SCM, at the author's request. Each contributor of these reflections is a trained theologian or historian who also knows well both the ICC/CC and CCa and Trinitarian theology, whether the doctrine is being approached from the perspective of biblical theology, systematic theology, the classical creedal statements, or the history of Trinitarian thought. Those from whom reflections were solicited included John Castelein, PhD, professor of contemporary Christian theology at Lincoln Christian University; Douglas Foster, PhD, professor of church history at Abilene Christian University; John Mark Hicks, PhD, professor of theology and historical theology at David Lipscomb University; Ron Highfield, PhD, professor of religion at Pepperdine University; Mark Love, PhD, director of missional leadership at Rochester College; Mark Powell, PhD, associate professor of theology at Harding School of Theology; and Johnny Pressley, PhD, professor of theology at Cincinnati Christian University. The following question was posed to each respondent:

> I am of the impression that most Christians in ICC/CC and CCa are generally Trinitarian, although in some cases ignorantly so, often simply following our evangelical friends in being, for the most part, in line with the traditional ecumenical creeds, even if they do not articulate their positions in extra-biblical language. Would you say the same?

Although there is insufficient space here to record the full, verbatim texts of the responses, these full texts may be found in the PhD dissertation on which the current work is based.[6] An examination of these anecdotal contributions would lead to the conclusion that they unanimously agree with the assessment offered in the question. The various anecdotal reflections differently nuance the exact course the Movement followed to get to its current general position, but even here there is substantial agreement that over time Barton Stone's nontraditional assessment of the Trinity was generally rejected and a position in line with traditional Trinitarianism was adopted. Those in the SCM may not articulate their Trinitarian positions in the extra-biblical language of the creeds, and they may reject the whole notion of creedal formulation, but the scholars listed above perceive SC views of the Trinity ultimately as little different from the Trinitarian positions of the ecumenical creeds, especially as these are in line with the contemporary theology of most North American evangelicals.

Statements of Faith

The ICC/CC and CCa have no denominationally applicable statements of faith that serve as authoritative documents defining the beliefs of constituent churches. Therefore, a careful analysis of a standard statement of belief cannot be conducted. However, in a relatively new phenomenon, many SC churches now prepare for themselves congregational statements of faith, which often will include a statement or two about the Trinity. These statements of faith began to be seen as recently as the late 1980s or early 1990s, and they usually exist as part of the organizational strategies and self-identifications of larger churches in urban centers. Large, notable, influential churches most frequently have developed statements of faith, although my sense is that the phenomenon is becoming more widespread. A practical fact is that as churches develop individual websites, they often wish to identify something about themselves there. A statement of faith, then, can function as much as a marketing tool as it does for establishing dogma. Indeed, statements of faith in SC churches often are intentionally descriptive, rather than prescriptive, so that such statements often carry little authority, even though they accurately describe what any particular church believes and thinks should be believed.

Representative statements can easily be assembled, compared, and evaluated, and they have the advantage of being both up-to-date and specifically representative of what individual faith communities believe. For the purposes of this study, duplicates of material were taken from congregational websites. I consider the chosen statements as representative examples for what may generally be said about Trinitarian doctrine within ICC/CC and CCa.

As was the case with the additional anecdotal submissions considered above, there is not room here to reprint the various statements of faith evaluated during research for this chapter; however, the full texts may be found in my doctoral dissertation.[7] It is also an easy thing to assemble the statements of faith that were evaluated, which derive from the fall 2012 statements of faith as published on the websites of:

- Bammel Church of Christ (www.bammel.org)—Houston, Texas
- Calgary Church of Christ (www.calgarycofc.com)—Calgary, Alberta, Canada
- Central Christian Church (www.centralchristian.com)—Henderson, Nevada
- Christ's Church of the Valley (ccvonline.com)—Peoria, Arizona
- Edmond Church of Christ (www.edmondchurchofchrist.com)—Edmond, Oklahoma
- Fairfax Church of Christ (www.fxcc.org)—Fairfax, Virginia
- Greenville Oaks Church of Christ (www.greenvilleoaks.org)–Allen, Texas
- Northside Christian Church (northsidechurch.com)—Clovis, California
- Otter Creek Church of Christ (www.ottercreek.org)—Brentwood, Tennessee
- Providence Road Church of Christ (www.prcoc.org)—Charlotte, North Carolina
- Richland Hills Church of Christ (www.thehills.org)—North Richland Hills, Texas
- Real Life Ministries (reallifeministries.com)—Post Falls, Idaho

- Southeast Christian Church (www.southeastchristian.org)—Louisville, Kentucky
- Southland Christian Church (southlandchristian.org)—Lexington, Kentucky
- The Branch (www.thebranch.org)—Farmer's Branch, Texas

As is the case with the anecdotal reflections presented in the previous sections, an examination of the above statements of faith generally supports the conclusion that ICC/CC and CCa are today typically orthodox Trinitarian. The statements vary in terms of their specificity and how they express language reflecting the carefulness of the ecumenical creeds, but clearly the congregations represented by these statements of faith are mostly in line with traditional Trinitarian orthodoxy. Perhaps what is most remarkable is that such statements of faith are even in existence, which indicates something of significance concerning the present capacity of ICC/CC and CCa to follow the trend of contemporary evangelicalism, where statements of faith are typical. Of course, this is a very small sample of the many statements of faith that now exist among ICC/CC and CCa, and the conclusion reached here may be challenged on this basis. Additionally, thousands of ICC/CC and CCa have not written statements of faith. The assessment here is based on the premise that the Trinitarian positions exemplified in the sample are representative of SC Trinitarian belief. Most often those churches that have constructed statements of faith include some proposition among their beliefs concerning the persons of the Father, the Son, and the Spirit. When they do, these statements are substantially in accordance with the positions of the classical creeds, traditional Trinitarian doctrine, and pervasive Trinitarian thought in contemporary evangelicalism.

Three Important Articles

As mentioned above, church historian Douglas Foster has written a paper, "Christology in the Stone-Campbell Movement: An Exploratory Survey," on the nature and person of Christ within the SCM. Although using in the title of his article a term typically reserved for addressing the doctrine of the two natures of Christ—"Christology," the relationship between the humanity and divinity of Jesus—Foster also chronicles in his overview both a history of Trinitarian thought in the SCM and the moves made by some among them toward christocentricity. Obviously, there are points at which Christological, Christocentric, and Trinitarian elements overlap; and Foster in his article chooses not to make a fine distinction between them.

Foster's Historical Theology

Foster's article constitutes historical theology. In considering the nineteenth century, he focuses on the whole of the Movement; in considering the twentieth century, he focuses exclusively on the CCa. He finds that what has been written christologically, especially after the era of the Campbells and Stone, has been mostly reactionary, with little that has been proactively constructive. Further, he finds that what has been done christologically has often been secondary and serendipitous to a primary focus on ecclesiology and soteriology. Foster's comments at this point are focused more on the second and third generations of thinkers in the Movement, but he identifies a definite turn toward christocentricity in CCa beginning in the last quarter of the twentieth century. This Christ centeredness, according to Foster, is being reflected hermeneutically, ecclesiologically, and soteriologically.[8]

While much of Foster's article is descriptive of the Christological/Trinitarian positions of Barton Stone and Alexander Campbell, similar to Chapters Two and Three in this book, he offers a valuable description of the Trinitarian thought that followed on the heels of the progenitors of the SCM.[9] In keeping with the direction of the anecdotal evidence and the statements of faith presented above, Foster describes the generations after the founders as "particularly orthodox in all their writings."[10] He does mention that some literature among CCa counters this trend, including some of Max Lucado's published work, which Foster labels "Antiochean," but Lucado's work, along with that of Mike Cope and Rubel Shelly, is both more popularly written and more centered on christocentricity than on rigorous Trinitarian theology. Foster also mentions two articles written by members of the noninstitutional branch of the CCa that he views as "astounding," in that they overtly deny the real humanity of Christ, emphasizing in an unusual and nontypical manner the exclusive divinity of Christ.[11]

Foster found more of a specifically Trinitarian emphasis in several authors of both the nineteenth and twentieth centuries, including C. L. Loos

(1823–1912). Loos was aware of and followed the Christological/Trinitarian position of Jan Jacob van Oosterzee (1817–1882), and because he was reared in a home where both French and German were spoken, was familiar with much of the theology of his day.[12] He was also an academic, serving as professor in at least three colleges and universities and eventually becoming president of Kentucky University.[13] W. K. Pendleton (1817–1899) also held to an orthodox Trinitarian theology; as a somewhat rare exception among SC writers, Pendleton actually deals with the results of the Council of Chalcedon and mentions from the Council of Nicea the *homoousios* controversy.[14] Consistent with the traditional orthodoxy of Loos and Pendleton, Foster also cites J. M. McCaleb (1862–1953), along with those who came later, like F. C. Sowell (1859–1951) and W. W. Otey (1867–1961).[15] Moving closer to the present day, Foster also mentions J. J. Turner and Edward P. Myers's *Doctrine of the Godhead* and references the April 1987 issue of *The Spiritual Sword* in which Ray Hawk, Hugo McCord, and Thomas Warren contribute articles that argue for the divinity of Christ and against United Pentecostalism and Jehovah's Witnesses.[16] Because Foster submitted his article in 1999, the last specifically Trinitarian reference that he mentions is Ron Highfield's contribution to *Theology Matters*.

While Foster admits that his delineation of the literature is brief, calling it an "exploratory survey," he supports what has been seen in the anecdotal material and statements of faith included above: although they have not been classically Trinitarian, CCa churches have generally taken a Trinitarian stance. Biblical language, especially the claims that Jesus is the Son of God, the Messiah, who is one with the Father, is used in the place of traditional Trinitarian jargon, but the views expressed are far more in line with classical Trinitarian expressions of the Three-in-One and the divinity of Christ than with any other perspective.

Segments of History from Hicks

John Mark Hicks schematized the history of Trinitarian thought in CCa in a 1999 unpublished paper written for the Restoration Theological Research Fellowship, in response to Foster's effort. Essentially in line with Foster's conclusions, Hicks divides SC history into four segments, with the most recent segment being far more inclined to emphasize the need for the establishment of an overt Trinitarian theology. Hicks says, "Trinitarianism has been (re)born among us";[17] "an emergent Trinitarianism is evident among us";[18] and that the CCa has been moving toward "the full embrace of a Trinitarian incarnational theology that focuses on the ethical life."[19]

Previous eras should also be identified with a Trinitarian perspective, although speculative theology is consistently avoided in favor of language centered on Jesus as the Son of God.[20] Whereas T. W. Brents (1823–1905) took a position similar to that of Barton Stone and Benjamin Franklin (1812–1878) desired to be neither Unitarian nor Trinitarian, Hicks finds that Hiram Christopher (1819–1901), Isaac Errett (1820–1888), and later Fred O. Blakely (1910–2001) and Roy Lanier Sr. (1899–1980) all represented a traditional Trinitarian position, mostly without relying on creedal, nonbiblical language and speculation.[21] Most valued, according to Hicks, is "biblical language and a minimalist Christology that is rooted in the factuality of Christ's redemptive work."[22]

The compendious surveys by Foster and Hicks are certainly helpful in elucidating how Trinitarian doctrine has played a role in the SCM despite the Movement's tendency to avoid the creedal affirmations and specific language and categories of classical Trinitarian theology. They confirm that the SCM has most typically been Trinitarian and has tended with time to become more consciously Trinitarian, even if there have been exceptions and a hesitancy on the part of many to make this specific admission.

Highfield's Overview

Ron Highfield, professor of religion at Pepperdine University and who specializes in systematic theology, in 1998 wrote the first chapter in a *feschrift* for Harold Hazelip, then-president of David Lipscomb University. In contexts outside the SCM the question asked in the title of Highfield's chapter, "Does the Doctrine of the Trinity Make a Difference?" would seem superfluous.[23] However, Highfield, in briefly offering historical background to the treatment of the Trinity in the SCM, shows why the question is meaningful. Following his brief historical comments, Highfield discusses the biblical foundations for orthodox Trinitarian doctrine, describing the basic dilemma of one God who presents himself to humans in three Persons. He then describes the earliest reaction of Christians to this dilemma, describing briefly the fourth-century events and the conclusions from Nicea and Constantinople.

Four elements make Highfield's brief chapter noteworthy for the purposes of this book.

1. It is found in a volume that is essentially a work of systematic theology, although it is a *feschrift* that includes chapters by numerous contributors. Volumes of systematic theology are rare in the SCM, and this one is indicative of the change in attitude about theology that has been happening within CCa.
2. It is encouraging that discussion about the Trinity is included in this book, an obvious choice in a volume dedicated to the importance of theology, but one not so obvious given SCM history. Equally encouraging is that the initial chapter of the volume focuses on the Trinity.
3. Although the parameters of the volume necessitated only a brief treatment of the Trinity, Highfield's overview includes classical Trinitarian discussion, offering to CCa readers a glimpse into how classical systematic theology can be juxtaposed in a meaningful way with SC theology.
4. Highfield's own position is clearly classically orthodox.

In fact, it is this last element that I find particularly interesting. Highfield specifically, intentionally and overtly defends the content of the Niceno-Constantinopolitan Creed to an extent that I have found nowhere else within the ICC/CC and CCa. He argues for the language "of the same essence." He argues for *homoousios* against *homoiousios*. He argues for the connection between the language of the creeds and biblical language. Highfield says:

> Being a Restorationist myself and firm believer in the exclusively normative nature of the Bible, I'm not saying that contemporary Christians must confess their faith with the postbiblical Trinitarian vocabulary. I'm not even saying that a Christian must raise the question of the Trinity, i.e., of how the Bible's message about the Father, Son, and Holy Spirit can be understood in

a way that preserves the unity of God as well as the difference among the Father, Son, and Spirit. But I am saying that if you do raise the subject, if you do form an opinion on the relationship among the Father, Son and Spirit, you'd better come up with something like the historic doctrine of the Trinity.[24]

With this I concur, and I find it satisfying that Highfield sees and states the issue so clearly. Highfield's position comes from his own careful study and his awareness of both historical theology and Scripture; thus, it would be inaccurate to say he has simply adopted the Trinitarian position of North American evangelicalism. Nonetheless, his Trinitarian perspective supports the contention that the classically orthodox view of the Trinity is the position most widely held within the ICC/CC and CCa.

Trinitarian Monographs

A handful of studies by those in the ICC/CC and the CCa have focused exclusively, or to a large extent, on the Trinity. The Trinitarian theology presented in most of these works is essentially orthodox.

Turner and Myers on the Godhead

In 1973, J. J. Turner and Edward P. Myers published *The Doctrine of the Godhead: A Study of the Father, Son, and Holy Spirit.*[25] It is to be commended as an attempt to bring the doctrine of God and the Trinity into the study life of members of the CCa, although this goal both contributes to and detracts from the value of the work. The work was intended to be used for individual Bible study and Sunday School classes in a fellowship little influenced by the doctrine of the Trinity, and it briefly mentions numerous Trinitarian issues that have received significant attention from theologians, including God's essence and attributes; his eternality; the deity of the Son; the oneness of Father, Son, and Spirit; their common nature; the doctrine of three Persons; the pre-existence of the Son; the personality of the Spirit; and arguments for traditional Trinitarian doctrine against Tritheism, Arianism, and Sabelleanism.

Unfortunately for anyone interested in substantial Trinitarian study, Turner and Myer's scope is extremely limited. The entire second edition is only 137 brief pages, with Chapter 5, "The Triune Godhead," and Chapter 8, "The Pre-Existence and Deity of Christ," covering a total of fifteen pages. There is no attention given to contemporary Trinitarian theology, little discussion of the history of Trinitarian doctrine, and no treatment of the doctrine of the Trinity within the SCM. Even the treatment given to biblical foundations for Trinitarian concepts is relatively brief, with little attention being given to the numerous exegetical issues that arise while proof-texting one's way through Paul or John to defend traditional Trinitarian belief.

For our purposes, the greatest value of *The Doctrine of the Godhead* is that it supports the claim that conservatives within the SCM since at least the latter half of the twentieth century have been generally traditionally orthodox Trinitarian, which Turner and Myers certainly are. Edward Myers, who holds a PhD in theology from Drew University, currently teaches undergraduates in the areas of doctrine and ministry at Harding University, an institution in many ways representative of CCa. J.J. Turner has been an instructor, preacher, and leader in institutions and churches well-known within the mainstream CCa. While there is no mention here of *homoousios*, while Athanasius is not mentioned (although Arius does receive mention in a footnote), and while there is no reference here to Constantinople or any wrestling with creedal language, the general discussion Turner and Myers offer of there being three equal, divine persons in one divine essence definitively links their position with traditional Trinitarian orthodoxy.

It is unfortunate that Turner and Myers make no references to the disagreement on the Trinity between Alexander Campbell and Barton Stone or to positions on the Trinity held by others in the SCM, and therefore, they give no historical context for their own position. Outside of references to Charles Hodge, Benjamin Warfield, Augustus Strong, Louis Berkof, Herman Bavinck, and some standard exegetical tools, there is little evidence offered here for why Turner and Myers traveled down the traditionally orthodox Trinitarian path. They would no doubt argue that they are simply delineating the biblical position on the Trinity, stemming from their own inductively exegetical assessment of the biblical evidence. There would be some validity to this claim, even if they could be accused of missing how much North American evangelicalism (certainly represented by Hodge, Warfield, Strong, and Berkof) has shaped their own perspectives.

Roy Lanier's Timeless Trinity

Roy Lanier Sr. (1899–1980) received his BA from Abilene Christian College in 1922 and an MA from Hardin-Simmons University in 1950. He ministered in CCa and taught in various institutions in Churches of Christ for over sixty years, and his *The Timeless Trinity for the Ceaseless Centuries* is the most thorough CCa treatment of the Trinity. It is noteworthy not only because of its length and thoroughness, but because it stands with Lonzo Pribble's *Theology Simplified* and Turner and Myers's *The Doctrine of the Godhead* as one of only three full-length monographs focusing on the Trinity that have been written by those from CCa.

For the most part, Lanier's work represents what one would expect a CCa theologian to have written about the Trinity in the middle of the twentieth century. The book is biblically centered, hermeneutically inductive, and there is virtually no mention or interaction with previous Trinitarian theologians. Surprisingly, neither Thomas Campbell, Alexander Campbell, nor Barton Stone are even mentioned in the volume, but Lanier freely and frequently makes reference to a few conservative systematic theologians, including Presbyterians Charles Hodge and B. B. Warfield and two Baptist theologians, Walter T. Conner and Augustus Strong. This is noteworthy because writers of Lanier's era were often reticent to quote theologians from other denominational streams, although Lanier's degree from Hardin-Simmons University would have acquainted him with the work of Conner and Strong. More typical is the fact that the majority of Lanier's references are to New Testament commentaries, word studies, or theological dictionaries, indicating the biblically centered, inductively exegetical approach Lanier takes to presenting Trinitarian doctrine.

Despite being titled *The Timeless Trinity,* more than specifically traditional Trinitarian issues are addressed in this volume. The work is neatly divided into three sections, one for each person of the godhead, and attention is given to the issues of their relationship, their common nature, and their roles in the divine economy. But Lanier's work is more accurately depicted as a comprehensive statement about the nature and attributes of God, including those of his Son and Spirit, than it is specifically about traditional Trinitarian issues. Lanier does examine traditional concerns about how there can be one God revealed in three persons, their common substance or nature, and the divinity of the Son and the Spirit, but this is done in the context of a larger discussion about who God is as he is revealed in Scripture. There is some mention of Sabellianism, modalism, and Arius, but Lanier's references to these and to Nicea, Constantinople, and Chalcedon occur only in passing.[26] The word *homoousios* does not occur in the entire volume, although there are references to essence, nature, substance, and personhood. There is no discussion of Athanasius, the Cappadocians, or Augustine, to say nothing of Schleiermacher, Scheeben, Dorner, Barth, or Rahner.

Timeless Trinity, *The Existence and Attributes of God*. There are eleven chapters in section one of this volume, but only one of these chapters, "The Unity of God," includes discussion of specifically Trinitarian issues. The remainder of the chapters discuss human knowledge of God, the truth of God's existence, his attributes, and his truth, love, holiness, justice, righteousness, omnipotence, omnipresence, and omniscience. When Lanier does address specifically Trinitarian issues, his conclusions are essentially classically orthodox Trinitarian. For him, "the term 'Son of God' means that he is of the same nature and essence as the Father, that he is the true God and eternal life."[27] Countering modalism Lanier says, "We must not view the personal relations, or distinctions, Father, Son, and Holy Spirit, as being three attributes of God. Each of these Persons in the Godhead is called God; each has all the attributes of God; but neither should be depersonalized and called an attribute of God."[28] God possesses personhood because Jesus was a person, because he is both God and reveals God, and because he came from God, meaning that God, too, must be a person.[29]

In chapter 5, "The Unity of God," Lanier organizes his thoughts around three concepts: (1) that there is but "one God; one infinite, self-existent, omnipresent spirit essence";[30] (2) that "within that one essence there are personal distinctions, Father, Son, and Holy Spirit. Each is called God; each has all the attributes of God; each must in many passages of scripture be distinguished from each other";[31] and (3) that the identity between the Son and Spirit is such that the presence of the Holy Spirit in the life of a Christian is the presence of the Son.[32] Lanier closes chapter 5 with four lengthy quotes that support his traditionally orthodox view. He references two Baptists, Walter Conner and Augustus Strong; and two from the SCM,

C. C. Crawford and H. Leo Boles.[33] In so doing, Lanier obviously links his own Trinitarian perspective as well as the perspectives of Boles and Crawford with conservative evangelical scholarship. Even one as informed on the issues as Lanier was apt to be significantly influenced by the traditional Trinitarian orthodoxy of North American evangelicalism. Thus, whether Trinitarian theology is given specific, thoughtful, written, clear delineation in a monograph, or it simply appears in the conversations of Christians in a Bible study, SC Trinitarian theology runs parallel to that of typical North American evangelicalism.

Timeless Trinity, A Study of Jesus Christ. This section consists of eight chapters in which both Trinitarian and christological issues are addressed, although between 85 and 90 percent of the works referenced in these chapters are commentaries, lexicons, or word studies. Of the eight chapters, the first four focus on preincarnational and pre-New Testament-era issues and literature. Three of the last four chapters focus on the deity of Jesus in a way more closely linked to traditional Trinitarian discussion, and chapter 8 focuses on christological questions concerning two natures doctrine. Chapter 1 defends the pre-existence of the Son by simply referencing biblical texts. Interestingly, at this point, Lanier will only say that Christ is pre-existent; there is no reference to His eternality, so that one wonders at the end of chapter 1 if Lanier will take a position similar to Isaac Watts and Barton Stone concerning the Son's existence and pre-existence or if he will defend Alexander Campbell's hesitancy about the eternality of the Son. Ultimately, he leaves his readers frustrated, never really specifying what exactly he believes it means for the Son to be pre-existent.

Chapters 2 and 3 in Part 2 are discussions of the λόγος and his work prior to the incarnation. Here Lanier begins by identifying the λόγος with Jehovah, using the connections that exist between Old Testament events and their fulfillment in the ministry and teaching of Jesus, so that "we must conclude that the Jehovah of the Old Testament is Jesus of the New Testament."[34] He then spends what seems an inordinate amount of space identifying Jesus with the "angel of Jehovah" who makes appearances in numerous Old Testament settings, such as Genesis 16:7–13. This angel is both Jehovah and distinguished from Jehovah. He appears as a man and as an angel. He withheld Abraham's hand and prevented him from killing

Isaac. He wrestled with Jacob. He is God Almighty, but he is nowhere referred to as the Father, therefore, he must be the Second Person.³⁵ This angel of Jehovah interacted with Moses, met him at the burning bush, and interacted with Joshua as a man. Lanier finishes Part 2, chapter 2 by saying:

> Since the "angel of Jehovah" is himself Jehovah, yet is distinguished from the Father; and since "Jehovah our God is one Jehovah," as stated by Moses (Deut. 6:4), and by Jesus (Mark 12:29), it follows that we must accept the doctrine that there is but one eternal, self-existent, infinite Spirit Being, but within that Being there are three Persons possessing the essence and attributes of deity.³⁶

While I may not entirely agree with Lanier's logic and his interpretations, his point is clear: the Son is to be identified with Jehovah. Further, "the visible temporary form of Jehovah associating with men for their benefit may be looked upon as a type of the invisible spiritual presence of God with us today in the person of the Holy Spirit, which is the presence of Christ with us," which is the identical point Lanier made about Jehovah and the Son, but here making it about the full divinity of the Spirit who is identified with Jehovah.³⁷ Chapter 3 extends the discussion of the λόγος in the pre-Christian period, connecting the λόγος to creation, in which he had a foundational role and which he continues to uphold and sustain.³⁸ He reveals the Father to creation, makes covenants with creation, escorts God's people through the wilderness, and—prior to the dispensation of Christ—is abundantly active through what Lanier calls the "dispensation of God."³⁹

The next four chapters of Part 2 amount to Lanier's assertion and defense of the full deity of the Son. Here he cites prophetic witness, evaluates Scriptures in the New Testament, assesses the titles applied to the Son (e.g., alpha and omega, author of salvation, the "effulgence of His Glory," "the very image of His substance," son of God, only begotten son of God), and then turns to the Pauline witness of Christ's divinity. These four chapters comprise the most direct evidence in his volume for the divine character of Christ. One striking element is how similar these chapters are with what is seen in some eighteenth-century British writers as they argue for the full divinity of the Son against those like Samuel Clarke, who took the opposing view. My suspicion is that Lanier is in touch with this style of argumentation about the Trinity through Trinitarians like H. P. Liddon rather than from his own reading of Isaac Watts or others from that era. At least, Lanier makes no reference to these earlier writers.

Timeless Trinity, Part 3. Lanier devotes this section of the book to the ministry of the Holy Spirit, with several of the chapters more generally examining the role the Holy Spirit plays in the life of the church and the believer. But chapters 1–3 and chapter 9 are quite specific in asserting and defending the full deity of the Holy Spirit; clearly in Lanier's view, when the Holy Spirit is present and active in the life of Christians and the church, God is present. Lanier is emphatic concerning the full deity of the Holy Spirit, whether discussing the ways the Spirit interacts with creation in the Old Testament period (chapter 1), examining the status of the Holy Spirit as one Person among the divine Three (chapter 2), arguing for the full divinity of the Spirit (chapter 3), or linking the work of the Spirit to the revelation of God through the divine Word (chapter 9).

Although classical creedal language is largely absent, there is no question of Lanier's alignment with what is essentially a classically orthodox Trinitarian position. Although Lanier did what Alexander Campbell and many of his followers refused to do—write at length about the Trinity and defend a traditional orthodox position—his position is in agreement with theirs and with the general tenor of Trinitarian thought within the SCM. Some exceptions to this do, however, exist, with Lonzo Pribble being one of the most prominent.

Lonzo Pribble's Theology Simplified

No other volume written by anyone in the ICC/CC and CCa focuses so exclusively on Trinitarian doctrine as does Lonzo Pribble's *Theology Simplified: God, His Son, and His Spirit*. However, in contrast to the works of J. J. Turner and Edward Myers, Roy Lanier Sr., Jack Cottrell, and C. Leonard Allen and Danny Gray Swick, Pribble's work is decidedly non-Trinitarian/anti-Trinitarian in its intention.[40] The cover of Pribble's volume includes the description, "Why the doctrine of the Trinity is neither reasonable nor biblical." This, of course, sets a polemical tone for the work, which is certainly manifested throughout Pribble's volume. Countless times he announces that he has proven the Trinitarian position to be in error, or that his arguments are undeniable, often including the Unitarians among those whose positions he has—in his mind—decimated.

The volume positively asserts and affirms minimal amounts about the Father, Son, and Spirit in comparison to the critical evaluation Pribble makes of traditional Trinitarian doctrine, including a critical verse-by-verse analysis of passages Trinitarians typically use to make their case that Jesus is the one true God. The majority of Part 1's forty-five chapters are simply brief examinations of passages typically used by Trinitarians, with the subjects of many chapters being just one or two particular verses. He additionally critiques the language of the creedal statements formulated at Nicea and Constantinople and that of the Athanasian Creed (although he strangely says little negative about Nicea). His positive support affirms what he terms the biblical position, one that he repeatedly says is so simple that any child or novice Christian can understand it.

Pribble defines the divinity and divine nature of the Son in terms less than the Father's full divinity; the Son is equal with God in possessing divinity, but not in a way that asserts for the Son full equality with the Father.[41] There is equality in status for Father and Son with reference to everything aside from their own relationship, where there is neither equality in nature nor in substance.[42] The Son for Pribble is not eternal, and his pre-existence refers to some time prior to creation when the Son was born—not created—rather than to the Son's eternality. In fact, for Pribble, the Fatherhood of God and Sonship of Christ are taken quite literally, with the Father/Son relation constituting the paradigmatic relationship by which the existence of the Three together is defined. For Pribble it is all so simple; just accept the Father/Son relationship as the chief identifier of the divine communion, and leave it at that. He says:

> Trinitarianism has declared, without even one single passage of Scripture that so states, that "the one God is a triune being composed of three coequal and coeternal persons—God the Father, God the Son, and God the Holy Spirit."
>
> But since the truth of the matter is so well established in Scripture in such simple terms that even children or a novice

can understand, we must now proceed to show how other evidence being used to the contrary does not in fact support either Trinitarianism or Unitarianism as have been defined, but rather, when properly understood, adds credence to the truth already established—that the one God is the Father, and that Jesus Christ is his only begotten divine Son. . . . Jesus said, "I am God's Son. That makes Jesus *God* in the sense that any son who is actual substance offspring possesses the same nature as his father. As Adam was human, so Cain is human. As Jesus' Father is divine, so Jesus is divine. But such does not mean that Jesus is that one, supreme self-existent God and Father of whom he is the Son. . . . There is still just one God absolute; and that is the Father.[43]

The resemblances between Lonzo Pribble and Barton Stone are striking, and this is not coincidence. On the first two pages of his "Introduction," Pribble specifically references Stone, saying, "Inspiration for the title, *Theology Simplified* was suggested in a statement by Elder Barton W. Stone . . . in *An Address to the Christian Churches*."[44]

He continues:

Without necessarily giving sanction to all of Stone's theology, we hereby give credit to his writings for removing some of those mysteries about God and his Son, which had so long plagued this author's curiosity, and for serving as an encouragement to take Stone's simple and understandable point of view, expand and elaborate upon it, and show how the resulting point of view, more than any other, withstands the scrutiny of divine Scripture.[45]

It is not surprising, then, that Pribble takes a view of the exclusive singularity of the Father as the one true God that is similar to Stone's view; he follows Stone's view of Christ's pre-existence without accepting the Son's eternal nature; believes the Son is divine but not equal to the one true God, and asserts that the doctrine of the Spirit's specific personhood is extra-biblical and, therefore, is to be rejected as a manmade accretion to authentic Christianity.[46]

Perhaps his most startling idea, in which Pribble separates even from Stone, is that the Son Jesus is not literally the divine λόγος who became flesh; the Son is only symbolically God's Word, in that he came to speak God's words to the world. λόγος is not who Jesus was, but is what Jesus spoke, so that he is called the Word of God because he was God's revealer speaking God's words. Pribble says:

> To conclude that the eternal word of God, God's infinite wisdom, reason and comprehension, his word, is a personal entity distinguished from God himself, is as illogical as it would be to conclude that a man's *logos* is a personal entity distinct from the man it is the word of. It would be hard to imagine that the almighty Jehovah God, the Father, did not have as a part of his being a *logos,* a word, or divine infinite reason. And if Jesus were actually the personal *logos* of God, then by what *logos* did the voice speak from heaven at Jesus' baptism (Matt 3:17) and at his transfiguration (Matt 17:5), "This is my Son, whom I love"? If the *logos* of God had become flesh, then by what *logos* were those words spoken? It had to be by the word of God, the Father, because he called Jesus his beloved Son. Does God have another word by which he speaks, in addition to his word that supposedly became flesh and was baptized in the River Jordan? . . . The only reasonable conclusion is that God, who is the Father, has an infinite *logos* which is not a personal entity distinct from the God it is the word of, just as he has a Spirit which is also not a personal entity distinct from the God it is the Spirit of. But God does have a Son who is the person distinct from the God he is Son of. It was the Son (called The Word of God) who "became flesh and dwelt among us." He was not literally God's word, but came to declare that word by the message he proclaimed.[47]

While one may question the basis of Pribble's own logic and some of his exegesis, nonetheless, one cannot fault Pribble for ignoring many of the key elements among the traditional biblical arguments in favor of the Trinity. He covers a great deal of Trinitarian ground. Unfortunately, what he covers is governed almost entirely by his polemic against classical Trinitarian doctrine, so that, as indicated above, he develops only a very circumscribed positive delineation of the Father, Son, and Spirit, with most of this coming in "Part 2. God and His Spirit."

Most noteworthy for our purposes is that *Theology Simplified* stands in such direct contrast to the direction that contemporary Trinitarian thought has typically taken within the ICC/CC and CCa. Pribble's perspectives on the relation between the Father and Son, the Son's subordination to the Father, his separation from the one true God, his divinity, his nature as firstborn and begotten, his eternality, the limitations of his pre-existence, his being only figuratively and symbolically called the Word of God, and the rejection of the Spirit's personhood place Pribble outside the mainstream of contemporary SC Trinitarian thought. Through personal experience I am aware there are others within SC churches who hold views similar to Pribble's or take other Trinitarian positions that are not traditionally orthodox. However, it is my assessment that views like Pribble's are an aberration, amounting to only a very small minority of the Trinitarian perspectives held among those ministering for and attending SC churches and an even smaller percentage of views held by those serving as instructors in SC universities and colleges.

Jack Cottrell's Traditional Trinitarianism

Several factors indicate the value of citing Jack Cottrell as a representative voice for SC Trinitarian thought, specifically with reference to the ICC/CC. Cottrell holds a PhD from Princeton Theological Seminary, has been teaching and writing at what is now Cincinnati Christian University since 1967, and is considered by many to be the dean of theologians within the ICC/CC. He is the only scholar in the ICC/CC and CCa of whom I am aware that has attempted anything like an individually written systematic theology, having published *What the Bible Says About God the Creator, What the Bible Says About God the Ruler,* and *What the Bible Says About God the Redeemer,* totaling over 1,500 pages.[48] This series has been the inspiration for another six-volume series in theology, in which Cottrell is responsible for *What the Bible Says About the Holy Spirit* and *What the Bible*

Says About Grace.[49] For our purposes, Cottrell—informatively and with a surprising thoroughness given the section's brevity—covers the doctrine of the Trinity in a section of just over fifty-seven pages in *What the Bible Says About God the Redeemer,* touching on the majority of questions addressed by classical Trinitarian thought in a way that illustrates well the traditional orthodoxy characteristic of contemporary conservatives within the SCM.

Much of Cottrell's analysis of Trinitarian doctrine in *What the Bible Says About God the Redeemer* offers a standard evangelical depiction of Trinitarian issues, including the way he applies biblical revelation to Trinitarian questions. He begins by grounding the Trinity in the divine economy, viewing the redemption of humankind in the person and ministry of Jesus as the decisive origin of Trinitarian thought. From there he moves into the basic problem of God's unity and triunity, presenting the biblical content that both creates and speaks to the matter of the primary Trinitarian dilemma. Following a section on Trinitarian heresies, he sets forth basic, traditional Trinitarian doctrine, citing numerous key figures in Trinitarian thought, including a brief history that references B. B. Warfield, Arthur Wainwright, Christopher Kaiser, James Hastings's *Encyclopedia of Religion and Ethics,* Robert Crossley, Louise Berkhof, Carl F. H. Henry, Gordan Clark, James Buswell, Robert S. Franks, Edmund Fortman, Geerhardus Vos, and Carl Brumback, almost all of whom make evangelical Trinitarian contributions.

Cottrell, Leonard Allen, and Danny Swick, are the only writers examined in this chapter who address the doctrine of the Trinity with contemporary Trinitarian thought in view. In Cottrell's work, the Trinity is considered in light of precritical, Enlightenment, and post-Enlightenment critically aware scholarship, including the modern and postmodern discipline of Trinitarian theology. Even as he remains staunchly evangelical in his orientation, his perspective is informed by both ancient and contemporary Trinitarian theology, so that his Trinitarian discussion encompasses more than just biblical narrative.

For instance, Cottrell is aware of Barth's contribution to what others term the current Trinitarian revival, and he is aware of the tendency at the end of the nineteenth century to identify Trinitarian thought with Hellenic philosophical categories and cites Bernard Lonergan's work as a welcome refutation of this approach.⁵⁰ He begins his discussion of the Trinity by indicating the necessity of the economic Trinity and the grounding of biblical Trinitarianism in the redemption that comes with Jesus Christ.⁵¹ Cottrell addresses the topic as a historically aware systematic theologian, rather than as a New Testament scholar or biblical theologian, like many of the others in the ICC/CC and CCa who have written on the Trinity. Further, Cottrell refers to the works of Barth and Lonergan and discusses Karl Rahner, all in the context of a discussion referring to Trinitarian *persons*.⁵² Although this has been an issue since antiquity, it is refreshing to see someone from the SCM aware of writers who have participated in the contemporary discussion. In private correspondence with me in June 2012, Cottrell, now in his mid-70s, indicated continued interest in contemporary Trinitarian scholarship.

As are most from the ICC/CC and CCa who have written on the Trinity, Jack Cottrell is typically orthodox Trinitarian, with a clear penchant for evangelical scholarship that upholds traditional Trinitarian theology. His willingness to interact with major figures in Trinitarian studies—Barth, Rahner, Lonergan—is refreshing even if his overview is not as detailed as the monograph of Roy Lanier. However, Cottrell's brief overview of Trinitarian doctrine ultimately displays a breadth of understanding, especially regarding contemporary scholarship that makes it comprehensively more valuable than any other single piece devoted to the Trinity from ICC/CC and CCa writers.

Allen and Swick's *Participating in God's Life*

One of the most encouraging signs that Trinitarian renewal could be taking place among some SC churches is *Participating in God's Life: Two Crossroads for Churches of Christ* by C. Leonard Allen and Danny Gray Swick.⁵³ Allen was recently named the dean of the College of Bible and Ministry at Lipscomb University; he earned a PhD in Christian thought from the University of Iowa and previously taught theology at Abilene Christian University. Danny Swick is his former student, having studied for a PhD in systematic theology at the University of Toronto.

Interestingly, Allen and Swick intentionally remove themselves from traditional Trinitarian discussion; they make no attempt to define the Trinity, delineate the divine mystery of the Three-in-One, or wade through historical Trinitarian positions, whether ancient or modern. They are not writing for those familiar with Trinitarian jargon and argumentation, but for the interested church public, particularly those interested in renewal among SC churches, and they say this about traditional Trinitarian discussions:

> So let us begin with a disclaimer: we find such discussions every bit as boring and irrelevant as you probably do. Our focus here is not to make the Trinity "make sense" and we have little at stake in the actual term "Trinity." Understanding how God is Three and at the same time One according to the rules of logic is as irrelevant as it is boring. The word "Trinity" itself is as good as any other word for describing what we are getting at and so we have opted to keep it. We want to be candid about exactly what we think of the word: it is not a revealed word, but the history and dynamics of Divine relationships that it describes is indeed revealed in Scripture. As one major theologian put it, Trinitarian doctrine "simply states explicitly what is implicit already in God's revelation in Jesus Christ." We therefore use the word as a helpful way to summarize the basic biblical revelation of God's nature and as a useful tool for expelling some very unbiblical concepts.[54]

Thus, rather than being a monograph focused on the Trinity and Trinitarian theology, *Participating in God's Life* is more a plea written to SC churches, especially the CCa, encouraging them to embrace and experience ecclesiastical and spiritual renewal by rediscovering the Trinitarian life of God and the ramifications God's Trinitarian existence holds for the church. The material in Parts 1 and 2, up through page 134, constitutes historical description, not of SCM Trinitarian theology, but of SC spirituality (or the lack thereof), detailing the impact of modernism and Lockean empiricism upon the Movement. Citing a controversy from the 1850s featuring Robert Richardson and Tolbert Fanning, Allen and Swick describe the controversy that arose over whether the Holy Spirit works separate from inspiration and application of the written Word. Does the Spirit indwell the believer? Is there connection and relationship between God and humans, constituted by personal interaction, subjectively experienced through the inner consciousness and affections of the soul?

Tolbert Fanning and those who came after him were emphatic that the answer to such questions was "no!" and declared that one spirit may influence another only by direct contact of one of the five senses or by argumentation using propositional language. God himself now communicates with humans only through words, according to Fanning's camp, and these words are incorporated in the pages of the Bible. For Robert Richardson, this dependency upon Enlightenment rationalism and empiricism was nothing less than a distortion of biblical doctrine and a denial of Christian spirituality, inhibiting divine immediacy. For those who followed Locke, faith became the acceptance of facts revealed about God, while faith for Richardson entailed trusting relationship, participatory interaction, and communion with the heart of God.

In the 1850s and decades following, a large segment of the SCM opted for the rational/empirical approach to faith, so that the devotional, affective side of spirituality was significantly minimized within most SC churches, especially in the southern part of the United States. Allen and Swick document some of this history, including places at which contrary voices arose. They also chronicle the collision that took place at the end of the twentieth century as postmodernism began significantly to influence spiritual life and attitudes, leading many to begin questioning the lack of experienced spirituality within SC churches. For Allen and Swick, Robert Richardson's functional doctrine of the Spirit would make possible a spiritual renewal manifested in at least two major areas of thoughtful reflection: (1) rejecting the modernistic view of a human being as an autonomous self in order to see each person as a relational self and prioritize genuine connection with others, including God; and (2) viewing God in terms of his intrapersonal Trinitarian relationality.

Allen and Swick say:

> The notion that the self is autonomous and founded in its own ability to reason is actually a new idea. An older idea that is gaining precedence again in our age is that the self is created through relationships. The self is not a given based on reason,

> but the self is something that is always being gained, expanded and reshaped through our relationships. In other words, I am not a self by myself; I become a self in and through my relationships with others. We become who we are as we interact with other people, seeing ourselves a little differently through the eyes of others, and gaining more of an identity in a community of our peers. More particularly, as we learn to love others, to give of ourselves, to relinquish our pretensions to autonomy we come closer to being selves in the true sense of the word. . . . in community we learn to see ourselves as part of a whole, with individuality to be sure, but an individuality that only comes alive in the midst of the whole.[55]

Faith for each individual self, then, is not the reception of facts and the maintenance of an individualized intellectual stance; it happens as communion, as oneness with another, where there is participation in the life of God. Here Allen and Swick borrow from the Eastern church the term *theosis*—becoming godlike as God's nature is spiritually infused into an evermore purified relationship between the believer and God—indicating the process whereby the Christian becomes all he or she was intended to be, so that to be fully human means to be communally associated with another, even as one draws close to the heart of God.[56]

The specifically Trinitarian turn taken by Allen and Swick involves viewing God in terms of his intrapersonal Trinitarian relationality.[57] Where others view God in terms of his attributes, the personal, relational nature of his attributes must be prioritized so that the relationality that it is to be Father and Son may specifically impact the nature of Christian life. Whereas in prior times, God's nature as Father or Son was considered metaphorical and analogous, biblical descriptions and titles should instead be taken seriously, without fear that we are simply identifying God with projections of ourselves. Far from being anthropomorphic, taking full account of God's relationality in his Trinitarian nature provides a distinctly theological foundation for understanding who God is in his nature as relationships.[58] In summary, Allen and Swick call the church fully to participate in the life of God:

What then do we hope to attain by using the word "Trinity?" In the broadest of strokes we can say that the Trinity summarizes the following biblical themes about God:

- God's relational nature;
- God's historical self-revelation as Father, Son and Spirit;
- The unique love that binds Father, Son and Spirit into a unity;
- God's movement toward us in the story of salvation, spanning from creation to consummation; and
- The way God's Life flows out to us—partially now and fully later.

When we affirm the doctrine of the Trinity we recall all of these biblical themes. More succinctly, the term "Trinity" is a human way of underscoring the fact that God's nature is such that we can "participate" in Him and He in us. Throughout the centuries use of the term "Trinity" has recalled this biblical fact about God's nature. This usage commends the term to us as shorthand reminder of God's relational nature and self-giving character. . . . The doctrine also reminds us that God's relationality is not merely His own: we participate in the Trinitarian Life of God, and through His Spirit we begin to live in Trinitarian fellowship with one another. The expression "Trinitarian Life" not only describes God's nature but also the way His relational nature is partially realized in our relationships when seen through the eyes of faith.[59]

Although Allen and Swick do not intend to provide an exhaustive look at Trinitarian doctrine in *Participating in God's Life,* for at least three reasons their work is as significant for the church as anything written about the Trinity by SCM authors. First, their work recognizes the value in Trinitarian theology and seriously considers its significance. There is not merely an acknowledgement here of the tendency of SC churches to be orthodox Trinitarian, nor an argument that they should be, but there is also an appreciation of the serious need to think *as Trinitarians,* to allow the influence of God as Trinity to greatly impact the ethos of the church.

Theirs is an initial attempt to specifically apply the Trinitarian nature of God to church life in a way that moves beyond intellectual understanding and comprehension of doctrinal propositions. Hopefully, Allen and Swick's work will provoke others to do the same. It would be of lasting value to the church if their work sparks a movement among ICC/CC and CCa to focus on Trinitarian spirituality and God's relationality.

Second, although they make minimal references to contemporary Trinitarian theologians, it is clear that Allen and Swick are conversant with contemporary Trinitarian scholarship and that they can apply the fruits of their understanding to current church life. This is immensely important because there has been great ignorance of contemporary Trinitarian trends among ICC/CC and CCa. While some in the academies are quite aware of current Trinitarian doctrine, the leadership of the average church is not. Allen and Swick have written with church leadership in mind and have made some of current Trinitarian discussion available to nonscholars, hopefully motivating church leaders to begin taking seriously the value of Trinitarian reflection.

Third, Allen and Swick offer evidence that the ICC/CC and CCa should be considered to possess at least a generally orthodox Trinitarian ethos. The Trinity may have been largely ignored in the shaping of SC ecclesiology, soteriology, eschatology, etc., but this is not because the Movement is non-Trinitarian or anti-Trinitarian. The SCM has simply not been overtly Trinitarian. Allen and Swick have offered reasons why this must change.

The Impact of Previous Stone-Campbell Trinitarian Perspectives on Contemporary Churches

The history of thought within ICC/CC and CCa demonstrates that the SCM has generally been orthodox Trinitarian in its theological orientation. Although there have been exceptions, Restorationists have typically been Trinitarian, albeit hesitant to use traditional Trinitarian language and speculative argumentation, especially when it contributes to disunity between Christians. What has been shown thus far in this book is that SC Trinitarian theology has been largely understated and certainly not overtly influential on the ethos of SC churches, demonstrating little impact on either SCM theology or ministry. Although in recent decades, most obviously in CCa, a Christocentric influence has significantly impacted the thinking, preaching, teaching, and practice of SC churches, explicitly Trinitarian doctrine has not been a shaping force of doctrine or practice.

Thus, an overt, intentional renewal of focus upon Trinitarian theology is called for among SC churches and institutions, such as undergraduate departments of Bible and graduate departments of theology, and among the scholars who represent the Movement. Thankfully, some of this is currently happening, as has been shown in this chapter. *This must continue to take place!* Those of us in the SCM are in many ways recipients of a rich heritage, but not necessarily in the specific discipline of theology, systematic theology, Trinitarian theology, or even biblical theology. Our expertise as a movement has come in the areas of biblical studies and patristics, and these areas of Christian scholarship have most significantly impacted the thinking and practice of SC churches.

The next two chapters are intended to move in an introductory way toward what I suggest are the next steps necessary to allow Trinitarian theology to influence the SCM, especially ICC/CC and CCa. Where Trinitarian thought in the SCM has been formulated *in reaction to* ecclesiological realities and soteriological priorities, suggestions will be made as to how ecclesiology and soteriology, including theological praxis, can flow *from* an overtly stated Trinitarian theology. Where there are ecclesiological and soteriological inadequacies in SC churches, overt Trinitarian thought can proactively work to move them forward by prioritizing Trinitarian doctrine and formulating influential Trinitarian doctrinal conceptions.

Notes

[1] See the discussion in Chapter Two. As late as 1861, Alexander Campbell wrote comments reflecting on his father's Trinitarian views, but his 1846 series in *The Millennial Harbinger* constitutes his final lengthy treatment of the Trinity.

[2] For example, in the three full-length monographs on the Trinity published by Roy Lanier, Ed Myers and J. J. Turner, and Lonzo Pribble there are no references to or mentions of any writers who today are typically linked to Trinitarian theology. In these works, the only references made to commonly recognized theologians are to the Presbyterian Charles Hodge (1797–1878), the Anglican H. P. Liddon (1829–1890), the Baptist Augustus Strong (1836–1921), the Dutch Reformed Herman Bavinck (1854–1921), the Presbyterian B. B. Warfield (1851–1921), the Baptist E. Y. Mullins (1860–1928), the Baptist Walter T. Conner (1877–1952), the American Reformed Louis Berkof (1873–1957), and the Presbyterian Lorraine Boettner (1901–1990). Thus, aside from Berkhof and Boettner, no references are made to theologians writing after the first half of the twentieth century, although these three monographs were published in 1973, 1974, and 2001. Allen and Swick's *Participating in God's Life*, is the only published material I know of from those in CCa that references and recognizes the value of contemporary Trinitarian writers. In their book, they mention Catherine LaCugna, Jürgen Moltmann, Wolfhart Pannenberg, James B. Torrance, and John Zizioulas. Jack Cottrell, who writes as a member of the ICC /CC takes more note of some who had written about the Trinity up through 1987, when his *What the Bible Says About God the Redeemer* was published.

[3] Douglas Foster, "Christology in the Stone-Campbell Movement"; John Mark Hicks, "Christological Reflections."

[4] I am defining *contextual description* as a combination of experiences and knowledge that form a comprehensive perspective and understanding of a recognized intellectual position held by an identified group. Typically in religious studies, theological positions are identified and evaluated based upon understandings of texts that communicate the positions. But when someone is describing and evaluating his or her own theological position, a wider range of data is available, including all the experiences and interactions that occur in living out faith together. Corporate prayer, worship, community service, study, and everyday conversations can significantly contribute understanding of a communally held teaching, so that anecdotal experiences can be material for surmising an intellectually held position by an identified group. This is an important element in reaching conclusions about the intellectual positions of groups, and in this case facilitates conclusions about Trinitarian doctrine in the ICC/CC and CCa, given their relative scarcity of published Trinitarian works.

[5] However, a distinction between Campbell and many of his followers today would be found on the question of the eternality of the Son. Most Restorationists today would accept the typical evangelical assessment that the Son is eternal, where, as seen in Chapter Two, Campbell did not.

[6] Carter, "The Trinity in the Stone-Campbell Movement," 278–82.

[7] See Carter, "Trinity," 284–91.

[8] This christocentricity appeared in the 1980s and 1990s in the writings of Leonard Allen, Max Lucado, Thomas Olbricht, Rubel Shelly, and many others, and it was also evident in the lectureship programs held on the campuses of the various universities and colleges of the CCa, most importantly the Pepperdine Bible Lectures from 1983 through the present. This Christocentric movement constitutes a paradigm shift in the ethos of

the CCa, and the focus of this work is to some extent an affirmation and outgrowth of that paradigm shift. In line with the anecdotal, contextual description delineated above, I witnessed this paradigm shift firsthand, attending the Pepperdine Bible Lectures twenty-three times between 1982 and the present, and hearing numerous leaders in CCa extol the benefits of a Christocentric view. I also heard at Abilene Christian University at the end of the 1970s and at the beginning of the 1980s the lectures of Thomas Olbricht, which included a strong christological emphasis, derived partly from his reading of Barth. I discovered in a private conversation with Dr. Olbricht in the early 1990s that his studies had taken him evermore in the direction of a Trinitarian emphasis, even beyond the christocentricity I had learned from him as a student. Olbricht's direction coincided with my own interests, and it all seemed a natural progression that fit perfectly with where many in CCa were headed at the time. This emphasis and movement is certainly still bearing fruit in this portion of the S-CM.

[9] Foster also discusses the orthodox Trinitarian position of Walter Scott, which is not included in this book largely because Scott gives little attention to the classical issues of Trinitarian theology. He simply assumes an orthodox Trinitarian view and applies it to practical theology. Foster's comments are valuable in that they clarify Scott's allegiance to an orthodox position that fits with the general S-CM direction. For Scott, Christ is fully divine. See Foster, "Christology in the Stone-Campbell Movement," 12–16.

[10] Ibid., 16.

[11] Ibid., 22. Foster mentions George P. Estes, "The Deity/Humanity Controversy," 258–59; and Gene Frost, "Jesus: Fully God or Fully Human?," 166–71.

[12] See W. T. Moore, "Charles Louis Loos, 445–46.

[13] Loos's orthodox Trinitarian position is expressed in his article, "Christ—His Two-Fold Nature," 133–34.

[14] Ibid., 16–17. See W. K. Pendleton, "The History of the Doctrine of Christology," 95.

[15] Foster, "Christology in the Stone-Campbell Movement," 19–20.

[16] Ibid., 21–22.

[17] Hicks, "Christological Reflections," 1.

[18] Ibid., 3.

[19] Ibid., 4.

[20] As examples, Hicks cites Loos, Pendleton, Franklin, and L. L. Pinkerton, 2–3.

[21] Ibid., 2–4. Fred Blakely is definitely an exception here, as Hicks points out that Blakely specifically mentions the Council of Nicea in his *The Apostle's Doctrine*, accepts its conclusions, and takes a position quite in line with traditional Trinitarian doctrine.

[22] Ibid., 1.

[23] Ron Highfield, "Does the Doctrine of the Trinity Make a Difference?," 15–26.

[24] Ibid., 25.

[25] J. J. Turner and Edward P. Myers, *Doctrine of the Godhead*. Also see the second edition, from 1985, which includes only minor corrections of spelling and format, with the content remaining the same.

[26] See Roy H. Lanier, *The Timeless Trinity for the Ceaseless Centuries*, 254.

[27] Ibid., 14.

[28] Ibid., 24.

[29] Ibid., 38.

[30] Ibid., 54; cf. ibid., 45.

[31] Ibid., 54; cf. ibid., 45–54. Lanier treats at length the subject of there being separate, distinct Persons within God, stating emphatically that the Father and Son must be viewed as separate persons. He is so emphatic that one must wonder what source of Sabellianism or modalism Lanier is so intent on refuting.

[32] Ibid., 54–55.
[33] Ibid., 56–58.
[34] Ibid., 166.
[35] Ibid., 171.
[36] Ibid., 178.
[37] Ibid., 179.
[38] Ibid., 180–81.
[39] Ibid., 190.
[40] Lonzo Pribble, *Theology Simplified: God, His Son, and His Spirit*.
[41] Ibid., 17–18.
[42] Ibid., 18.
[43] Ibid., 13, 15.
[44] Ibid., i.
[45] Ibid., ii.
[46] Ibid., 198ff.
[47] Ibid., 185–86.
[48] Jack Cottrell, *What the Bible Says About God the Creator*; *What the Bible Says About God the Ruler*; *What the Bible Says About God the Redeemer*.
[49] Jack Cottrell, *Power From on High: What the Bible Says About the Holy Spirit*; *Set Free: What the Bible Says About Grace*.
[50] Ibid, 167–69.
[51] Ibid., 118. He discusses some of the contemporary debate concerning the immanent and economic Trinity, noting Barth, Rahner, and Bernard Lonergan as three writers who speak to the issue. Because he wrote *What the Bible Says About God the Redeemer* in 1987, his work does not mention writers such as Catherine LaCugna or Paul Molner, but Cottrell's work is a welcome advance beyond most others from the ICC/CC and CCa in that he addresses contemporary Trinitarian issues, at least in an introductory manner. For his discussion on the economic Trinity and what he calls the ontological Trinity see 159–67.
[52] Ibid., 158–59.
[53] C. Leonard Allen and Danny Swick, *Participating in God's Life: Two Crossroads for Churches of Christ*.
[54] Ibid., 138.
[55] Ibid., 147.
[56] Ibid., 150.
[57] Ibid., 151ff.
[58] Ibid., 156.
[59] Ibid., 159.

6

The Need for Reassessing Stone-Campbell Trinitarian Perspectives

In Chapter One, I briefly mentioned my hope that this book could offer constructive suggestions for how an overtly delineated Trinitarianism could benefit SCM churches and its theologies. A significant place for Trinitarian doctrine could offer widespread and abundant theological, ecclesiological, missional, soteriological, pneumatological value, and enhance the effectiveness of SC churches as they work in and for the Kingdom of God.

The simple fact is that further *restoration* is needed. Growth is in order. Theological development and maturation in certain areas—preeminently Trinitarian theology—would greatly assist the SC cause. Theological inadequacies must be addressed if SC churches are to move forward in their desire to assist with establishing God's kingdom in the present world. This chapter will examine the needs that may be met by giving Trinitarianism not only a more significant place in SC theology, but also the premier place.[1]

Trinity as Theological and Hermeneutical Starting Point

Historically, the starting points—the theological presuppositions—most directly impacting the SCM have been those centered on the need for obedience to God's expectations regarding the beliefs and practices of the church in response to the propositionally revealed Word of God, namely, Scripture. Scripture as apostolic, propositional, plenary truth, in combination with empirical induction and logic as *the* means of interpreting and applying biblical "facts," has provided the hermeneutical context in which the church is to obediently conform to God's will and bear witness to God. When SC churches inductively search Scripture for biblical commands and apostolic examples, their efforts are grounded in the perception that the essence of the church's identity and mission lies in efforts to obediently conform to propositionally revealed divine expectations, as seen first in the early church's obedience to the instructions and examples offered by the apostles and, therefore, by Christ and the Holy Spirit. This hermeneutical context makes unity in the church possible as all Christians reach a common understanding concerning the biblically revealed priorities and practices that should characterize God's people as they seek obedience to God. These central tenets have constituted the theological and hermeneutical nexus for those in the SCM, especially those in the ICC/CC and CCa.

However, focusing on obedience to God's *expectations* as conveyed through Scripture, is not the same as focusing on God's *nature, attributes,* and *actions*, allowing God, himself, to be the dominant hermeneutical influence on the church's identity and mission. To focus on Scripture as propositionally revealed truth is not equivalent to making the living, dynamic, Trinitarian Word of God the core revelatory construct. To inductively search for biblical facts and to interpret them using the most consistent logic possible is not to hermeneutically apply Trinity as *the* presupposition that must govern the interaction between Scripture and the church. To focus on the possibility of ecclesiastical unity reachable through a common understanding and practicing of what God expects is not the same as allowing the epitome of communal cohesiveness exemplified in the Trinity to create a relational longing for unity within the church. Taking a clue from Karl Barth, the thesis of this book is that properly prioritizing the Trinity—which for Barth is most directly and significantly experienced as the Word of God—can provide the SCM with an orientation capable of significantly altering their theology and praxis in a way more consistent with God's revelation of himself than what they have historically experienced.

Several prominent theologians, most notably Barth, have in the last hundred years accepted Trinitarian theology as the starting point for their theological projects. In fact, for Barth, a Trinitarian perspective with special emphasis given to the Word of God as the revelation of God to humankind serves as *the* theological prolegomena. Instead of beginning with a prolonged epistemological explication of theological method, hermeneutics, and the role Scripture is to play in theology, Barth essentially begins with the Word of God as the crucial *Trinitarian* theological premise. Theology properly initiated will begin with the Trinitarian God manifested through his Word as the central revelatory reality. Theology, including the Word preached, the Word found in Scripture, and, preeminently, the Word as revelation of God must be controlled by more than just a Trinitarian theological perspective that stands as background to our understanding. Instead, the actual Trinity, and not just Trinitarian theology, must be the governing force and influence impacting all of reality, so that the actions and revelations of the Trinitarian Word sustain and hold together all things, and all theological, philosophical, historical, ethical, social, and scientific perspectives must be evaluated against it. The Trinity should serve as the primary presupposition in a Christian worldview. In addition, only a Trinitarian beginning can properly shape and fulfill the praxis of the churches living out the revelatory impact of their Trinitarian Lord on the world.

There is, of course, a sense in which the epistemological option exercised by Barth was unavailable to the Campbells, Barton Stone, and Walter Scott. Although during their lifetimes significant challenges to the precritical perspective were being made, especially in Germany, initiators of the SCM were little affected by these challenges, and their epistemological orientation placed the propositional revelation of the written Scriptures at the center of their perspectives concerning God's revelation of himself. This separates them from the role the Word of God plays for Barth, wherein God in any present moment of revelation speaks through Jesus Christ himself, offering the divine creation of light to those who hear.[2] Surprisingly, though, there is some semblance of correspondence between Barth's views and the Scripture-centered epistemology and theological orientation of early Restorationists. Barth, himself, says:

> Basically, the theme of dogmatic prolegomena as understood in this sense is obviously none other than that which the older Protestant theology, in its resistance to Roman Catholicism and then to incipient Modernism, treated under the title *De scriptura sacra*. We shall see that the cardinal statement of the doctrine of the Word of God which we shall try to develop in what follows is indeed materially the same as the assertion of the authority and normativeness of Holy Scripture as the witness to divine revelation and the presupposition of Church proclamation.[3]

Correspondence is seen between Restorationists and Barth with respect to God's revelation of himself as the core constituent in God's relationship to humankind. For Barth, Word of God—which includes but transcends the written witness of Scripture—is *the* authoritative witness to God's revelation of himself; Word of God is itself God's Trinitarian revelation that enlightens, informs, transforms, and governs the lives of those responding to the Word. For early Restorationists, the written witness of Scripture is *the* revelation of God available to humankind and serving as the revelatory Word of God that enlightens, informs, transforms, and governs the lives of those responding to the Word.

This correspondence in viewing God's revelation of himself through the Word as the center of the church's life is what should allow Restorationists to hear Barth and others who view Trinitarian revelation as the central narrative through which God shares himself with humankind. There is a need for those in the SC heritage to move beyond the early post-Enlightenment, Lockean presuppositions that prioritized the inductive interpretation of propositionally revealed Scriptural facts as (1) *the* means of experiencing God's revelation of himself; and (2) the source of instruction for obediently conforming to God's expectations for the church, and to move toward *Trinitarian theology as the crucial presupposition and hermeneutical criterion.* The church's theology, its application of Scripture, and its life as God's community must be Trinitarianly governed. In adopting such a perspective as *first theology*, SC churches could position themselves to live ecclesiastically under the influence of that which is biblically and theologically central.

Achieving Theological Clarity, Coherence, and Completeness Through a Trinitarian Emphasis

As was specifically seen in the preceding material detailing the history of Trinitarian thought among SC churches, no clearly articulated, generally accepted description of Trinitarian thinking can be said to represent the SC Trinitarian perspective. This, of course, leaves a void at a place where many within the Christian tradition have been compelled to expend great theological energy. What is needed in the SCM is a consideration of the nature and character of our Trinitarian God at a more profound and better delineated level than what SC theology has typically provided, allowing for more clarity, coherence, and completeness within SCM theology.

Interestingly, this lack of a duly considered, clearly articulated Trinitarian perspective is in contrast to what may be seen among many Restorationists with respect to some of the other doctrines of Christianity. While there is no historically accepted creedal position or official dogma that defines Restorationist belief, perspectives on several Christian doctrines have come to be commonly accepted and practiced, commonly explicated and taught, commonly scripturally defended and handed down from one generation to the next, becoming identifiable as that body of doctrine that stipulates what it means to be Restorationist or which is representative of the SC ethos. So, while the SCM has never participated in the fields of systematic theology or dogmatics at the same level as many other Christian fellowships, there is precedent among Restorationists for clearly establishing beliefs and distinct doctrinal perspectives.

For example, the two more conservative branches of Restorationists (ICC/CC and CCa) typically hold a common view on the sacraments (baptism by immersion for the remission of sins; weekly partaking of the Lord's Supper); on ecclesiastical polity (a plurality of elders in each autonomous congregation); on referring to individual bodies of believers ("Church of Christ" or "Christian Church"), on a noncharismatic style of daily Christian living, and of Scripture (inerrant, infallible, and plenary). ICC/CC and CCa are generally Arminian in their soteriology and amillenial in their eschatology. Additionally, for those in the most theologically conservative *a cappella* branch of the SCM, one can readily point to a commonly held list of practices to be included in corporate worship (prayer, preaching, praise through instrumentally unaccompanied song, financial support of the church's efforts, and the weekly celebration of the Lord's Supper) and to a generally held pattern describing the steps of conversion.[4]

Obviously, Restorationists have felt it important to solidify and set forth their commonly held positions on a significant number of doctrinal matters, and they have taken great pains to do so. Throughout their history, the practical realities of Christian life, especially in North America from about 1805 to 1960, pushed them to closely examine the Bible and to develop doctrinal positions and ecclesiastical practices that in their view served the dual needs of (1) providing a primitive, pristine original form of Christianity free from the distortions that accrued throughout the history of the church; and (2) offering to all believers a practical means of Christian unity. Unity, it was proposed, could occur as long as all simply subscribed to the primitive, pristine original form of the church discernible in the pages of the New Testament. Although Restorationists were convinced that confusion, lack of clarity, and disunity would result from formulating and accepting a particular form of *extrapolated, speculative* Trinitarian belief, they were convinced that there was great clarity on other biblical doctrines and that believers from outside the RM could easily see the clear and compelling evidence in the New Testament for those doctrinal positions. They were, then, motivated to give considerable attention to these doctrinal matters and to ask others to join them in becoming one unified body espousing their re-discovered, primitive form of the faith.

Of course, many have failed to see the clarity that Restorationists have claimed to find in the New Testament's depiction of the church's beliefs and practices. Even among Restorationists themselves, there has been abundant confusion, disagreement, and disunity on doctrinal matters that would seem to lie much further from the core of Christian belief than the nature of God, his Son and his Spirit. It is, therefore, ironic that even as Restorationists attempted to avert problems they saw inherent in attempts to delineate *Trinitarian* doctrine, they were embroiled in the same kinds of problems surrounding other doctrinal issues. Therefore, it is not just the case that their doctrinal history legitimizes the practice of summarizing what has become dogma for SC churches. It is not just the case that, despite their noncreedal stance, there *is* precedent within SC churches for a position to be reached on any number of doctrinal issues, making room for discussion of another significant doctrinal matter—the doctrine of the Trinity. Additionally, if Restorationists now "riskily" participate in clarifying discussions about the Trinity, even the worst-case scenario will not put them into a more confusing, divisive position than where they have previously been!

The opinion expressed throughout this book is that a widespread, indepth consideration of the Trinity is precisely what is needed to help move SC churches toward a more complete, more impactful theological position. Whatever other difficulties there may be in the Restorationist attempt to ground Christian unity in biblical primitivism, at least one large lacuna exists within SCM theology, and the centrality of a Trinitarian perspective in both the biblical revelation and the history of Christian thought warrants Restorationists working to fill this void with well considered, biblically grounded, clearly presented thoughts on the Trinity.

Essentially, a damaging theological choice was made early on among those propagating the Restorationist perspective. When the progenitors of the SCM refused to engage in constructive Trinitarian theology, they avoided developing an identifiable position on what has typically been presented in historical theology as *the* crucial Christian doctrine. Even those who over the centuries argued against what became the traditionally orthodox Trinitarian position recognized the centrality of Trinitarian doctrine. Currently, when systematic theologies are written, the doctrine of the Trinity often forms the foundation on which everything else is grounded.[5] Even when theologians for a time reduce their attention to Trinitarian doctrine, this theologically vital subject consistently returns to the forefront of dogmatic and systematic theology.[6]

Restorationists may not feel compelled to develop a clarified Trinitarian position or to exert great amounts of effort considering the doctrine of the Trinity simply because this has been the focus of so many throughout Christian history. However, the amount of attention given the Trinity within the Christian tradition indicates that Restorationists should at least ask if perhaps they have missed something centrally important by largely avoiding the subject. The early Restorationist caution about how Trinitarian discussions may instigate divisions within the faith is substantially justified as history has proved this to be the case. However, the risk is justified because of the crucial place of the Trinity within Christian thought and the theological centering SC churches may gain by giving Trinitarian doctrine its due. Virtually every area of Christian theological and ecclesiastical thought and practice has been greatly impacted when theologians and ecclesiasts employ serious reflection upon the Trinity. And, incontrovertibly, were SC churches seriously to consider the doctrine of the Trinity, they would find *their* system of belief and *their* praxis positively altered by Trinitarian reflection. Early Restorationists made a flawed choice when they relegated Trinitarian doctrine to a place of insignificance; we are justified in correcting that choice.

Trinitarian Discussion as a Point of Theological Engagement

The academic, scholarly influence of the SCM on the wider theological community has been somewhat limited, with Restorationist scholars excelling in biblical studies, patristics/early church, and ecumenism. This is not by accident but is the unavoidable result of the Movement being from the outset predisposed to viewing with suspicion the area of study typically associated with systematic theology. "Theology" and "theologians," even today, are terms that precipitate sidewise glances and disparaging remarks among some Restorationists about those who are more interested in humanly originated speculation than in the divinely revealed truths of Scripture.

It is hoped, then, that this book will help bring Restorationists more into the theological conversation, giving SC theological perspectives a voice in places where there has previously been silence and allowing Restorationists to interact with and be influenced by the voices of others. It has been a departure from the norm when those with a SC heritage have published something in one of the classical areas of systematic theology. Up until about 1980, it was extremely rare for conservative members of the SCM to intentionally allow the discipline of systematic theology and the accruements of theologians to play a significant role in SC churches. Even when Calvin or Luther or Hodge has been examined, the purpose typically has been to cite the places where such theologians and systematicians deviate from what Restorationists have taken to be the biblical norm.

What better place to help alter this pattern of theological reticence than with Trinitarian theology? The doctrine of the Trinity—essentially the doctrine of God—lies closest to the center of biblical revelation and is most needed for establishing the character and ministry of the Christian church. The doctrine of the Trinity can take those interested to the heights of theological discourse and discussion, and it can offer directly practical applications of theology to praxis. Trinitarian doctrine, then, is an appropriate choice as the place where the SCM can expand its engagement with systematic theology and the theological community.

The Need for Coherence with the Apostolic Tradition

As previously noted, the SCM from the beginning has been interested in what for them has become practically a separate category of historical theology, that of biblical primitivism. Biblical primitivism refers both to the effort to establish first-century (biblical) church belief and practice—the biblically presented primitive faith—and to efforts to emulate this practice in the contemporary church. Additionally, in keeping with a primitivistic preference for that which is earliest, Restorationists have been keenly interested in the very earliest *post-biblical* period of Christian historical theology and have paid abundant attention to the second through fourth centuries.

Unfortunately, three elements of Restorationism have compromised the value to SC Trinitarianism of this focus on earliest Christianity. First, while some SC historical theologians have referenced Trinitarian doctrine among writers of the second through fourth centuries, early Trinitarian doctrine generally has been a peripheral issue for them.[7] Second, because of the anticreedal Restorationist stance, interest in the fourth-century Trinitarian debates has been minimal compared to that shown by scholars and theologians concerned with the formulation of the earliest ecumenical creeds. Third, Restorationists' primitivistic concerns have typically delimited them from attending to the theology of subsequent centuries, so any interest in the development of Trinitarian doctrine would end prior to A.D. 450.

In fact, the primitivistic emphasis in the SCM has typically been linked to a denigrating portrayal of theology subsequent to the first century. As Restorationists undertake historical theology, their antipathy grows and their interest wanes as they chronologically advance past biblical teaching to postbiblical theologians. This is certainly the case as incipient Catholicism becomes full-blown Roman Catholicism after the fifth century. As is often seen in the writings of the Reformation and post-Reformation, early SCM writings vilify what became the Roman Catholic system of theological tradition. Biblical primitivism was viewed as the exclusive source for church doctrine, and the value of the developing apostolic tradition (even that of the second century) was effectively repudiated and relegated either to a role verifying what is found in the Bible or as antithesis to biblical doctrine. In the latter case, the developing apostolic tradition, especially after the second century, became the foil for Restorationist distillations of the biblical picture of the church and its teaching.

A considerable amount of what became the postapostolic tradition, including the notion of the rule of faith, was devoted to Trinitarian discussion and the doctrines of God and Christ. Yet, because Restorationists have relegated both Trinitarian theology and postapostolic tradition to places of relative insignificance, something vital has been missed: the SCM has been little influenced by what God was working through the presence of his Spirit in the postapostolic tradition of the developing church.

Perhaps the repudiation of the postapostolic tradition could be partially overcome if a general interest in Trinitarian doctrine were to coincide with a focus by SC historical theologians on Trinitarian theology during the first 400 years after the biblical era. An examination of the earliest forms of Trinitarianism within the primitive church would coincide with and support the basic primitivistic orientation that comprises the ethos of the SCM. Then a birth of interest in Trinitarianism during the first five centuries, as one aspect of a more general Trinitarian focus, could serendipitously allow for synergy between the SCM and the postapostolic tradition. I believe this renewed interest and focus would be valuable to the SCM, fostering not only an *appreciation* for the postapostolic tradition, but creating actual *coherence* between the postapostolic tradition and SC theology.[8]

The Need for Coherence with Biblical Orthodoxy

Chapters Two and Three examined in detail the perspectives on Trinitarian doctrine held by three of the four most influential early Restorationists. It was demonstrated that although Thomas and Alexander Campbell held essentially orthodox Trinitarian views, they tended to avoid giving the Trinity a place of significance in their writings because they felt the doctrine of the Trinity was largely divisive, specifically because there was insufficiently clear biblical teaching about the nuances of Trinitarian belief. Thus, the Disciples' side of the SCM grew to be orthodox Trinitarian, in an unarticulated, undisclosed, almost clandestine way, with little attention given to grounding Trinitarian doctrine in biblical revelation.

As detailed in Chapter Three, Barton Stone was influenced by the development of a widespread non-Trinitarianism and at one point believed the biblical perspective actually pointed away from classical Trinitarianism toward a quasi-Arian position. Later, following communication with Alexander Campbell in the course of bringing their two movements together, Stone chose for the sake of unity to no longer voice strong opinions about the Trinity.

I believe the Campbells and Stone were in error in: (1) concluding that Trinitarian positions must be unacceptably speculative because the *biblical* teaching about the Trinity is insufficiently clear; (2) concluding that discussions about the *biblical* defensibility of Trinitarian doctrine must always end in ecclesiastical disunity; (3) disallowing a place in Restorationist doctrine for a *biblically* grounded Trinitarianism; (4) missing or ignoring the *biblical* centrality of the doctrine of the Trinity; and (5) failing to see the positive ramifications for the church that could be found in a clearly developed, *biblically* grounded doctrine of the Trinity. I also contend that Barton Stone erred in defending a quasi-Arian Trinitarian perspective, that the classically orthodox Trinitarian view espoused in the Nicean Creed of AD 325 and the Constantinoplian Creed of AD 380–381, while not using specifically biblical language or finding direct support in Scripture, nonetheless better summarizes and explicates the biblical position.

My argument is simply that an overtly stated, biblically grounded, orthodox Trinitarianism would better align those of the SCM with what the Bible reveals about God. A biblically coherent, biblically presented Trinitarian position would allow SC churches to be in line not just with traditional Christianity but also with what the Bible points to as what should be the Christian view of the relationship between Father, Son, and Spirit.

This, of course, raises the question of what constitutes a legitimate biblical grounding of Trinitarian doctrine. Historically, the SCM's biblicism properly places them within fundamentalism. Their traditional way of construing and interpreting Scripture, their maintenance of traditional doctrinal positions in the face of historical criticism, and their fervent desire to find direct biblical justification for all doctrinal decisions and ecclesiastical practices secures their position among the most theologically conservative groups of Christians. This is not to say that the SCM is monolithic, but there is among Restorationists a general style of doing theology, of living ecclesiastically, and of construing, interpreting, and applying the Bible, especially in the ICC/CC and CCa.[9] Therefore, *any argument for theological change among them must be biblically grounded if there is to be any chance that such a change will be accepted.*

The task of reorienting those in SC churches toward an overtly Trinitarian theological perspective is made easier by the incipient, unarticulated Trinitarian tendencies present among them, as described in Chapter Five. However, it is crucial that a directly biblical foundation for a Trinitarian perspective be presented if what is incipient is to ever come to full fruition. The objectives of SC churches include the idea that a primitive, biblical way of being Christian always needs to be restored within the contemporary church. Therefore, if it can be shown that the Bible includes the Trinity as a central element in its revelation of God's interaction with humankind, Restorationists should consider themselves remiss if they avoid giving substantial attention to Trinitarian doctrine. Although a demonstration of *biblical justification* for giving a central place in Restorationist thought to the doctrine of the Trinity lies beyond the scope of the current project, it should be part of the process of developing SC Trinitarian theology, of which more will be said in Chapter 7.

The Role of Trinitarian Doctrine in Establishing Ecclesiastical Identity

Even before the 1906 U.S. Census recognized that the SCM had essentially split into two factions, the identity of the Movement's churches was quite clearly established. Restorationists were those historically linked to the Disciples of Christ of Thomas Campbell, Alexander Campbell, and Walter

Scott, and to the Christians of Barton W. Stone. They followed the originators of the Movement in turning to the Bible as their exclusive source for faith and practice, rejected the legitimacy of denominational divisions within Christianity, called for unity on the basis of what has become known as biblical primitivism, and rejected the formulated statements of belief represented by historical creeds. In addition, Restorationists consistently inculcated a rather fixed set of distinctive doctrines that had been established by applying to the Bible a hermeneutical method directly linked to the Baconian/Lockean logic and empiricism that was so prevalent prior to the onset of postmodernism. This trend toward distinctive doctrines continued, particularly in the CCa after 1906. Although there eventually developed several additional separations, especially within CCa, the majority of those in ICC/CC and CCa prior to the 1970s held a clear perspective about their respective fellowships.

However, like many Christian denominations, SC churches at the beginning of the twenty-first century have faced a partially debilitating loss of identity, especially in the CCa. As the modernism in the second half of the twentieth century began to give way to generally postmodern perspectives, Baby Boomers and those coming after them in CCa found it increasingly difficult to continue down the theological/ecclesiastical path established by their predecessors. The soundness of the modernistic logic used to establish doctrinal positions was routinely challenged, with many wanting to completely depart from what had been the hermeneutical norms for conservative Restorationists. The priorities of logical consistency, rational clarity, and directly grounding doctrinal positions in the propositionally revealed indicatives and imperatives of the Bible began to give way to a less-stratified and codified spirituality centered on the emotive and the intuitive that stressed less the need for doctrinal accuracy and more the need for relationships, community, and authenticity. For many, polemics and debating have been superseded by an ecumenically oriented acceptance of those with doctrinal positions that vary from SC perspectives.

Additionally, among the CCa there has been widespread alteration (1) in the level of significance given to doctrinal fidelity as many view doctrinal correctness as less important; (2) in the importance of several of the specific doctrines traditionally defended by CCa with some doctrinal positions previously viewed as vital now viewed as optional or even as having been repudiated; and (3) in the specific content of some doctrinal positions, with some aspects of the specific doctrines maintained by CCa now being conceived differently than they were even thirty or forty years ago.

The ramifications of these changes for SC churches are monumental. Many of the specifics that previously identified the churches of the Movement no longer apply. As was mentioned in Chapter One, even the way Restorationists may think of their formative intellectual history has been radically altered. Whereas some in the Movement have embraced, endorsed, and actively promoted these changes, others have rejected them as nothing less than the demise of Christianity.

Thus, Restorationists, especially those in the CCa, can be quite baffled with respect to their identity as a distinct fellowship of believers. What do they stand for? What do they believe? What should be their practices? How are they as a fellowship distinct from others? They do continue to exist as a distinct fellowship, but should they? Previously there was a certain intractability that characterized CCa; now, in many cases, there is ambivalence and timidity, even a loss of purpose and direction. What happens when a Movement that has viewed one of its primary purposes to be the conversion of doctrinally confused believers finds itself confused, with no distinct perspective? What then?

This book advocates the assertion of Trinitarian doctrine as a foundational premise on which ecclesiastical identity may again be achieved for those in the SCM, especially for CCa. Far from being the unbiblical, humanly originated doctrinal accretion that some early Restorationists took Trinitarian doctrine to be; far from being an intangible, impractical set of highly speculative assertions; far from being just a substantial obstacle to Christian unity, overtly stated Trinitarian doctrine may serve as a foundational pillar for SC identity. To use language well known in CCa, Trinitarian doctrine should become one of the (if not *the*) *identifying marks of the church*. Were this to be the case, SC churches could find their identities grounded at the center of biblical theology, with the possibility that other identifying features of their life and ministry could cluster around and be derived from this theologically central pillar.

The Trinity as Antidote to a Fracturing Ecclesiology

Seriously considering the nature of the Trinity could actually take SC churches closer to achieving their original goal of creating Christian unity than what they attempted through the establishment of primitive Christian faith and practice. Although early in the Movement's history large numbers of Christians did unite upon the principles of biblical primitivism, the ferment of Restorationism after the U.S. Civil War, particularly in the twentieth century, was largely disastrous with reference to Christian unity. Although the Disciples of Christ played a role in the ecumenical movement that arose in the first half of the twentieth century and culminated in the World Council of Churches, the SCM of the last century was characterized by division far more often than by unity.

With respect to the RM as a whole, the April 1865 edition of *Lard's Quarterly* listed as sources of controversy: (1) the assumption of pastoral power by preachers, (2) the use of musical accompaniment in worship, (3) the tendency toward philosophical speculation, and (4) the issue of open communion.[10] To these were soon added discussions about "the pastorate," the use of ministerial titles, the presence of choirs in worship, the propriety of missionary societies, re-baptism for those coming from other fellowships, and the presence of Christians within other fellowships. Of these issues, the one that eventually caused the greatest separation was the incorporation of musical accompaniment into public worship, and this division, officially recognized in 1906, saw the CCa separated from the Disciples of Christ.

The later division that separated the Disciples of Christ from the ICC/CC is not as easily attributed to one issue. Edwin Hayden lists four causes for the split: (1) federation in interdenominational activities; (2) the acceptance of higher criticism applied to the Bible, beginning in the last decade of the nineteenth century; (3) controversy over open membership; and (4) the limitation of missionary fields and activities through comity agreements.[11] Of these, Leroy Garrett cites "federation" as the principal cause of the division, with some wishing to cooperate with other denominations despite differing views on baptism; the Disciples desired unity so strongly that they felt sacramental agreement was unnecessary.[12] However, the rancor caused by the introduction of theological liberalism, especially the association of the Disciples with higher criticism as it appeared at the University of Chicago in the early twentieth century, must be viewed as equally significant in bringing about the split. Those in what became the ICC/CC consistently upheld the inerrancy of Scripture and continued to defend miracles, the virgin birth, and the bodily resurrection of Christ. Those among the Disciples were open to the results of biblical and historical criticism. The refusal of the two sides to compromise on what they perceived to be crucial to their self-understandings led to a division that was clearly evident by 1950, after brewing throughout much of the first half of the century.

In addition to the two major splits within this Movement that had insisted Christian unity was its major reason for existence, divisions continued to multiply within each of three separate fellowships, most abundantly within CCa. Because there is no denominational structure, organizational constitution, bylaws, or hierarchy, it is difficult to know exactly when a division has occurred between different segments of the RM. Anecdotal evidence shows CCa congregations commonly cease to have fellowship with one another on the basis of many different issues, including the use of musical accompaniment in worship. They have separated over whether multiple cups may be used during the Lord's Supper because biblical primitivism suggests only one cup was used at the original institution of the Supper. They have separated over whether congregations may cooperate with one another's ministries by pooling financial resources under the oversight of a single congregation. Other issues causing congregations to limit or cease fellowship with others in the SCM include located ministers, kitchens in church buildings, Sunday School ministries, support for church schools and colleges, women serving as deacons or elders, the subject of marriage and divorce, and methods used in evangelism and discipleship. For the most part, this fracturing has been minor, so that there has always been a "mainline" Church of Christ (a cappella), but in other cases, such as the cooperation controversy of the 1950s, major sections of CCa have separated.

What seems clear is that the fracturing of the SCM has occurred because of both the inconsistent application of biblical primitivism and the constant challenge of living out a primitive faith whose original beliefs and practices are considered perpetually paradigmatic, in a world that has not remained the same as it was in the first century. The effort which began with the question, "How do we for the sake of unity restore the original and essential faith and practice of the church?" has been constantly challenged by the question of "How can we appropriately incorporate into the life of the church the alterations in thought and practice which the church will inevitably face in a world that constantly changes?" The result has been frequent tension and division over the answers given to those two questions.

This book proposes, as an alternative to the kind of biblical primitivism applied in the SCM, that a reconsideration of the Trinity be used as a theological starting point for ecclesiastical unity. Instead of grounding ecclesiastical unity in uniformity or agreement upon a list of essentials, Christian unity may be experienced in light of a consideration of the nature of the Trinity. Thus, unity—and essentially an entirely new ecclesiology—may be theologically constructed and nuanced in light of Trinitarian theology.

The Trinity as Soteriological Corrective

There are those who stand removed, critically observing from a distance the SCM's soteriology, and those from the inside who criticize the Movement's approach to reconciliation, atonement, and forgiveness. There are lingering doubts from within, and open denigration from without, concerning SC soteriology, despite the consistent claim by Restorationists that their soteriology is free of legalism and that they, although firmly Arminian, are no closer to Pelagianism than are any of the other denominational fellowships deriving from the Reformation. The crux pertains to the SC perspective on baptism and to the necessity—according to some in the CCa—of obediently emulating the "five steps of salvation" and the ecclesiological patterns they see in the New Testament.

Baptism is essentially sacramental for Restorationists, so that it is certainly not only an "outward sign of an inward grace" but is soteriologically efficacious. To be baptized puts the believer in touch with the sanctifying blood of Christ in a way that most Protestants believe is the provenance of faith alone. Many, therefore, perceive that Restorationists think of baptism as a *meritorious work,* and even some Restorationists have taken this to be their own Movement's position. I take this to be an incorrect evaluation of the SC view of baptism and its relation to salvation. For Restorationists, at their best, baptism is no more a work leading to salvation than is faith itself. Both come as responses to the grace of God shown in Christ and function *at much the same level*, a fact that it seems hard for many critics to grasp, given their aversion to works righteousness. For Restorationists baptism is *inherent in* faith, not a separate action *in addition to* faith. Thus, in my view it is incorrect for either those within or outside of the SCM to cite baptism as a major point of soteriological difficulty. Admittedly, the SC position on baptism has in the mouths of a certain group of preachers been legalistically and meritoriously developed, but I take this to be an aberration, not the standard SC position. If SC baptism is a major area of soteriological concern for others, it is because they have incorrectly construed the SC perspective on baptism, not because of the way the doctrine typically has been espoused by those in the SCM.

Almost from the beginning, the SCM has placed significance not on baptism alone, but on baptism as part of the "five steps of salvation," especially as formulated and taught by Walter Scott. It was apparently Scott who first introduced Thomas and Alexander Campbell to the notion that by orienting their Movement in the direction of biblical primitivism they had restored *the* biblical formula for Christian conversion.[13] The formula Scott first preached was originally "believe, repent, be baptized, receive remission of sins, and receive the gift of the Holy Spirit." The five-fingered exercise eventually was altered to either "hear, believe, repent, confess, and be baptized" or "believe, repent, confess, be baptized, and go on to live a new life." In all three formulas, although baptism was the "step" that received the most attention from Restorationists, salvific importance was attached to the convert's participation in all five steps. While it is difficult to imagine the fullness of Christian conversion not including the hearing of the gospel, the believing of it, repentance of one's sins, confession of Christ as Lord, baptism, reception of the indwelling Holy Spirit, and the living out of the new life, the uniqueness of the Restorationist presentation consists in the soteriological import of the process *qua* process. Those coming to Christ are taught that there can be no omission of any of the five steps, otherwise one's salvation is not secured.

The biblical primitivism of the SCM has also led some—principally the CCa—to assert the necessity of adhering to a specific pattern of belief and practice discernible in the New Testament. For some, salvation is not only dependent upon the personal faith response of those who accept Christ as

Lord and Savior, but also upon whatever elements are essential to biblical ecclesiology become soteriologically crucial because salvation is only found among those belonging to the CCa. To coin a phrase, this may be referred to as *soteriological ecclesiastical patternism*. To be an adherent of a church doctrinally or practically removed from the church presented in the New Testament is to step outside the protective veil of the body of Christ. It is, therefore, vital to a believer's salvation that membership in the body of Christ be maintained by living, worshipping, and serving in a church that in a number of specific details emulates the practice of the primitive church. Preaching the biblically correct steps in the conversion process, calling each congregation by the biblically correct name, baptizing correctly, correctly participating in the Lord's Supper, participating in the correct liturgical practices in biblically correct ways—all these verify participation in the true body of Christ, assuring that one has been appropriately added to and then has continued in the *Lord's* body of the saved.[14]

Even citing the importance of the apostolic tradition, it would seem impossible to legitimately make the case that a person's salvation in Jesus depends upon exactly following a formulaic conversion process or whether the person's church family exactly replicates the characteristics of the early church. Romans 8:15-17, Romans 10:8-13, Galatians 4:4-6, Ephesians 1:3-14, Colossians 1:19-22, and other portions of the New Testament point in an entirely different direction. In each of these Scriptures, salvation and the assurance of believers about the life they share with God comes from God's Trinitarian working of salvation in the lives of Christians. The Trinitarian economy has provided spiritual adoption, redemption, reconciliation, forgiveness of sin, and a life of joy because of what we have received as God graciously extends to us salvation through Christ and new life in his Spirit. Perhaps the clearest and most prolonged single statement of God's Trinitarian salvific work is in Ephesians 1:3-3:21, where God's work of salvation is detailed in a series of statements that link together the work of Father, Son, and Spirit. The culmination of this salvific work comes in 3:14-21:

> For this reason I bow my knees before the Father, from whom every family in heaven and on earth takes its name. I pray that, according to the riches of his glory, he may grant that you may

> be strengthened in your inner being with power through his
> Spirit, and that Christ may dwell in your hearts through faith, as
> you are being rooted and grounded in love. I pray that you may
> have the power to comprehend, with all the saints, what is the
> breadth and length and height and depth, and to know the love
> of Christ that surpasses knowledge, so that you may be filled
> with all the fullness of God. Now to him who by the power at
> work within us is able to accomplish abundantly far more than
> all we can ask or imagine, to him be glory in the church and in
> Christ Jesus to all generations, forever and ever. Amen.

Like the rest of the first half of Ephesians, these verses are entirely Trinitarian, describing the salvation given through the Trinity's joint investment in humankind. They express the relational inner working, the indwelling, and the overflowing fullness present in the person who belongs not to a particular fellowship, but who lives in a particular relationship with the Trinity through the love of Christ. Quite simply, there is no mention of the need to belong to a fellowship that expresses life in Christ as a specifically patternized response extending from core theological matters to beliefs and practices that are peripheral to Christianity and the biblical witness.

A strikingly new experience of reconciliation, including the abundant life available through the Spirit, could be gained in SC churches—particularly the CCa—through an understanding of the Trinitarianly relational way of salvation provided by God's sending of His Son. For approximately forty years, a gradual turning toward this way of grace has been occurring in CCa, but progress is slow in many churches, and in some cases there has been a backlash. What is called for is a deepening understanding of Trinitarian soteriology, so that CCa may have the power to comprehend, with all the saints, what is the breadth and length and height and depth, and to know the love of Christ that surpasses knowledge, so that they may be filled with all the fullness of God. Under this influence, the formulaic series of five salvific steps and the soteriological ecclesiastical patternism that have at times greatly hindered the alignment of the church with the grace of Christ may be *theologically* superseded (but not rejected or replaced!).

The Need for Pneumatological Renewal

In Alexander Campbell's initial setting forth of the plea for restoration, found in his journal *The Christian Baptist*, 1823–1830, he included little mention of the Holy Spirit. Neither Campbell nor his early theological descendants gave the Holy Spirit a prominent place in their restorative efforts for several reasons:

1. Their reaction against what Campbell termed "enthusiasms," most prominently displayed, ironically, at the 1801 Cane Ridge Revival in which Barton Stone played a prominent role;
2. Their response to John Locke's emphasis on reason, logic and empiricism;
3. Their view of the New Testament's witness to the Holy Spirit—including their view of the Spirit's role in conversion vis à vis that of the Reformed position;
4. The way they viewed the witness of church history to the activity of the Holy Spirit.

Ignorance concerning the work of the Holy Spirit and an inadequate pneumatology have been the result. Restorationists have often either essentially ignored the Holy Spirit or, in response to the rising prominence of Pentecostalism and the charismatic movement, have intentionally avoided giving pneumatology and the person of the Holy Spirit the same level of attention that they have given the Father and Son. And, of course, no specific impetus coming from an explicit Trinitarianism has been available to move Restorationists toward developing an adequate pneumatology.

An inadequate pneumatology has negatively affected the SCM at several points, starting with the existence of few monographs—especially those pitched at an advanced level—specifically devoted to the work of the Holy Spirit in the life of the church. Restorationists have given little intensive scholarly attention to the Spirit's role within Christianity. However, the greatest negative impact of the underdeveloped pneumatology has been the insufficiency of the place given to the Spirit in the life of the church. The mission and ministry of the church have been little driven by the presence of the Holy Spirit, and the role of the Holy Spirit in conversion has been neglected. The Spirit as a source of relationship between believers and God has been inadequately nuanced, so that the church's teaching on the Holy Spirit has had little influence on personal piety, God-dependency, and even the vocabulary of Christians as they describe God's interaction and impact on their personal spiritual lives. The Spirit's role in worship has been largely ignored, so that Jesus's admonition concerning true worshipers in John 4:24 finds Restorationists giving significant attention to worshipping in "truth" but little to worshipping in "s[S]pirit." Sanctification as a characteristic of the Spirit's presence in followers of Christ has been neglected, along with the assurance and peace available to those who have received the guarantor of their inheritance in Christ.

Clearly, renewal and revitalization is called for regarding the Spirit's work in the life of the church. In addition to the need for extensive, specific delineation of a theology of the Spirit, attention given to the *Trinitarian* Holy Spirit could bring life both to the inner Spirituality of SC churches and to their praxis. Delineated and nuanced from a Trinitarian perspective, especially in connection with God's *perichoretic* presence and activity in the world, an adequate Trinitarian pneumatology would provide Restorationist churches opportunities to assist in transforming the lives of individual Christians and of society and culture in the direction of life in the Spirit. The specifics regarding renewal and transformation as aspects of an adequate Trinitarian pneumatology are beyond the scope of this book, but it is hoped that the encouragement here for giving the Trinity a proper place in SC theological and ecclesiological reflection will initiate within the Movement additional focus upon the life-giving presence in the church of the Holy Spirit of God.

Trinitarian Influence on Liturgical Practice

In addition to the "five steps of salvation," the practice of corporate worship is the place where soteriological ecclesiastical patternism has figured most prominently in Restorationist especially in CCa. It would not be an overstatement to say a kind of utilitarianism has dominated the application of biblical instruction and first-century ecclesiastical practice to the liturgical practices of the contemporary church. There is a sense, of course, in which this has served Restorationists well. Replication of first-century worship practices connected SC churches to a liturgy that was at least initially theologically—even Trinitarianly—driven. Unfortunately, with soteriologial ecclesiastical patternism, the grace-filled movement of God toward humanity that worked to create the church's liturgical responses to God quickly became a human-to-God, truly Pelagian, and, in some cases, "cheap knock-off" copy of the original, missing the depth and theological centering of the apostolic prototype. Replication, even when a desire to be obedient to divine instruction stands behind the effort, is perched ready to become sterile and perfunctory, deteriorating into a shallow formality compared to worship consistently directed not only by Trinitarian theology but also by the actual Trinitarian presence of God in the planning, preparation, and practice of a Trinitarian-centered liturgy.

When utilitarianism and the duplication of liturgical acts dominate corporate worship, preaching often becomes a shallow defense of the choices made by the church in the course of fulfilling soteriological, ecclesiastical patternism. The significance of the sacraments becomes merely their actual replication and the fact that such actions actually take place when and how they are supposed to, and their theological import and connectivity become vague notions alluded to without sufficient thoughtfulness. Singing becomes a required step in the liturgical process rather than the spontaneous pouring out of Spirit-driven gratefulness in response to the good news of God's Trinitarian grace extended in Christ. Prayer becomes an invocation and benediction, opening and closing a meeting during which a series of steps are to be conducted as part of an agendum to be accomplished.

At first glance, such an assessment of worship in some Restorationist contexts will seem harsh. After all, the faith and sincerity of congregants must be given a place in conducting worship; their attitudes as they approach the Christian assembly are decisive in actual practice, creating an environment in which the most ritualistic of acts is more than perfunctory patternism. However, without an overt recognition of the theological impetus needed to infuse the life of the Spirit and profound gratitude to God into worship, human deficiencies will tend toward the lowest common denominator, in this case taking the church toward the perfunctory.[15]

Trinitarian theology is the appropriate remedy to the effects on corporate worship of soteriological ecclesiastical patternism. When the Trinitarian acts of God in history, as given a central place by Barth or G. E.

Wright, are intentionally recounted and rehearsed in worshipful acts and attitudes, congregants are brought face to face with God's nature and character, drawing from them grace-centered gratitude and devotion. Focus on Trinitarian community as explicated by John Zizioulas can bring to corporate worship a sense of the communal identity experienced within God and which Jesus prayed would be part of the church's κοινωνία. Spirit-mediated prayer and Spirit-fostered praise, when recognized, permits entrance into a pneumatologically governed corporate experience that, when juxtaposed beside a christologically centered participation in the Eucharist, brings the worshipper into contact with the fullness of the Trinity's redeeming activities. If the goal of worship is engagement with God, then redefining, rearranging, and reorchestrating the acts of worship around Trinitarian focal points prevents God from being a distant planner of an agendum; spiritually effective contact can be experienced with the One who Trinitarianly reveals himself and has Trinitarianly acted on humankind's behalf.

Trinitarian influence on worship, then, will have tangible impact at several vital, very practical fronts:

1. A theologically based measuring stick instantly becomes available to evaluate worship. Does worship effectively bring congregants into touch with the Trinity?
2. Because the Restoration churches are part of the free church tradition, they (at least ICC/CC and CCa) typically give little or no attention to the liturgical calendar. Incorporating a Trinitarian focus into worship can provide a way of introducing the balance that is provided by following a liturgical calendar in a manner that is theologically informed, theologically driven, and more complete than soteriological, ecclesiastical patternism could ever be.
3. Trinitarian reflection can provide a theological basis on which to make God-honoring choices about worship styles, choices of songs to be sung, topics to be covered in preaching, and the legitimacy of adding creative worshipful elements.
4. If certain practices are considered essential to Christian worship, how can these be shaped to reflect Trinitarian influence, and

how can the actual list of essentials be lengthened or shortened in light of Trinitarian grace? Clearly there will be abundant value to the church in a Trinitarianly centered formulation of liturgical forms, symbols, and practices.

Trinity and Sacramental Renewal

In addition to biblical primitivism, a plea for the unity of all believers, and the *a cappella* worship of CCa, the SCM is best-known for the uniqueness of its historical perspective on baptism. In traditional SC theology, there is clear sacramental value to believers' baptism by immersion, so that others sometimes describe the view of "Campbellites" as baptismal regeneration. While this is an overstatement, it is true that baptism has possessed salvific significance for Restorationists, and it is common for those in ICC/ CC and CCa to speak of baptism as being a *necessary* component in Christian conversion. Believers' baptism by immersion for the forgiveness of sins has been for many Restorationists a precept used as a test of Christian fellowship, so that many in SC churches would consider unchristian and unsaved those who have not experienced Christian baptism by immersion for the forgiveness of sins.

While it goes beyond the bounds of this book to make a case for or against the place of baptism in SC theology, it is important to point out the value that would be gained in this significant area of church life were Restorationists to take seriously the import of Trinitarian doctrine on the church's understanding of baptism. For example, since its inception, the SCM has rightly pointed to Romans 6:3 and following verses and the identification with Christ that takes place as believers are immersed with Christ into the watery grave of baptism. But what is typically at stake for Restorationists is the physical parallel between immersion and the entombment of the physical body of Jesus. One physically goes down into the waters of baptism and is spiritually buried with Christ just as Christ was immersed into a tomb upon his physical death. One then physically and spiritually arises from the watery grave just as Christ physically arose and left the tomb. The image is fitting and soteriologically significant, but the *physical* parallel of going down in and arising out, the central point on which Restorationists have focused as they argue for baptism by immersion, hardly encompasses the full identification with Christ that the believer experiences through and because of Christian baptism. For Restorationists, too often baptism functions merely as a step in the process of soteriological ecclesiastical patternism; it is a physical action to be emulated.

To speak of baptism as possessing a symbolic, metaphorical significance quickly triggers defensiveness among Restorationists regarding the manner of baptism, so that the focus on physical parallelism prevents the development of the profound significance of the *spiritual* identification with Christ that one experiences in immersion. Trinitarian theology can speak to this identification, not only with respect to Romans 6, but by, for example, viewing the baptism of Jesus not just as an example to be followed but as entry into the fullness of the life of the Messiah, an initiation into the fullness of the Trinitarian life intended for him by his Father and sealed at his baptism by the coming of the Spirit.

In the same way, to be baptized in the name of Father, Son, and Spirit addresses the authority of the Trinity over the life of the believer; it makes a claim upon the baptized, initiating him or her into life experienced in and with the Trinity. The SCM has chiefly applied Matthew 28:18 and the following verses as depicting the necessity of the church including Trinitarian baptism as part of its evangelistic plea. Should the church include the tripartite formula in its preaching and as baptisms actually occur? Of course. But too often for Restorationists the Trinity becomes little more than part of a correctly uttered, formulaic baptismal liturgy. The *actual influence of the Trinity* on the life of the believer—and not just the influence of the *concept* of the Trinity, or the *nominal identification* as a Trinitarianly baptized Christian, or the enforcement of *obedience* to the imperative of preaching Trinitarian baptism—is richer than Restorationists can conceive when their Trinitarian conceptions are truncated because Trinitarian doctrine is absent from SC theology.

Likewise, Restorationists should allow Trinitarian theology to influence how they observe the Lord's Supper. There is frequently mentioned in the celebration of the Supper its communal aspect, with respect to both communion between God and the individual and also between Christians. However, for many, what seems to matter most is the actual taking of the meal as a fulfillment of the command to "*Do this* in remembrance of me."

At that point, communion is most significant as a completed ritual that fulfills an obligation. The order in which the Supper's events should occur, the question of leavened or unleavened bread, the character of fermented or unfermented wine, the frequency of the taking of the Supper, the number of cups used for the wine, whether prayers should be said between the passing of each emblem, whether the bread and wine are to be thought of as something more than emblems—these are the kinds of issues that have often captured the attention of Restorationists.

Missing is the depth of relationship experienced by communicants as they representationally share a meal in which Jesus declares, "This is my body" and "This is my blood." What does it mean to participate in the sharing of the body and blood, not just with Christ, but with the Trinitarian presence of God as he manifests himself in the meal and in the union he offers to his children? How are participants affected by such fellowship with God experienced through the meal? Is there sacramental efficacy in the Supper because in Christ the fullness of God is incarnationally present, both in his personhood and in the meal that he says represents his personhood? And is this level of oneness with the Trinity, experienced in the meal, paradigmatic for the type of fellowship available between believers, not just because fellowship has been modeled within the Trinity but because fellowship has been modeled in the relationship between Divine Trinity and redeemed communicant?

These are questions seldom raised among a people unused to ruminating on Trinitarian relationships and the subtleties of Christian communion influenced by Trinity. But perhaps a stirring may occur upon consideration of the Trinitarian relations and processions, making the sharing of the Lord's Supper far less ritualistic, perfunctory, and legislated than it typically is. It is an event in which genuine communion may be shared, a relational act made possible by the Trinitarian God's sharing of self with those who now enter into communion with the Trinity, through faith. Giving significant consideration to Trinitarian doctrine will only enrich and deepen the experience of God in the Lord's Supper, an event already liturgically central across the breadth of the SCM. Perhaps, "*Do this* in remembrance of me" may become a Trinitarianly influenced reflection—"Do this *in remembrance of me.*"[16]

The Potential of Trinitarian Influence on Ecclesiastical Praxis

There is a sense in which the ministry and mission of SC churches have always been Trinitarianly motivated. In typical Restorationist fashion, the mission of the contemporary church has centered on emulating the mission of the primitive church, which in turn emulated Christ. The Christ-directed mission derived from Matthew 28:18–20 or from Acts 1:8 has compelled the church to go into all the world with the good news of Christ. To minister to the unfortunate ones and preach the good news about what God has done in Christ is to participate in the Father-originated ministry and mission of the Son through the presence and power of the Holy Spirit.

And of course the biblical example of Jesus has significantly figured in the mission of the church, which exists to "seek and save that which was lost" (Luke 19:10) as Christ did. The church is called to wash one another's feet in response to the example set by Christ (John 13:14) and to love one another just as they have been loved by him (John 13:34). It is not uncommon to hear Restorationists teaching on actualizing in the church the presence of the kingdom and on the will of God being done on earth as in heaven. God sent the Son into the world not to condemn the world, but to save the world (John 3:17), so the church responds by attempting to achieve the same. Nonetheless, because of the disparagement of Trinitarian doctrine within the SCM, there has been little opportunity for the Triune God *qua* Triune to directly and overtly influence mission within SC churches.

Largely missing is the sense that the church's mission is not to be viewed as activity that has merely *originated* in God, but as the ongoing mission of unity and cooperation *with* and *in* God. Although Restoration churches have followed the example of God and Christ, there has been little direct expression of the church participating in a cooperative mission with God. The church has been *sent out* by God as Christ was, but without the mutual working *with* God in the mission that is part of the Son's *existence in* the Father's mission. The Son is sent, but the sending occurs in mutual participation with the Father, rather than as an isolated monarchical action. Further, the sending of the Son includes incarnational participation with those to whom the mission is directed, so that the church, if following after Christ and with Christ, will find itself participating both with God and with the world, even as it is sent into the world.

Additionally, Restoration churches have largely missed, as was discussed above, the cooperation with the Spirit in the mission of the kingdom of God, including the realization that the ministry of the Spirit is at the center of the ministry of the Word of God in the world. Reciprocal relations between Father, Son, *and Spirit* constitute the fullness of the communal, cooperative mission they share in redeeming humanity, but discussion of this kind of Trinitarian reciprocity is simply missing in a fellowship unfamiliar with allowing Trinitarian theology to directly and intentionally influence its praxis.

Conclusion

My view is that an overt, clearly stated, classical Trinitarianism that falls in line with the traditional ecumenical creeds will benefit the SCM more than either the Trinitarian reticence of the Movement's progenitors or the merely implicit and largely innocuous Trinitarianism of those who followed them, and I wrote this chapter to outline some of those benefits. Of course many other positive benefits of developing an overt Trinitarianism position, and its impact for the ministry of the church, could be added to those discussed here. My contention is that by adopting this kind of Trinitarian stance, Restorationists will better align themselves with biblical teaching and with the historic Christian faith, which will greatly enhance the church's efforts to glorify God in the world.

Notes

[1] Much of the material in this chapter will apply most specifically to the CCa, although much will also be applicable to the two other large branches of the SCM. All three branches characteristically share a void with reference to Trinitarian doctrine, and the current study aims to correct what amounts to a theological error across the entirety of the Movement. However, I am most familiar with the CCa and also believe it most needs theological reorientation.

[2] Karl Barth, *The Doctrine of the Word of God*, 41.

[3] Ibid., 43.

[4] Although not true to the original five-step pattern developed by Walter Scott, by the middle of the twentieth century, the conversion pattern found among the CCa was typically stated as "hear, believe, repent, confess, and be baptized."

[5] E.g., Karl Barth, Robert Jenson, Jürgen Moltmann, and Wolfhart Pannenberg all begin their systematic theologies with a volume devoted to an explication of the Trinity.

[6] It is commonly asserted that there was a great curtailment of Trinitarian theology in the nineteenth and early twentieth centuries and that Barth set this right. In some sense this may be true, but post-Schleiermacherian Protestantism was not the only theology conducted after Schleiermacher, and historical theologians are remiss if they ignore those such as Matthias Scheeben, who continued to write significant Trinitarian theology during this period. That said, the amount of Trinitarian theology presented during the last forty years has been strikingly abundant in comparison to the previous 150 years.

[7] For example, Everett Ferguson in *Early Christians Speak: Faith and Life in the First Three Centuries* devotes chapters to baptism, the Lord's Supper, worship, polity, prayer, church discipline, and acts of mercy within the early church. But he gives little attention to Trinitarian doctrine, even in a chapter on "The Faith Preached and Believed."

[8] It would be a departure from the specific direction of this book to elaborate on how the SC tradition could benefit from giving the postapostolic tradition its due. I believe repudiating the postapostolic tradition in favor of biblical primitivism has had both its advantages and disadvantages. At the very least, the Movement has suffered from not taking advantage of the potentially positive influence of the first few centuries upon the formation of SC doctrine: the maturation that comes with reflecting on the thoughts of others; the correction of one's errors and imbalances; the creativity that derives from an exposure to a broad range of thinking. More than this, the postapostolic tradition may be viewed not as an aberration from true Christianity but as the fruition of the Holy Spirit's continued watchfulness and guidance over the church. In this case, coherence with the postapostolic tradition benefits the church's effort—and may be crucial for the church's effort—to adhere to and explicate the faith once for all delivered to the saints.

[9] Conversations with ministerial and academic colleagues about whether SC churches may accurately be labeled "fundamentalist" indicate the danger of making such generalizing statements. Some of my ministerial friends reflect upon the ongoing changes in perspective evident within CCa (see Chapter One) and think it an anachronism to refer to contemporary SC churches as fundamentalist. Some of my academic friends reflect upon the historical separation of Restorationists from the rise of fundamentalist evangelicalism and upon their own critical perspective and will not accept that the term "fundamentalist" could ever have been accurately applied to the SCM. My own sense is that while there are definitely theologically conservative Restorationists who are not also fundamentalists, (1) there was and still is a strong

correspondence between the Restorationist ethos and the tenets of fundamentalism; and (2) there still is a significantly higher number of Restorationists who approach the Bible and traditional beliefs in a way similar to fundamentalists than there are those who do not.

[10] Moses E. Lard, "The Work of the Past," 257–62.

[11] Edwin V. Hayden, *50 Years of Digression and Disturbance*, 6.

[12] Leroy Garrett, *The Stone-Campbell Movement*, 626.

[13] See Alexander Campbell, "*Statistics of Great Britain*," 480.

[14] This is the point where the Restorationist perspective on baptism can most legitimately be criticized. Baptism has become part of the ecclesiastical pattern to which churches and individuals must adhere in order to be part of *the* church of Christ. The soteriological difficulty with baptism so conceived is, in my view, not that it is a *meritorious work*, but that it forms part of the list constructed as part of soteriological ecclesiastical patternism.

[15] The obvious example of this is when Christians participate in a church assembly only long enough to participate in the Lord's Supper, then quickly exit, their most important liturgical requirement having been met. Soteriological ecclesiastical patternism creates opportunity for just such an attitude, so that those who experience the entirety of a worship service may be doing little more; they just stayed longer, participating in a lengthier series of worshipful acts.

[16] It is not uncommon for those in Restoration churches to ask what exactly they are to think about in the taking of the Supper as they "Do this in remembrance of me." A people unused to thinking theologically, who tend to focus on the replication of physical acts of worship, have trouble getting much past the mere envisioning in their minds of the body of Christ on the cross. Mel Gibson's *The Passion of the Christ* may be helpful here, but the ability to expand one's thoughts to the entirety of the Trinitarian history of God's efforts in Christ to reconcile the world to himself will be more helpful.

7

Toward a Stone-Campbell Trinitarian Theology: A SUMMARY PROPOSAL

Previous chapters have documented the roots and history of Trinitarian theology within the SCM, particularly the ICC/CC and the CCa. Included in the book has been the recommendation that Restoration churches make explicit their commitment to a doctrine of the Trinity that is essentially in line with that found in the classic ecumenical creeds of Nicea and Constantinople because these statements are in line with biblical Trinitarian doctrine. Chapter Six identified how the development of an overtly stated, theologically nuanced, praxis-oriented Trinitarian theology would be valuable both to the ICC/CC and CCa and to the Kingdom of God.

But what course should be followed in actually developing a vibrant Trinitarianism in SC churches? How will they actually become explicitly Trinitarian? This chapter will attempt to answer those questions by making several suggestions—some of which are theologically and hermeneutically oriented while others are exceedingly pragmatic—indicating how

Trinitarian theology can come to directly impact the lives and ministries of SC churches.

A primary attitudinal change must take place within the SCM that will allow them to develop a perspective different from that of their theological ancestors, who—for reasons examined in previous chapters—were hesitant to focus on explicit Trinitarian doctrine.

I contend that Alexander Campbell and some others did not take a stronger position on the Trinity largely because he capitulated before contemporary events and understandings, not because the biblical witness to the Trinity is weak. There was so much controversy and ecclesiastical disunity over the Trinity that Campbell concluded through his empirically considered, propositionally oriented evaluation of the biblical witness that the Bible's language about the Trinity was insufficiently clear to develop a highly nuanced Trinitarian focus. Part of what today makes possible a different approach to Trinitarian doctrine is that the entire climate of Western epistemology has changed, not only from what it was two hundred years ago, but also from what it was sixty years ago, bringing with it changes in the theological/ecclesiastical milieu for Christianity.

There is now a freedom and a need to reach new conclusions regarding the biblical foundations of Trinitarian doctrine, and there is no longer the worry among many adherents of the SCM that rampant disunity will be propagated if an overt Trinitarian stance is espoused. Postmodern acceptance of differences of opinion and the loss of confidence in foundationalistic truth claims mean alternative perspectives can more easily coexist. In such a context, overtly expressed belief in a particular Trinitarian perspective is less threatening and less polemical, allowing for new conclusions to be freely entertained without pressure.

Therefore, in the remainder of this chapter, I put forth a ten-part proposal of steps that need to occur in order to develop a more robust Trinitarian doctrine in SC churches.

1. Interest must be renewed in the biblical foundations of Trinitarian doctrine, including an analysis of Scripture's testimony to the triune God. Those in ICC/CC and CCa will seriously entertain any doctrinal proposal only within the context of a biblically grounded position. Therefore, many of those in the SCM, intrigued by the suggestion to reinvestigate our position on the Trinity, will insist that Trinitarian renewal should begin with a detailed, exhaustive examination of Scripture. Additionally, a biblical foundation supporting traditional Trinitarian doctrine must be delineated if that doctrine is to play a significant role in SC churches. The question is not whether the specific terminology of the classical creedal formulations can be justified specifically by Scripture (a difficult task), but whether there is sufficient correspondence between the conceptual framework of classical formulations of the Trinity and the biblical depiction of a God who reveals himself as Father, Son and Spirit. Does the presentation of God in Scripture sufficiently connect to classical Trinitarianism so that those of the SCM could view a strengthened support of classical Trinitarianism as a *biblically* justifiable theological move? I believe there is biblical evidence for such a move, as I discussed in Chapter Six. It is crucial that those who wish to see SC churches become overtly Trinitarian be willing to offer anew the required biblical justification for Trinitarian doctrine.

In addition, as Scripture is assessed with respect to the Trinity, it will be important to specifically deal with the Trinitarian writings of Barton Stone, the most prominent place in SCM theological history where the biblical foundations of Trinitarian doctrine are questioned. This book has sought to make available the information needed to address Stone's position and his arguments, but no attempt has been made to refute Stone. Stone's arguments must be directly addressed for those in the SCM to construct for themselves an overtly orthodox Trinitarian stance.

2. New perspectives must be developed concerning the nature and authority of Scripture, Scriptural interpretation, the use of the Bible in formulating Christian doctrine, and what constitutes the center of biblical revelation.

Some in the SCM have changed their perceptions regarding the nature and authority of Scripture and approaches to its interpretation, and these new perspectives could alter the conclusions of Restorationists regarding the Trinity. Enlightenment rationalism and empiricism have, to an extent, been superseded by postmodern, nonfoundational epistemological perspectives. Inductive searches for specific propositions and the logical, syllogistic sorting out of biblical premises have been at the very least supplemented, if not replaced, by theological-contextual evaluations of texts and narratival reading.

The entirety of the biblical theology is being taken more seriously, as is an enhanced understanding of variances of genre and the historical character of biblical texts. The central elements of the biblical theology are allowed to have more controlling influence in the assessment of doctrinal priorities. More people accept the idea that traditional and contemporary Trinitarian doctrine can be biblical, even though the language used in Trinitarian doctrinal formulations does not directly reflect the plain language of the Bible. Biblical justification of Trinitarian doctrine just needs to be attempted in a way that is more theologically informed.

Early Restorationists viewed the Bible as the divinely inspired compilation of "facts" to be inductively analyzed, an approach George Lindbeck terms the propositional-cognitive construction of doctrine from Scripture[1] and that David Kelsey identifies as the view that doctrine is the same as its content, as in Benjamin Warfield's doctrinal constructions.[2] Thomas and Alexander Campbell, Barton Stone, Walter Scott, and most of their theological descendants applied Scripture as verbal, plenary revelation to be interpreted rationalistically and empirically, with an inductive assemblage of biblical, propositional evidence constituting the chief means of doctrinal formulation. All the biblical references that support some aspect of God's revelation of himself and his activity could be compiled and presented as a lawyer would present evidence before a jury. From such evidence, inductively derived conclusions could be reached, with other truths being deduced from what could inductively be shown.

However, this is not the strongest basis on which Trinitarian doctrine (or most any other major biblical doctrine, for that matter) may be constructed, nor is this the best procedure to follow in order to access the Bible's revelatory value *in a way that matches with its nature as authoritative, sacred literature.* The propositional-cognitive construal of Scripture in constructing doctrine is dependent upon the accuracy, clarity, and explicitness of the propositions, and there are relatively few of these with respect to the Trinity in the Bible. In addition, while Scripture does contain propositional revelation, the basic perspective on Scripture in which the propositional-cognitive view is considered to be *the* character of biblical revelation has been largely superseded since the early years of the SCM. Hermeneutical perspectives and views concerning the authority and nature of Scripture have changed so much since the beginning days of the SCM that the majority of scholars today view the applying of nineteenth-century, empirically inductive interpretive procedures to the Bible as problematical. Although some in ICC/CC and CCa have gradually moved away from perceptions regarding the use of the Bible as a witness for Christian doctrine, others interpret the Bible and develop doctrinal precepts in essentially the same ways as did their spiritual forefathers in the first half of the nineteenth century. Contemporary perspectives on Scripture need to be more widely understood and adopted, and significant alterations must continue in the ways that many apply the Bible to the formulation of doctrine.

The approach to Scripture taken by early Restorationists is inadequate in at least five ways: (1) it is insufficiently theological or conceptual; (2) it tends to view and to treat all biblical content as propositional, factual data; (3) it in a very direct way applies the entirety of the Bible to doctrinal formulation, so that the impact of Scripture on theology resembles the impact of data collection in supporting hypotheses in the various fields of scientific inquiry; (4) it is insufficiently critical—which was understandable in the progenitors of the SCM but is now a hindrance to the adequate construction of biblically grounded ecclesiastical doctrine; (5) It does not take adequate account of the nature of the Bible as literature or of postmodern understanding of hermeneutical processes.

These realities require that SC formulators of doctrine be willing to apply other models of construing the Bible and using it for doctrinal construction. This is not to say that it is never appropriate or legitimate for a Warfield/Campbell style of viewing Scripture to be unapologetically applied by Restorationists to the formation of Trinitarian doctrine, as the multivalent character of Scripture and the revelational value of the fullness of Scripture variously construed and applied by theologians in constructing doctrine allows this to sometimes be an acceptable procedure. But there is significant room for perceptions about Scripture to be altered among those in the SCM, whereby theological moves and doctrinal construction can develop in ways that are both theologically and intellectually more justifiable.

At the very least, there are conservative models of doing theology that should satisfy those of the SCM who wish to remain intimately connected to traditional ways of doctrinally construing the Bible, and yet which permit the classically orthodox view of the Trinity to be accepted as biblically coherent. For example, conservatives like Clark Pinnock first look in Scripture for cognitive content that has been rationally revealed, much like Alexander Campbell would have done. Pinnock applies induction and looks for "facts," "evidence," and "data" that must be assembled. However, in contrast to what has often been done in the SCM, he also looks for coherence, canonical wholeness, and calls for cognitive reflection in discerning the system of truth and wholeness that represents the summation of the facts.[3] Karl Barth, T. F. Torrance, and G. E. Wright would also look for a certain coherence that stands beyond the biblical "facts"; for Barth, Torrance, and Wright, along with John Howard Yoder and Donald Bloesch, the coherence is not primarily identified as or with the direct summation of the facts. Instead, coherence stands behind the narratival history of Jesus and God's revelation of himself in the history of Jesus Christ.[4] In this case, one penetrates beyond the historical form to the divine content that is the living Word of the Trinity. Thus, theological, conceptual readings of the Bible, as advocated by Pinnock, Barth, Torrance, G. E. Wright, Yoder, and Bloesch need to have a place in the doing of SC theology. William Manson's "depth exegesis" and N. T. Wright's critical realism should speak to those who are still fundamentalist biblicists in their theological and doctrinal orientation,[5] as should the advocacy of theological interpretation from Stephen Fowl,[6] Christoper Seitz,[7] Francis Watson,[8] and Kevin Vanhoozer.[9]

It should be noted in the case of each of these writers that this is more than just empirically discerning the "forest" of the various propositional "trees" discerned in the Bible. It includes seeing in the cumulative message of biblical statements the divine message that comes with illumination and fullness of understanding. In the case of the Trinity, the biblical narratives about Jesus constitute a truth far greater than the sum of the parts of his history, with a divine impulse of the Spirit able to provide a sense of the wholeness of the message about Christ. Unfortunately, recognizing the presence of the Spirit in reading Scripture, too, is an element of biblical interpretation inadequately emphasized among those of the SCM—not surprising in a Movement that is inadequately Trinitarian from the outset.

3. A new generation of scholars, ministers, and leaders of SC churches should assess the contributions the early church fathers made toward Trinitarian theology, including the first two ecumenical creeds, building on the laudable heritage of patristic studies that has characterized scholarship within ICC/CC and CCa.

I have in mind two related areas of study that should be undertaken. The first closely builds on the work of Abraham Malherbe, Everett Ferguson, Fred Norris, Thomas Olbricht, and others who have been experts in patristics and authorities on the Greco-Roman world of the early church. Their attention to the earliest period of post-apostolic Christianity has been of immense value to SC churches and practically created a niche in which SC scholars have specialized and excelled. Such scholars of earliest Christianity have established a model for working with ancient texts and applying them to contemporary church life, and Fred Norris has included a specific focus on the Trinity, which is the specific area of concentration within patristics where I suggest more attention be paid. SC churches need more scholars who are familiar with the Trinitarian emphases of writers in the first four hundred years of Christianity.

A second area of studied focus that requires the attention of SC scholars concerns the fourth-century ecumenical creeds of Nicea and Constantinople. Although reading Ferguson, Norris, and an account of Thomas Olbricht's familiarity with Basil the Great shows SC patristics scholars have significant familiarity with the fourth century, there has not been a sufficiently widespread familiarity with, or explicit acceptance of, the actual content of the ecumenical statements formulated by the early church. Typically, those of the SC heritage have been so diligent about pitting themselves against the authoritative application of creedal statements that they have not stopped to adequately consider the creeds formulated at Nicea and Constantinople, especially their sufficiency as summaries of biblical doctrine. The question asked of the creeds should not be, "What do the creeds say that is extrabiblical; to what extent are they grounded only in human opinion?," so that we may be justified in rejecting them. Rather, we should ask, "Do the creeds present Trinitarian doctrine in a way that sufficiently coheres with biblical content? Are there points of Trinitarian doctrine that should characterize the thinking of those within the SCM?"

Although it is true that extrabiblical language is found within the ecumenical creeds and that application of the creeds has at times fostered disunity and sectarian, judgmental attitudes within the church, these facts should not obscure the carefully worded statements about the Trinity that were constructed by the early church. The creeds of Nicea and Constantinople were created through processes whereby Christian leaders gave their attention to the Trinity at a level that cannot be ignored, even if we say nothing of the possibility of the Spirit's influence during these processes. To admit the value of the creedal content does not have to equate with the sectarian disavowal of other positions, and such an action could lead to clearer, more biblical understanding of foundational theological premises. There is room here for accepting in principle the conclusions of the early church about the Trinity, or at least accepting conclusions that are in line with theirs. Since SC adherents have recognized for 200 years the value of the Campbells', Scott's, and Stone's positions on various topics (such as destructiveness of sectarianism, the plan of salvation, baptism, the Lord's Supper, the autonomous authority of elders in the local church, etc.), it would only make sense that dialoging with or even accepting the ideas of the early church with reference to the Trinity would be an acceptable practice.

Clearly those in the SCM think it possible for Christians at certain points of history to formulate doctrine in a way that should be followed by those who come after them. I argue that what the fourth-century church did in the case of the Trinity can be viewed in just this way. Their conclusions deserve our careful attention and, I assert, our acceptance—not as authoritative means for inclusion and exclusion, but as helpful, theologically sufficient conclusions reached by our predecessors that warrant our adherence today. Thus, those in the SCM should turn their attention to the early creedal formulations from Nicea and Constantinople, evaluating their content against biblical content, and adopting as doctrinally sufficient an orthodox, classically Trinitarian position. To do so would align SC churches with biblically defensible Trinitarian doctrine.

4. A wider implementation of statements of belief, combined with the intentional inclusion of explicitly Trinitarian doctrinal positions, may over time significantly, constructively shape the thinking and praxis of SC churches.
While I am not advocating the promotion of a particular creedal formulation as a test of faith for Restorationist churches, autonomous summary statements of belief, which have been recently formulated among some ICC/CC and CCa, could include statements that reflect a traditional Trinitarian perspective and be adopted by a wider number of individual congregations. At the very least, individual congregations and their leaders should give due consideration to being intentionally Trinitarian in their theological identities, missions, and ministries. The relative weakness of Restorationists with respect to an explicitly Trinitarian perspective has been ecclesiastically and pastorally damaging, and correction of this thinking could enhance the efforts of Restorationist churches on several fronts, as described in Chapter Six.

The idea of churches adopting any sort of belief statements beyond the Scriptures is likely to produce resistance on the parts of many church members and leaders who view such actions as a move toward creedalism and sectarianism. This will make the official adoption of a Trinitarian position, including any documentation that would assert for such a position, a difficult sell in many congregations.

However, it is simplistic and inaccurate to indiscriminately label a congregation's efforts to summarize its beliefs as formulating sectarian creeds. The kinds of summary statements of belief suggested here should be primarily descriptive, not prescriptive, and can be applied in line with the SCM's characteristic principle of congregational autonomy. For some, even this amount of doctrinal prescription may seem to be too much. However, they fail to recognize the gross inconsistency of summarily rejecting all belief statements while adamantly holding to a set of unwritten or summarized beliefs used to perpetually evaluate the theological positions of others. To have framed a summary statement of beliefs, while intentionally avoiding using it as a creed, is at least as legitimate as having an unwritten set of beliefs that is used as a creedal formula—a phenomenon that has taken place far too often.

5. The ICC/CC and CCa should intentionally formulate and write Trinitarian theology, including an understanding and incorporation of contemporary Trinitarian theology.
The ICC/CC and CCa need to move from being little influenced by Trinitarian doctrine to being significantly shaped by the *doctrine* of the Trinity and by the *direct influence* of the divine Trinity. This requires theological understanding and creative application of Trinitarian theology. Unfortunately, much of what has been written on Trinitarian theology has not only been ignored, but has been intentionally pushed to the periphery in the course of developing ecclesiastical belief and practice, to the significant detriment of Restorationist theology and practice.

Although there are indications that this mistake is gradually being recognized by contemporary SC adherents, the problems created by avoiding an overt Trinitarianism continue to negatively impact the contributions of ICC/CC and CCa toward the realization of the proleptic presence of God's kingdom in the world. I suggest that there are those in the Movement who should become intimately familiar with the works of contemporary Trinitarian theology that potentially will be the most helpful in assisting the Movement to formulate overtly stated Trinitarian perspectives.

Of course, there will be some hesitancy to take this step as some worry that turning to contemporary theology for guidance regarding the Trinity will expose the ICC/CC and CCa to the kind of humanly originated, potentially divisive theologies that they perceive have caused so much trouble for the church in the past. And, they ask, as contemporary theology greatly suffers from the impact of the Enlightenment, theological liberalism, and historical and biblical criticism, should not any theology from the last two centuries be suspect with respect to its fidelity to the gospel and Scripture?

Four factors should mitigate such fears. First, there is simply a significant need for those in ICC/CC and CCa to acquaint themselves with contemporary theology generally and contemporary Trinitarian theology in particular, if only to be aware of contemporary trends. Although I believe those who reflect on the history of Trinitarian thought have tended to exaggerate the hiatus of Trinitarian reflection during the approximately 100 years between Hegel's death and Barth's key assertion of the centrality of the Trinity in the opening volume of his *Church Dogmatics*,[10] it is true that the amount of literary attention given to the Trinity since Barth has been momentous when compared to the last few decades prior to Barth. Both the number of Trinitarian works published and the general profile of Trinitarian thought on the larger theological scene have markedly increased in the last forty years. However, the impact of all this work has been minimal on those in the ICC/CC and CCa; little has been written on the Trinity by those in the ICC/CC and CCa, and very few of the works annotated in Chapter Five actually consider theology's recent focus on the Trinity. Those in the ICC/CC and CCa need to reflect on the works of those who have created the Trinitarian renaissance in order to understand current Trinitarian trends and most informatively shape Trinitarian doctrine for SC churches.

Second, to have its greatest impact, theology must be more than just biblically or patristically *descriptive*, centered only on what God has revealed in Scripture or what may be discerned in a study of the early church. Although biblical theology and a form of theological description must serve as *the* crucial foundation for theology and ultimately dominate what is said with respect to the Trinity, more is needed than simply a description or restatement of what is in the Bible. Biblical description should be *primary*, but it must not be *exclusionary*. Theology must also be *relevantly constructive* and *prescriptive*, helpful for those reading it today, so that they may take what they read and incorporate it into the life of the church. Theological construction in the SCM has often entailed description and then replication, amounting to a simplistic examination of biblical theology and practices and anachronistically applying the fruits of such research to the contemporary church without permitting the questions and issues of today to influence the ways theology addresses the realities of the current church in the world. Studying contemporary Trinitarian theology will help prevent ICC/CC and CCa from ineffectually replicating and describing biblical doctrine in a way that is detached from the contemporary needs of church and world. The goal of restoring the biblical church *today* must include significant emphasis on the *today* side of theology.

Third, Trinitarian theology is no longer dominated by liberalism nor by radically negative biblical criticism, if it actually ever was. Many—if not most—of those who since Barth have participated in constructive Trinitarian theology have done so from a perspective of faithfulness to traditionally orthodox Christianity. Stanley Grenz, Colin Gunton, Jürgen Moltmann, Wolfhart Pannenberg, Thomas Torrance, Miroslav Wolf, John Zizioulas, and numerous others have written on the Trinity from positions of faith, adding legitimacy to the practice of assimilating their positions into Trinitarian perspectives within the SCM. Adopting elements from the Trinitarian theologies of these and other writers has great potential to help Restorationists frame for themselves Trinitarian theology that is both defensibly orthodox and significant for SC church life.

Finally, as in any age, there must be era-specific understanding, construction, and application of theology for the gospel to bring about transformation *for that day*. ICC/CC and CCa need to become familiar with the particular contemporary Trinitarian proposals that offer the greatest potential for shaping Trinitarian thought among SC churches, so that they can have a significant impact on the current world that needs the triune God. The need for relevant Trinitarian construction means others beyond those who influenced the Campbells and Stone must be consulted for insights that can positively impact SC theology and praxis.[11] Those writing about the Trinity in the last seventy years or so speak to the subject in a way that is most relevant for those living on this side of the Enlightenment/modernist/postmodernist divide. Their suggestions regarding the influence of the Trinity have a notably contemporary sense about them, in that they are postcritical, post-Constantinian and oriented toward a world that is post-Christian. It is appropriate, then, to enquire about how the works of recent contributors to Trinitarian discussion could best inform and enable ICC/CC and CCa to meet the numerous needs listed in Chapter Six. Intentional reflection on *contemporary* Trinitarian theology will help move ICC/CC and CCa from an initial, imperative stating of their commitment to orthodox Trinitarian doctrine toward nuancing their own beliefs along the lines of some whose Trinitarian theologies are enabling the church to have an enhanced transformative impact on society.[12]

6. Intentional instruction of Trinitarian thought and the history of Trinitarian theology should be added to Bible colleges, university departments of Bible and religion, and seminaries within the SC movement. Although it might be surprising to those unfamiliar with postsecondary education among ICC/CC and CCa, some SC institutions of learning have only quite recently begun using the term "theology" to describe a field of instruction or to include courses titled systematic theology in their curriculum. Even rarer—if in fact it has ever occurred in these schools—would be a course specifically designed to address Trinitarian doctrine. In previous eras, there have been courses in biblical doctrine, and I hold a master of arts degree from Abilene Christian University with a specialization in "doctrinal studies." To use Abilene Christian as an example, the word "theological" was first used in the 1990s to describe an area of specialization within its graduate school, and it was also in that decade that the graduate division for studying Bible and theology at ACU was named the "The Graduate School of Theology." During my graduate studies at ACU in the 1980s there were no courses labeled "systematic theology"; content typically associated with systematics was presented only in "Introduction to Doctrinal Studies" and "Restoration Doctrine." Even at the MDiv level, students, like me, who were interested in systematics, were forced to attend institutions outside the CCa to take a concentration in systematic theology.

Curriculums have changed, and theology proper is now being taught in several SC institutions. However, deans, departments, curriculum committees, and professors of theology must intentionally include courses and concentrations that will include the study of the Trinity in order to ensure that the centrality of the Trinity takes root in the minds of those preparing for ministry in ICC/CC and CCa. Such courses will allow for the gradual dissemination into SC churches of an explicitly Trinitarian perspective capable of influencing ecclesiastical life and ministry and the personal spiritual perspectives of SC adherents.

7. Trinitarian curriculum that includes both theoretical and ministry-oriented practical components should be developed for church instruction. Congregational Bible classes should teach Trinitarian doctrine. Small group curricula should include applications of Trinitarian theology to church life and to the church's witness to the world. The concept of missionality, so closely linked to discussions of the Trinity in the last couple of decades, should become part of regular church instruction. This will require that a generation of church leaders and teachers beyond just the lead ministers become familiar with at least the rudimentary elements of Trinitarian theology and the more practical ramifications of Trinitarian thought for the church.

This challenge is an exciting one, not a burden. When Bible class teachers pass on both biblical Trinitarian instruction and ideas about the application of Trinitarian doctrine to church ministry, the church will move toward fulfillment of its mission and develop a missional attitude.

8. Stone-Campbell churches can greatly increase the influence of Trinitarian doctrine by incorporating Trinitarian preaching that is missionally oriented.

Jack Cottrell draws attention to the relative absence in SC churches of preaching about the Trinity, referencing Gordon Clark's parallel claim that in thirty years of visiting all kinds of evangelical churches from coast to coast he had never once heard a sermon on the Trinity.[13] Although more has likely been said from pulpits about the Trinity than Cottrell and Clark suggest, an increase in Trinitarian preaching would undoubtedly help move the church toward both Trinitarian understanding and Trinitarian praxis.

The doctrine of the immanent Trinity must be given its proper place and not lost in the midst of a flurry of Trinitarian ministry. Churches must heed the insistence of Karl Barth, Thomas Torrance, and Paul Molnar that the immanent Trinity not be relinquished, so that the immanent, ontological Trinity continues to serve as the basic theological principle undergirding all theology and, therefore, all preaching. But more is needed than simple theoretical expositions of biblical texts explicating and defending Trinitarian doctrine. Just as crucial is preaching that calls congregants to reflect upon the economic Trinity, permitting God's Trinitarian outreach to humankind to influence the thoughts and actions of those average Christians who everywhere participate in church life.

In our time, those reflecting most directly on the influence of the Trinity on the mission of the church are those who stress the importance of being *missional*. Despite the unfortunate status of "missionality" as a current buzzword, Leslie Newbigin, John Flett, George Hunsberger, and others who have written about the *missio dei* have done much to draw attention to the value of Trinitarian doctrine for the church's ministry to the world. Contemporary preaching should point churches toward the kind of missional implications that today's missional theorists derive from the economic Trinity.[14]

9. Trinitarian reflection should more often be placed on the programs of Stone-Campbell lectureships and conventions.
Certain large gatherings of SC adherents in recent decades have been as influential in shaping the general ethos of the Movement's churches as any other experience. Previously, popular journals and books were quite significant, giving editors of journals and magazines much influence over shaping ecclesiastical thought and practice; however, in many ways, lectureships and conventions have superseded the influence of publications. Thousands from the SCM annually attend the North American Christian Convention; the lectureships of Abilene Christian University, Pepperdine University, and other colleges and universities associated with CCa; and the Tulsa Workshop (formerly the Tulsa Soul Winning Workshop). The format of each of these includes numerous individual classes where Trinitarian theology could be considered, and plenary sessions could intentionally incorporate a specifically Trinitarian focus, just as such gatherings have in the past done with ecclesiology, missiology, and eschatology.

10. Christian Scholar's Conferences and working groups should periodically, if not regularly, include or be devoted to Trinitarian doctrine.
The SCM's sizable void with respect to the Trinity will require significant amounts of Trinitarian theological construction. In addition, the centrality of the Trinity to the Christian faith necessitates frequent and abundant reflection on the Trinity, especially where Trinitarian doctrine most directly impacts the church's ministry to the world. The rapidly expanding Christian Scholar's Conference could make the Trinity a plenary theme at one of its annual conferences; a working group of the American Academy of Religion or the Society of Biblical Literature could be established for those from the SCM interested in the Trinity; independent gatherings could be organized

to promote Trinitarian reflection among SC scholars. The Trinity could be set as a primary theme by journals such as *Restoration Quarterly* and *Stone-Campbell Journal,* and by the *Stone-Campbell Journal* annual conference. Although Trinitarian reflection should routinely be present among members and leaders in SC churches, scholarly reflection by Restorationists will be crucial in advancing a Trinitarian ethos for SC churches.

Notes

[1] George Lindbeck, *The Nature of Doctrine*, 16.
[2] David H. Kelsey, *The Uses of Scripture in Recent Theology*, 16–24.
[3] See Clark Pinnock, "How I Use the Bible in Doing Theology," 18–34; and *The Scripture Principle*.
[4] Cf. T. F. Torrance, *The Christian Doctrine of God*, 37–50. For Barth and G. E. Wright, David Kelsey's summaries are helpful, especially his chapter 3 on "Recital and Presence" in *The Uses of Scripture in Recent Theology*, 32–55. Also, cf., Donald G. Bloesch, "A Christological Hermeneutic," 78–102; and John Howard Yoder, "The Use of the Bible in Theology," 103–20.
[5] See William Manson, *Jesus and the Christian*, 174–83; N. T. Wright, *The New Testament and the People of God*, 32–46, 61–67.
[6] Stephen E. Fowl, *Engaging Scripture*.
[7] Christopher Seitz, *Prophecy and Hermeneutics*.
[8] Francis Watson, *Text, Church, and World*.
[9] See Kevin Vanhoozer, *Is There a Meaning in This Text?*
[10] See, for example, Grenz, *Rediscovering the Triune God*, 7–16, 32–33. As a corrective to this, see Samuel M. Powell, "Nineteenth-Century Protestant Doctrines of the Trinity," 267. Powell says:

> There is a well-known narrative about nineteenth-century theology: the doctrine suffered a grievous blow at the hands of the rationalistic theologians of the Enlightenment, that Friedrich Schleiermacher provided the *coupe de gráce*, that the doctrine consequently lay moribund throughout the nineteenth-century, and that its vitality today is due only to the efforts of Karl Barth and those who followed his lead. As with all narratives made familiar by retelling, there is a pith of truth here. . . . But the simplicity of the narrative warns us against its plausibility. Schleiermacher's view of the Trinity resists easy summarizing and, far from being moribund, the doctrine was vigorously discussed and employed throughout the nineteenth century by Protestant theologians of all types. The Barthian renewal of Trinitarian theology, accordingly, was no recovery after a period of neglect; it was instead the recovery of a dialogue underway for more than a century before the appearance of *Church Dogmatics*.

[11] Of course, anyone reflecting on the history of the SCM should realize that the Campbells, Stone, and Scott applied contemporary theology and philosophy to the problems of church and society in hopes that these new insights could help the church have great impact for the Kingdom of God. They were adopting and adapting contemporary insights in ways that influenced their constructions of doctrinal precepts, including their perspectives on the Trinity. It is remarkably ironic that the progenitors of the SCM were considered significant innovators in their day, and many felt orthodox Christianity should be suspicious of them. It is further ironic that thousands of Christians reflected upon the new style of being the church that typified early Restorationists, and that their applications of the Bible and Christianity were influential just because they so fit the needs of the church and society at the time. From the outset, then, it was part of the SC ethos to apply the insights of contemporary theological and philosophical trendsetters to the needs of the church and society, actually becoming

trendsetters on whom others were dependent. For today's Restorationists to apply the insights of contemporary thinkers in constructing new theological positions is quite in line with the historical SC ethos, especially in the case where a seemingly "lost" central theological construct, like the Trinity, now has a chance to be *restored* to its proper place in the thinking and life of the church.

[12] Not only is there a need to look at the most contemporary relevant Trinitarian contributions published to date, but there is some need to expand the definition of "contemporary" because the well-known course of Trinitarian studies over the last eighty years or so is not well-known among Restorationists. There is good reason, then, to include Karl Barth among those "contemporary" writers warranting our attention, although Barth has been dead for nearly 50 years. Barth's continuing relevance requires his work to be given a prominent place in a discussion of contemporary Trinitarian theologians who must be allowed to influence Trinitarian doctrine for ICC/CC and CCa. Further suggestions concerning the ways in which contemporary Trinitarian theology—specifically the contributions of Karl Barth, Jürgen Moltmann, and John Zizioulas—may positively impact SC theology are included in Chapter 7 of Kelly D. Carter, "The Trinity in the Stone Campbell Movement."

[13] Cottrell, *What the Bible Says About God the Redeemer*, 170.

[14] Cf. George Hunsberger, "Missional Vocation," 77–109; John Flett, *The Witness of God*, 196–239.

Bibliography

Abbey, C. J. and John H. Overton. *The English Church in the Eighteenth Century.* London: Longmans, Green, and Co., 1878.———. *The English Church in the Eighteenth Century.* rev. ed. London: Longmans, Green, and Co., 1896.

Abernathy, George Ross. *The English Presbyterians and the Stuart Restoration, 1648-1663.* Philadelphia: American Philosophical Society, 1965.

Ahlstrom, Sydney E. *A Religious History of the American People.* New Haven, CT: Yale University Press, 1972.

Allen, Leonard. *The Cruciform Church: Becoming a Cross-Shaped People in a Secular World.* Abilene, TX: Abilene Christian University Press, 1990.

Allen, Leonard and Danny Swick. *Participating in God's Life: Two Crossroads for Churches of Christ.* Orange, CA: New Leaf Books, 2001.

Babcock, William S. "A Changing of the Christian God: The Doctrine of the Trinity in the Seventeenth Century." *Interpretation* 45 (1991): 133-46.

Barkan, Elazar and Ronald Bush, eds. *Prehistories of the Future: The Primitivist Project and the Culture of Modernism.* Stanford, CA: Stanford University Press, 1995.

Barth, Karl. *The Doctrine of Reconciliation.* Translated by Geoffrey W. Bromiley. Vol. 4, no. 2, *Church Dogmatics.* Edinburgh: T&T Clark, 1958.

———. *The Doctrine of the Word of God: Prolegomena to Church Dogmatics.* Translated by Geoffrey W. Bromiley. Vol. 1, no. 1, 2nd ed., *Church Dogmatics*. Edinburgh: T&T Clark, 1975.

Beckwith, Roger T. "The Calvinist Doctrine of the Trinity." *Churchman* 115, no. 4 (2001): 308–15.

Blakely, Fred O. *The Apostle's Doctrine.* Vol. 1, 2nd ed. Highland, IN: Author, 1962.

Bloesch, Donald G. "A Christological Hermeneutic: Crisis and Conflict in Hermeneutics." In *The Use of the Bible in Theology: Evangelical Options,* edited by Robert K. Johnston, 78–102. Atlanta: John Knox Press, 1985.

Boas, George. *Essays on Primitivism and Related Ideas in the Middle Ages.* Baltimore: Johns Hopkins Press, 1948.

Bourn, Samuel. *An Address to Protestant Dissenters; or an Enquiry into the Grounds of Their Attachment to the Assembly's Catechism; Whether They Act Upon Bigotry or From Reason: Being a Calm Examination of the Sixth Answer in the Assembly's Shorter Catechism. By a Protestant Dissenter.* London: Printed for J. Roberts in Warwick-Lane, and sold at pamphlet-shops, 1736.

Bozeman, Theodore Dwight. *To Live Ancient Lives: The Primitivist Dimension of Puritanism* Chapel Hill: University of North Carolina Press, 1988.

Brownlow, Leroy. *Why I Am a Member of the Church of Christ.* Fort Worth, TX: Brownlow Publishing, 1945.

Calvin, John. *Commentary on the Gospel According to John.* Translated by William Pringle. Vol. 1. Grand Rapids, MI: William B. Eerdmans, 1949.

———. *Institutes of the Christian Religion.* Library of Christian Classics, Vol. 20. Edited by John T. McNeill. Translated by Ford Lewis Battles. Philadelphia: Westminster Press, 1960.

Campbell, Alexander. "A. Campbell to Elder A. Broaddus—*No. III.*" *The Millennial Harbinger* New Series 6, no. 5 (May 1842): 209–11.

———. *Campbell-Rice Debate on the Holy Spirit: in the Great Debate on "Baptism," "Holy Spirit," and "Creeds," Held in Lexington, Kentucky Beginning November 15, 1843 and Continuing Eighteen Days Between Alexander Campbell, Christian and N. L. Rice, Presbyterian.* Cincinnati, OH: F. L. Rowe, 1901.

———. *Christian Baptism, with Its Antecedents and Consequents.* Bethany, VA: Author, 1851.

———, ed. *The Christian Baptist.* Revised by D. S. Burnet from the second edition, with Mr. Campbell's last corrections. 7 vols. St. Louis, MO: Christian Publishing, 1835.

———. *The Christian System in Reference to the Union of Christians, and a Restoration of Primitive Christianity, as Plead in the Current Reformation.* Reprint of the Second Edition of 1839. Nashville: Gospel Advocate, 1974.

———. "Christian Union—No. V." *The Millennial Harbinger* Series 3, 3, no. 12 (December 1846): 686–95.

———. "From *The Christian Baptist*, To *The Christian Messenger*." *The Christian Messenger* 2, no. 1 (November 1827): 6–10.

———, ed. *Memoirs of the Elder Thomas Campbell together with a Brief Memoir of Mrs. Jane Campbell*. Cincinnati, OH: H. S. Bosworth, 1861.

———. "Mr. Broaddus." *The Millennial Harbinger* 4, no. 1 (January 1833): 8–10.

———. "Sermon on the Law." *The Millennial Harbinger* Series 3, 3, no. 9 (September 1846): 493–521.

———. "Statistics of Great Britain." *The Millennial Harbinger* 2, no. 10 (October 3, 1831): 479–480.

———. "To Brother Henry Grew." *The Millennial Harbinger* 4, no. 4 (April 1833): 154–60.

———. "To the Christian Messenger." *The Christian Baptist* 5, no. 3 (October 1, 1827): 378–81.

———. "To Timothy." *The Christian Baptist*, 4, no. 10 (May 7, 1827): 333–35.

———. "Union Among Christians." *The Millennial Harbinger* Series 3, 3, no. 4 (April 1846): 216–25.

———. "Unitarianism, Or, Remarks on Christian Union, No. II." *The Millennial Harbinger* Series 3, 3, no. 7 (July 1846): 388–94.

———. "Unitarianism as Connected With Christian Union—No. III." *The Millennial Harbinger* Series 3, 3, no. 8 (August 1846): 450–54.

———. "Unitarianism as Connected With Christian Union—No. IV." *The Millennial Harbinger* Series 3, 3, no. 11 (November 1846): 634–38.

Campbell, John P. *Vindex: Or the Doctrines of the Strictures Vindicated, Against the Reply of Mr. Stone*. Lexington, KY: Daniel Bradford, 1806.

Campbell, Thomas. "Christian Society." *Millennial Harbinger* Series 3, 4, no. 7 (July 1847): 394–400.

———. "Circular Letter, Address to the Redstone Baptist Association, 1816." In *Memoirs of Alexander Campbell Embracing A View of the Origin, Progress, and Principles of the Religious Reformation Which He Advocated*. Vol. 1, edited by Robert Richardson, 539–55. Philadelphia: J. B. Lippincott, 1868.

———. *Declaration and Address of the Christian Association of Washington*. Washington, PA: Washington Christian Association, 1809.

———. "The Direct and Immediate Intention of the Christian Institution, Essay I." *Millennial Harbinger* New Series, 3 (January 1839): 41–43.

———. "The Direct and Immediate Intention of the Christian Institution, Essay II." *Millennial Harbinger* New Series, 3 (February 1839): 92–93.

———. "The Direct and Immediate Intention of the Christian Institution, Essay III." *Millennial Harbinger* New Series, 3 (May 1839): 216–20.

———. *Prospectus of a Religious Reformation; The Object of which is The Restoration of Primitive Apostolic Christianity in Letter and Spirit—in Principle and Practice.* Cincinnati, OH: 1829.

———. "Trinitarianism, Arianism, & Socinianism." *Millennial Harbinger* 4, no. 4 (April 1833):153–60.

Cardale, Paul. *The True Doctrine of the New Testament Concerning Jesus Christ, Considered; Wherein the Misrepresentations That Have Been Made of It, Upon the Arian Hypothesis, and Upon All Trinitarian and Athanasian Principles, Are Exposed.* 2nd ed. London: J. Johnson, 1771.

Carter, Charles Sydney. *The English Church in the Eighteenth Century.* 2nd ed. London: Church Book Room Press, 1948.

Carter, Kelly D. "The Trinity in the Stone-Campbell Movement: Historical/Theological Analysis and Constructive Proposal." PhD diss., Southern Methodist University, 2012.

Childers, Jeff, Douglas A. Foster, and Jack R Reese. *The Crux of the Matter: Crisis, Tradition, and the Future of the Churches of Christ.* Abilene, TX: Abilene Christian University Press, 2001.

Clack, Spencer. "From the Baptist Recorder, 'Letters Addressed To A. Campbell.'" *The Christian Messenger* 2, no. 2 (December 1827): 28–29.

Clarke, Adam. *Containing the Gospels Matthew, Mark, Luke, and John.* Vol. 1 of *The New Testament of Our Lord and Saviour Jesus Christ Containing the Text, Take from the Most Correct Copies of the Present Authorized Translation Including the Marginal Readings and Parallel Text, with a Commentary and Critical Notes. Designed as a Help to a Better Understanding of the Sacred Writings.* London: J. Butterworth and Son, 1817.

Clarke, Samuel. *The Scripture Doctrine of the Trinity: Wherein Every Text in the New Testament Relating to that Doctrine is Distinctly Considered; the Divinity of Our Saviour, the Distinct Power and Office of the Father, the Son, and the Holy Ghost; and the Absolute and Incommunicable Supremacy of the Father, Proved and Explained from Scripture; with some Observations Added on the Sufficiency of the Apostles' Creed in Baptism, and Consequently in All Other Aspects.* 2nd ed. London: James Knapton, 1719. Reprinted by Deacon Morrell and Retitled *Clarke on the Trinity.* London: n.d. Reprinted again and edited by Dale Tuggy. Fredonia, NY: Dale Tuggy, 2007.

Cleland, Thomas. *Letters to Barton W. Stone, Containing A Vindication Principally of The Doctrines of the Trinity, the Divinity and Atonement of the Saviour, Against HIS RECENT ATTACK in A Second Edition of His "Address."* Lexington, KY: Thomas T. Skillman, 1822.

———. *The Socini-Arian Detected: A Series of Letters to Barton W. Stone, on Some Important Subjects of Theological Discussion. Referred to in his "Address" To the Christian Churches in Kentucky, Tennesse, and Ohio*. Lexington, KY: Thomas T. Skillman, 1815.

Coke, Thomas and Francis Asbury. *The Doctrines and Discipline of the Methodist Episcopal Church in America, with Explanatory Notes*. 10th ed. Philadelphia: Henry Tuckniss, 1798.

Colligan, J. Hay. *The Arian Movement in England*. Manchester: Manchester University Press, 1913.

Coomer, Duncan. *English Dissent Under the Early Hanoverians*. London: Epworth Press, 1946.

Cottrell, Jack. *The Faith Once for All: Bible Doctrine for Today*. Joplin, MO: College Press, 2002.

———. *Power From on High: What the Bible Says About the Holy Spirit*. Joplin, MO: College Press Publishing, 2007.

———. *Set Free: What the Bible Says About Grace*. Joplin, MO: College Press Publishing, 2009.

———. *What the Bible Says About God the Creator*. Eugene, OR: Wipf and Stock Publishers, 2000.

———. *What the Bible Says About God the Redeemer*. Eugene, OR: Wipf and Stock Publishers, 2000.

———. *What the Bible Says About God the Ruler*. Eugene, OR: Wipf and Stock Publishers, 2000.

Cragg, G. R. *The Church and the Age of Reason 1648–1789*. London: Penguin Books, 1960.

———. *Reason and Authority in the Eighteenth Century*. Cambridge: Cambridge University Press, 1964.

Creed, J. M. and J. S Boys-Smith. *Religious Thought in the Eighteenth Century*. Cambridge: Cambridge University Press, 1934.

Cunningham, David S. *These Three Are One: The Practice of Trinitarian Theology*. Oxford: Blackwell Publishers, 1998.

Davidson, Robert. *History of the Presbyterian Church in the State of Kentucky: With a Preliminary Sketch of the Churches in the Valley of Virginia*. New York: Robert Carter, 1847.

Davies, Horton. *Worship and Theology in England: From Watts and Wesley To Maurice, 1690–1850*. Princeton: Princeton University Press, 1961.

DeGroot, Alfred Thomas. *Disciple Thought: a History*. Fort Worth, TX: DeGroot, 1965.

Drysdale, A. H. *History of the Presbyterians in England: Their Rise, Decline, and Revival.* London: Publication Committee of the Presbyterian Church of England, 1889.

Estes, George P. "The Deity/Humanity Controversy." *The Preceptor* 41 (September 1992): 258–59.

Ferguson, Everett. *Early Christians Speak: Faith and Life in the First Three Centuries.* rev. ed. Abilene, TX: Abilene Christian University Press, 1987.

Flett, John. *The Witness of God: The Trinity, Missio Dei, Karl Barth, and the Nature of Christian Community.* Grand Rapids, MI: William B. Eerdmans, 2010.

Flynn, Carl F. "God, Christ, Soteriology in the *Declaration and Address*." In *The Quest for Christian Unity, Peace, and Purity in Thomas Campbell's Declaration and Address: Text and Studies,* edited by Thomas H. Olbricht and Hans Rollman, 323–39. Lanham, MD: Scarecrow Press, 2000.

Foster, Douglas. "Christology in the Stone-Campbell Movement: An Exploratory Survey." Paper presented to the annual meeting of the Restoration Theological Research Fellowship, Boston, MA, November 20, 1999.

Fowl, Stephen E. *Engaging Scripture: A Model For Theological Interpretation.* Hoboken, NJ: Wiley-Blackwell, 1998.

Frost, Gene. "Jesus: Fully God or Fully Human?" *The Preceptor* 43 (July 1994): 166–71.

Garrett, Leroy. *The Stone-Campbell Movement: An Anecdotal History of Three Churches.* Joplin, MO, College Press Publishing, 1981.

Garrison, W. E. *Alexander Campbell's Theology: Its Sources and Historical Setting.* St. Louis: Christian Publishing Company, 1900.

Garrison, W. E. and DeGroot, A. T. *The Disciples of Christ: A History.* St. Louis: Bethany Press, 1958.

Gibson, William, ed. *Religion and Society in England and Wales, 1689–1800.* London: Leicester University Press, 1998.

Gonzalez, Justo. *From the Beginnings to the Council of Chalcedon.* Vol. 1 of *A History of Christian Thought.* Nashville: Abingdon Press, 1970.

Grenz, Stanley J. *Rediscovering The Triune God: The Trinity in Contemporary Theology.* Minneapolis: Fortress Press, 2004.

Grew, Henry. "Trinitarianism, Arianism, & Socinianism." *The Millennial Harbinger* 4, no. 4 (April 1833): 153–54.

Griffin, Martin, Jr. *Latitudinarianism in the Seventeenth Century Church of England.* Annotated by Richard H. Popkin. Edited by Lila Freedman. New York: E. J. Brill, 1992.

Gunton, C. E. *The Promise of Trinitarian Theology.* Edinburgh: T&T Clark, 1991.

———. *The One, the Three and the Many: God, Creation and the Culture of Modernity.* Cambridge: Cambridge University Press, 1993.

———. *The Triune Creator: a Historical and Systematic Study.* Grand Rapids, MI: Eerdmans, 1998.

Hardy, Edward R., ed. *Christology of the Later Fathers.* Louisville, KY: Westminster John Knox Press, 1954.

Harris, Murray. *Jesus as God: The New Testament Use of Theos in Reference to Jesus.* Grand Rapids, MI: Baker Book House, 1992.

Harris, Randall J. and Rubel Shelly. *The Second Incarnation: A Theology for the 21st Century Church.* West Monroe, LA: Howard Publishing, 1992.

Hawley, Monroe E. *The Focus of Our Faith.* Nashville: 20th Century Christian, 1985.

Hayden, Edwin V. *50 Years of Digression and Disturbance.* Joplin, MO: Author, 1955.

Hicks, John Mark. "Christological Reflections in the Light of Doug Foster's 'Christology in the Stone-Campbell Movement.'" Paper presented to the annual meeting of the Restoration Theological Research Fellowship, Boston, MA, November 21, 1999.

Highfield, Ron. "Does the Doctrine of the Trinity Make a Difference?" In *Theology Matters: Answers for the Church Today,* edited by Gary Holloway, Randall J. Harris, and Mark C. Black, 15–26. Joplin, MO: College Press Publishing, 1998.

Hill, Samuel, Jr. "A Typology of American Restitutionism." *Journal of the American Academy of Religion* 44 (1976): 65–76.

Howell, Margaret A. and Charles F Mullett. *English Dissent: Catalog To An Exhibition Of Eighteenth Century Pamphlets, 18 October To 18 November 1979: On The Occasion Of The Annual Meeting Of The American Society For Eighteenth Century Studies, Midwestern Branch.* Columbia, MO: Ellis Library, University of Missouri-Columbia, 1979.

Huber, Richard T. *The Doctrine of the Trinity in the Thought of Thomas and Alexander Campbell—Including a Comparison with the Thought of Barton W. Stone and Walter Scott.* Master's thesis, Butler University, 1956.

Hughes, Richard T., ed. *The American Quest for the Primitive Church.* Urbana: University of Illinois Press, 1988.

———. "Christian Primitivism as Perfectionism: From Anabaptists to Pentecostals." In *Reaching Beyond: Chapters in the History of Perfectionism,* edited by Stanley Burgess, 239–45. Peabody, MA: Hendrickson Publishers, 1986.

———. "From Primitive Church to Civil Religion: The Millennial Odyssey of Alexander Campbell." *Journal for the American Academy of Religion* 44, no. 1 (1976): 87–103.

———. *Reviving the Ancient Faith: The Story of Churches of Christ in America.* Grand Rapids, MI: William B. Eerdmans, 1996.

Hughes Richard T. and C. Leonard Allen, *Illusions of Innocence: Protestant Primitivism in America, 1630–1875*. Foreword by Robert N. Bellah. Chicago: University of Chicago Press, 1988.

Hunsberger, George. "Missional Vocation: Called and Sent to Represent the Reign of God." In *Missional Church: A Vision for the Sending of the Church in North America*, edited by Darrell L. Guder, 77–109. Grand Rapids, MI: William B. Eerdmans, 1998.

Hunt, John. *Religious Thought in England: From the Reformation to the End of Last Century*. Vol. 2. London: Strahan, 1871.

Hylson-Smith, Kenneth. *The Churches in England from Elizabeth I to Elizabeth II: Volume II 1689–1833*. London: SCM Press, 1997.

International Standard Bible Encyclopedia. Edited by Geoffrey W. Bromiley. 4 vols. Grand Rapids, MI: William B. Eerdmans, 1988.

Jennings, W. W. *Origin and Early History of the Disciples of Christ*. Cincinnati, OH: Standard Publishing, 1919.

Jenson, Robert W. "Karl Barth." In *The Modern Theologians: An Introduction to Christian Theology in the Twentieth Century*, edited by David F. Ford, 2nd ed., 21–36. Malden, MA: Blackwell Publishers, 1997.

———. *The Triune God*. Vol. 1 of *Systematic Theology*. Oxford: Oxford University Press, 1997.

———. *The Triune Identity: God According to the Gospel*. Philadelphia: Fortress Press, 1982.Jones, Joe R. *A Grammar of Christian Faith: Systematic Explorations in Christian Life and Doctrine*. 2 vols. Lanham, MD: Rowman and Littlefield, 2002.

Jüngel, Eberhard. *The Doctrine of the Trinity: God's Being Is in Becoming*. Translated by Horton Harris. Grand Rapids, MI: William B. Eerdmans, 1976.

Kärkkäinen, Veli-Matti. *Trinity and Religious Pluralism: The Doctrine of the Trinity in Christian Theology of Religions*. Burlington, VT: Ashgate Publishing, 2004.

Kelsey, David H. *The Uses of Scripture in Recent Theology*. Philadelphia: Fortress Press, 1975.

Knight, G. A. F. *A Biblical Approach to the Doctrine of the Trinity*. Edinburgh: Oliver and Boyd, 1957.

LaCugna, Catherine Mowry. *God for Us: The Trinity and Christian Life*. San Francisco: Harper San Francisco, 1991.

Lanier, Roy H. *The Timeless Trinity for the Ceaseless Centuries*. Denver: Author, 1974.

Lard, Moses E. "The Work of the Past—The Symptoms of the Future." *Lard's Quarterly* 2, no. 3 (April 1865): 257–62.

Lebreton, J. *The Origins*. Vol. I of *History of the Dogma of the Trinity from Its Origins to the Council of Nicea*. London: Burns, Oates and Washbourne, 1939.

Lester, Hiram J. "The Form and Function of the Declaration and Address." In *The Quest for Christian Unity, Peace, and Purity in Thomas Campbell's Declaration and Address: Text and Studies*, edited by Thomas H. Olbricht and Hans Rollman, 173–92. Lanham, MD: Scarecrow Press, 2000.

Lindbeck, George. *The Nature of Doctrine: Religion and Theology in a Postliberal Age*. Philadelphia: Westminster Press, 1984.

Loos, C. L. "Christ—His Two-Fold Nature." *Millennial Harbinger* 36 (March 1865): 130–134.

———. "Glorifying in the Cross Only." In *The Living Pulpit of the Christian Church: A Series of Discourses, Doctrinal and Practical*, edited by W. T. Moore, 447–70. Cincinnati, OH: R. W. Carroll, 1868.

Lossky, Vladimir. *The Mystical Theology of the Eastern Church*. Translated from French. London: J. Clarke, 1957.

Luther, Martin. *Sermons on the Gospel of John: Chapters 1–4*. Vol. 22 of *Luther's Works*. Edited by Jaroslav Pelican. Translated by Martin Bertram. St. Louis: Concordia Publishing House, 1957.

Manson, William. *Jesus and the Christian*. Cambridge: James Clarke Publishers, 1967.

Martin, Robert. *The Doctrine of the Eternal Sonship of Christ Considered, Illustrated, and Defended and Fully Proved to Be A Truth Revealed in the Holy Scriptures; Including Also a Respectful Answer to All the Objections and Arguments Which Have Been Urged by the Rev. Dr. Adam Clarke Against Such a Filiation*. Oxford: J. Ham, St. Aldate's, 1821.

Mathes, James. *Works of Elder B. W. Stone*. Edited by John Allen Hudson. Rosemead, CA: Old Paths Book Club, 1953.

McAllister, Lester G. *Thomas Campbell: Man of the Book*. St. Louis: Bethany Press, 1954.

McAllister, Lester G. and William E Tucker. *Journey in Faith: A History of the Christian Church (Disciples of Christ)*. St. Louis: Bethany Press, 1975.

McGrath, Alistair. *Understanding the Trinity*. Grand Rapids, MI: Zondervan, 1988.

McLachlan, H. J. *Socinianism in Seventeenth-Century England*. London: Oxford University Press, 1951.

Miller, Samuel. *Letters on the Eternal Sonship of Christ: Addressed to the Rev. Prof. Moses Stuart, of Andover*. Philadelphia: 1823.

Molnar, Paul D. *Divine Freedom and the Doctrine of the Immanent Trinity: In Dialogue with Karl Barth and Contemporary Theology*. T&T Clark, 2002.

Moltmann, Jürgen. *God in Creation: A New Theology of Creation and the Spirit of God*. Translated by Margaret Kohl. San Francisco: Harper and Row Publishers, 1985.

———. *The Trinity and the Kingdom: the Doctrine of God.* Translated by Margaret Kohl. New York: Harper & Row Publishers, 1981.

Moore, W. T., ed. "Charles Louis Loos." In *The Living Pulpit of the Christian Church: A Series of Discourses, Doctrinal and Practical.* Cincinnati: R. W. Carroll & Co., 1868.

New International Dictionary of the Christian Church. rev. ed. Edited by J. D. Douglas. Grand Rapids, MI: Zondervan, 1978.

Nye, Stephen. *The Explication of the Articles of the Divine Unity, the Trinity and Incarnation.* n.p.: 1715.

O'Collins, G. *The Tripersonal God: Understanding and Interpreting the Trinity.* Mahwah, NJ: Paulist Press, 1999.

Office of Research, Evaluation, and Planning of the National Council of the Churches of Christ in the U.S.A. *Yearbook of American and Canadian Churches 2003.* Nashville: Abingdon Press, 2003.

Olbricht, Thomas H. "The Bible as Revelation." *Restoration Quarterly* 8, no. 4 (Fourth Quarter, 1965): 211–232.

———. "Continental Reformation Backgrounds for the *Declaration and Address.*" In *The Quest for Christian Unity, Peace, and Purity in Thomas Campbell's Declaration and Address: Text and Studies,* edited by Thomas H. Olbricht and Hans Rollman, 157–71. Lanham, MD: Scarecrow Press, 2000.

Overton, John H. and Frederic Relton. *The English Church: From the Accession of George I to the End of the Eighteenth Century (1714–1800).* London: MacMillan, 1906.

Parker, I. *The Dissenting Academies in England.* Cambridge: Cambridge University Press, 1914.

Payne, E. A. *The Free Church Tradition in the Life of England.* London: SCM Press, 1944.

Pelikan, Jaroslav. *The Emergence of the Catholic Tradition (100–600).* Vol. 1 of *The Christian Tradition: A History of the Development of Doctrine.* Chicago: University of Chicago Press, 1971.

Pendleton, W. K. "The History of the Doctrine of Christology: A Lecture." *Millennial Harbinger* 41 (February 1870): 86–98.

Phillips, Richard. "Thomas Campbell: A Reappraisal Based on Backgrounds." *Restoration Quarterly* 49, no. 2 (Second Quarter, 2007): 75–102.

Pinnock, Clark. "How I Use the Bible in Doing Theology." In *The Use of the Bible in Theology: Evangelical Options,* edited by Robert K. Johnston, 18–34. Atlanta: John Knox Press, 1985.

———. *The Scripture Principle.* San Francisco: Harper and Row, 1984.

Powell, Samuel M. ":Nineteenth-Century Protestant Doctrines of the Trinity." In *The Oxford Handbook of the Trinity*, edited by Gilles Emery and Matthew Levering, 267–280. New York: Oxford University Press, 2011.

Prestige, G. L. *God in Patristic Thought*. 2nd ed. London: SPCK, 1952.

Pribble, Lonzo. *Theology Simplified: God, His Son, and His Spirit*. Grapevine, TX: Star Bible Publications, 2001.

Rahner, Karl. *The Trinity*. Translated by Joseph Donceel. New York: Herder and Herder, 1970.

Richardson, Robert. *Memoirs of Alexander Campbell Embracing A View of the Origin, Progress, and Principles of the Religious Reformation Which He Advocated*. Vol. I. Philadelphia: J. B. Lippincott and Company, 1868.

Rosman, Doreen. *The Evolution of the English Churches, 1500–2000*. Cambridge: Cambridge University Press, 2003.

Rupp, Gordon. *Religion in England 1688–1791*. Oxford: Clarendon Press, 1986.

Rusch, William G., trans. and ed. *The Trinitarian Controversy*. Philadelphia: Fortress, 1980.

Schleiermacher, Friedrich. *The Christian Faith*. 2nd ed. Edited by H. R. MacKintosh and J. S. Stewart. Foreword by B. A. Gerrish. Edinburgh: T&T Clark, 1999.

Scott, Walter. *The Gospel Restored: A Discourse of the True Gospel of Jesus Christ, in which the Facts, Principles, Duties and Privileges of Christianity are ... Necessities of Man in His Present Condition*. Cincinnati, OH: O.H. Donogh, 1836.

Seitz, Christopher. *Prophecy and Hermeneutics (Studies in Theological Interpretation): Toward a New Introduction to the Prophets*. Grand Rapids, MI: Baker, 2007.

Shelly, Rubel and Randy Harris. *The Second Incarnation: A Theology for the 21st Century Church*. West Monroe, LA: Howard, 1992.

Skinner, R. F. *Nonconformity in Shropshire, 1662–1816; a Study in the Rise and Progress of Baptist, Congregational, Presbyterian, Quaker and Methodist Societies*. Shrewsbury, UK: Wilding, 1964.

Stone, Barton W. *An Address to the Christian Churches in Kentucky, Tennessee and Ohio, on Several Important Doctrines of Religion*. Nashville: M. & J. Norvell, 1814.

———. *An Address to the Christian Churches in Kentucky, Tennessee, & Ohio on Several Important Doctrines of Religion*. 2nd ed. Lexington, KY: Printed by I. T. Cavins, 1821.

———. *Atonement, The Substance of Two Letters Written to a Friend*. Lexington, KY: Joseph Charles, 1805.

———. *The Biography of Eld. Barton Warren Stone, Written by Himself, with additions and Reflections by Eld. John Rogers*. Cincinnati, OH: Published for the author by J. S. and U. P. James, 1847.

———. "The Creed of the Waldenses." *The Christian Messenger* 1, no. 3 (January 25, 1827): 54–56.

———. "History of the Christian Church in the West—VI." *The Christian Messenger* 1, no. 9 (July 25, 1827): 193–98.

———. "History of the Christian Church in the West—No. VIII." *The Christian Messenger* 1, no. 12 (October 25, 1827): 265–69.

———. *The Last Will and Testament of the Springfield Presbytery, in Observation on Church Government, by the Presbytery of Springfield, to Which is Added, The Last Will and Testament of That Reverend Body. With a Preface and Notes by the Editor.* Edited by Richard McNemar. N.p.:1808.

———. "Letter II—To Elder S. Clack." *The Christian Messenger* 2, no. 3 (January 1828): 52–57.

———. *Letters to James Blythe, D. D., Designed as a Reply to the Arguments of Thomas Cleland, D. D. Against My Address, 2d. Edition, On the Doctrine of Trinity, the Son of God, Atonement, &c.* Lexington, KY: William Tanner, Monitor Office, 1824.

———. *A Letter to Mr. John R. Moreland, In Reply to His Pamphlet.* Lexington, KY: Printed at the Office of the Public Advertiser, 1821.

———. "Objections to Christian Union Calmly Considered." *The Christian Messenger* 1, no. 2 (December 25, 1826): 25–37.

———. "Remarks on the Preceding Communication." *The Christian Messenger* 2, no. 6 (April 1828): 128–32.

———. "Reply." *The Christian Messenger* 2, no. 1 (November 1827): 10–13.

———. "Reply." *The Christian Messenger* 6, no 4 (April 1832): 118–21.

———. "Reply: To Elder Spencer Clack, Editor of the *Baptist Recorder*." *The Christian Messenger* 2, no. 2 (December 1827): 29–36.

———. *A Reply to John Campbell's Strictures on Atonement.* Lexington, KY: Joseph Charles, 1805.

———. "To *The Christian Baptist*." *The Christian Messenger* 1, no. 9 (July 25, 1827): 204–9.

———. "To Elder Thomas Campbell." *The Christian Messenger* 7, no. 7 (July 1833): 204–10.

———. Untitled Comment on an Article on the Trinity from the *Western Luminary*. *The Christian Messenger* 1, no. 4 (February 24, 1827): 83–86.

———. Untitled Editorial Comments. *The Christian Messenger* 1, no. 1 (November 25, 1826): 18–22.

———. Untitled Review of a May 1830 Article on the Trinity in the *Gospel Herald*. *The Christian Messenger* 4, no. 8 (July 1830): 169–73.

Stuart, Moses. *A Commentary on the Epistle to the Hebrews in Two Volumes*. Andover, MA: Flagg and Gould, 1827.

———. *A Commentary on the Epistle to the Romans, with a Translation and Various Excurses*. Andover, MA: Flagg and Gould, 1832.

———. *Letters on the Eternal Generation of the Son of God Addressed to the Rev. Samuel Miller, D. D. by Moses Stuart*. Andover, MA: Flagg and Gould, 1822.

———. *Letter to the Rev. Wm. E. Channing Containing Remarks on His Sermon Recently Preached and Published at Baltimore*. 3rd ed. Andover, MA: Flagg and Gould, 1819.

A Subscriber. "To the Editors of the Christian Messenger." *The Christian Messenger* 6, no 4 (April 1832): 118.

Tanner, Kathryn. *Jesus, Humanity, and Trinity: A Brief Systematic Theology*. Minneapolis: Fortress Press, 2003.

Thompson, J. *Modern Trinitarian Perspectives*. New York: Oxford University Press, 1994.

Thompson, Rhodes, ed. *Voices from Cane Ridge*. St. Louis: Bethany Press, 1954.

"Timothy." "The Spirit of Orthodoxy." *The Christian Messenger* 2, no. 6 (April 1828): 124–28.

Torrance, Thomas F. *The Christian Doctrine of God: One Being, Three Persons*. Edinburgh: T&T Clark, 1996.

———. *The Trinitarian Faith: The Evangelical Theology of the Ancient Catholic Church*. Edinburgh: T&T Clark, 1993.

———. *Trinitarian Perspectives: Toward Doctrinal Agreement*. Edinburgh: T&T Clark, 1994.

"The Trinity from Spark's Inquiry." *The Christian Messenger* 4, no. 4 (March 1830): 72–75.

Turner, J. J. and Edward P. Myers. *The Doctrine of the Godhead: A Study of the Father, Son, and Holy Spirit*. West Monroe, LA: Let the Bible Speak, 1973.

———. *The Doctrine of the Godhead: A Study of the Father, Son, and Holy Spirit*. rev. ed. Abilene, TX: Quality Publications, 1985.

Tyler, B. B. *A History of the Disciples of Christ*. Louisville, KY: 1895.

Vanhoozer, Kevin. *Is There a Meaning in this Text?: The Bible, the Reader, and the Morality of Literary Knowledge*. Grand Rapids, MI: Zondervan, 1998.

Volf, Miroslav. *After Our Likeness: The Church as the Image of the Trinity*. Grand Rapids, MI: William B. Eerdmans, 1998.

———. "'The Trinity Is Our Social Program': The Doctrine of the Trinity and the Shape of Social Engagement." *Modern Theology* 14, no. 3 (July 1998): 403–23.

Wainwright, G. "The Doctrine of the Trinity: Where the Church Stands or Falls." *Interpretation* 45 (1991): 117–32.

Ware, Charles C. *Barton Warren Stone: Pathfinder of Christian Union*. St. Louis: Bethany Press, 1932.

Warfield, B. B. "Calvin's Doctrine of the Trinity." *The Princeton Theological Review* 7, no. 4 (1909): 553–652.

Watson, Francis. *Text, Church, and World: Biblical Interpretation in Theological Perspective*. Grand Rapids, MI: William B. Eerdmans, 1994.

Watson, Richard. *Remarks on the Eternal Sonship of Christ; and Use of Reason in Matters of Revelation: Suggested by Several Passages in Dr. Adam Clarke's Commentary on the New Testament*. London: T. Cordeux, 1818.

Watts, Isaac. *The Arian Invited to the Orthodox Faith*. In Vol. 6 of *The Works of the Rev. Isaac Watts, D. D. in Nine Volumes*. 207–390. Leeds, UK: Edward Baines, 1813.

———. *The Christian Doctrine of the Trinity*. In Vol. 6 of *The Works of the Rev. Isaac Watts, D.D. in Nine Volumes*. 107–206. Leeds, UK: Edward Baines, 1813.

———. *An Essay on the True Importance of Any Human Schemes to Explain the Sacred Doctrine of the Trinity*. In Vol. 6 of *The Works of the Rev. Isaac Watts, D.D. in Nine Volumes*. 474–83. Leeds, UK: Edward Baines, 1813.

———. *A Faithful Enquiry After the Ancient and Original Doctrine of the Trinity, Taught by Christ and His Apostles, So Far as is Sufficient for Our Salvation*. Exeter, UK: J. Gresswell, 1745.

———. *The Glory of Christ as God-Man Displayed*. In Vol. 6 of *The Works of the Rev. Isaac Watts, D.D. in Nine Volumes*. 484–649. Leeds, UK: Edward Baines, 1813.

———. *Useful and Important Questions Concerning Jesus the Son of God*. In Vol. 6 of *The Works of the Rev. Isaac Watts, D.D. in Nine Volumes*. 391–473. Leeds, UK: Edward Baines, 1813.

Watts, Michael R. *The Dissenters: Volume I: From the Reformation to the French Revolution*. Oxford: Clarendon Press, 1978.

———. *The Dissenters: Volume II: The Expansion of Evangelical Non-Conformity*. Oxford: Clarendon Press, 1995.

West, W. G. *Barton Warren Stone*. Nashville: Disciples of Christ Historical Society, 1954.

Wiles, Maurice. *Archetypal Heresy: Arianism Through the Centuries*. Oxford: Clarendon Press, 1996.

Williams, D. Newell. *Barton Stone: A Spiritual Biography*. St. Louis: Chalice Press, 2000.

Williams, Rowan. *Arius: Heresy and Tradition*. rev. ed. Grand Rapids, MI: William B. Eerdmans, 2001.

Wrather, Eva Jean. *Alexander Campbell: Adventurer in Freedom: A Literary Biography.* 3 Vols. Edited by D. Duane Cummins. Fort Worth, TX: TCU Press and Nashville: Disciples of Christ Historical Society, 2005–2009.

Wright, N. T. *The New Testament and the People of God.* Minneapolis: Fortress Press, 1992.

Yeago, David. "The New Testament and Nicene Dogma." *Pro Ecclesia* 3 (1994): 152–64.

Yoder, John Howard. "The Use of the Bible in Theology." In *The Use of the Bible in Theology: Evangelical Options*, edited by Robert K. Johnston, 103–20. Atlanta: John Knox Press, 1985.

Zenos, Andrew C. *Presbyterianism in America: Past, Present and Prospective.* New York: Thomas Nelson and Sons, 1937.

Zizioulas, John D. *Being as Communion: Studies in Personhood and the Church.* Foreword by John Meyendorff. Crestwood, NY: St. Vladimir's Seminary Press, 1985.

———. "The Church as Communion." *St. Vladimir's Theological Quarterly* 38, no. 1 (1994): 3–16.

———. "Communion and Otherness," *St. Vladimir's Theological Quarterly* 38, no. 4 (1994): 347–61.

———. "The Doctrine of the Holy Trinity: The Signifcance of the Cappadocian Contribution." In *Trinitarian Theology Today: Essays on Divine Being and Act*, edited by Christoph Schwöbel, 44–60. Edinburgh: T&T Clark, 1995.

———. "Human Capacity and Human Incapacity: A Theological Exploration of Personhood." *Scottish Journal of Theology* 28, no. 5 (October 1975): 401–48.

———. "On Being a Person: Towards an Ontology of Personhood." In *Persons, Divine and Human*, edited by Christoph Schwöbel and Colin E. Gunton, 33–46. Edinburgh: T&T Clark, 1991.

www.ingramcontent.com/pod-product-compliance
Lightning Source LLC
Chambersburg PA
CBHW030436300426
44112CB00009B/1027